THE EVERYTHING.

LAW OF ATTRACTION
DREAM DICTIONARY

Dear Reader,

Since early childhood, my dreams have been thrilling adventures into a magnificent world of fantasy. My dreams not only lit my imagination but also my unending desire to get to know the world within. It is impossible for me to separate my dream world from my spiritual path. From my earliest days I felt the vibration of spirit hiding behind the imagery my dreams revealed. As an adult, I began to see that my dreams held the keys to understanding my unconscious fears, anxieties, hopes, desires, and beliefs. In my dreams I found the information I needed to release and heal old emotional experiences, so I could refocus my heart and mind toward my goals. I began to work consistently with my dreams, learning to interpret my unique dream language so I could co-create my life more consciously.

To me, dreams are windows into the very workings of our souls—deep, rich sources of self-knowledge and spiritual growth. If you allow it, your dreams will unerringly steer your course, lighting the way ahead; they are like a warm beacon of divine love illuminating the way home to your own precious heart.

Enjoy the journey!

Blessings,

Cathleen O'Connor

Welcome to the EVERYTHING® Series!

These handy, accessible books give you all you need to tackle a difficult project, gain a new hobby, comprehend a fascinating topic, prepare for an exam, or even brush up on something you learned back in school but have since forgotten.

You can choose to read an *Everything*® book from cover to cover or just pick out the information you want from our four useful boxes: e-questions, e-facts, e-alerts, and e-ssentials.

We give you everything you need to know on the subject, but throw in a lot of fun stuff along the way, too.

We now have more than 400 *Everything*® books in print, spanning such wide-ranging categories as weddings, pregnancy, cooking, music instruction, foreign language, crafts, pets, New Age, and so much more. When you're done reading them all, you can finally say you know *Everything*®!

QUESTION

Answers to
common questions

FACT

Important snippets
of information

ALERT

Urgent
warnings

ESSENTIAL

Quick
handy tips

PUBLISHER Karen Cooper

DIRECTOR OF ACQUISITIONS AND INNOVATION Paula Munier

MANAGING EDITOR, EVERYTHING® SERIES Lisa Laing

COPY CHIEF Casey Ebert

ACQUISITIONS EDITOR Lisa Laing

ASSOCIATE DEVELOPMENT EDITOR Hillary Thompson

EDITORIAL ASSISTANT Ross Weisman

EVERYTHING® SERIES COVER DESIGNER Erin Alexander

LAYOUT DESIGNERS Colleen Cunningham, Elisabeth Lariviere, Ashley Vierra, Denise Wallace

Visit the entire Everything® series at *www.everything.com*

THE
EVERYTHING®
LAW OF ATTRACTION
DREAM
DICTIONARY

An A to Z guide to using your dreams to attract
success, prosperity, and love

Cathleen O'Connor, PhD

Avon, Massachusetts

*For dreamers of all ages: May your most
treasured dreams bring light and joy.*

An Everything® Series Book.
Everything® and everything.com® are registered trademarks of F+W Media, Inc.

Published by Adams Media, a division of F+W Media, Inc.
57 Littlefield Street, Avon, MA 02322 U.S.A.
www.adamsmedia.com

Contains material adapted and abridged from *The Everything® Dreams Book, 2nd Edition*, by Jenni
Kosarin, copyright © 2005 by F+W Media, Inc., ISBN 10: 1-59337-336-8, ISBN 13:
978-1-59337-336-8, and from *The Everything® Law of Attraction Book*, by Meera Lester,
copyright © 2008 by F+W Media, Inc., ISBN 10: 1-59869-775-7, ISBN 13: 978-1-59869-775-9.

ISBN 10: 1-4405-0466-0
ISBN 13: 978-1-4405-0466-2
eISBN 10: 1-4405-0467-9
eISBN 13: 978-1-4405-0467-9

Printed in the United States of America.

10 9 8 7 6 5 4 3 2 1

Library of Congress Cataloging-in-Publication Data
O'Connor, Cathleen.
The everything law of attraction dream dictionary / Cathleen O'Connor.
p. cm.—(An everything series book)
ISBN 978-1-4405-0466-2
1. Dreams. 2. Dream interpretation. 3. Visions. 4. Success. 5. New Thought. I. Title.
BF1091.O26   2010
35'.3—dc22   2010009950

*This book is available at quantity discounts for bulk purchases.
For information, please call 1-800-289-0963.*

Contents

Acknowledgments

To Elizabeth Harper and Karen Paolino, who together opened the door of inspiration and opportunity. You helped me catch one of my biggest dreams. To Terah Cox, with whom I share so many dreams, for wonderful discussions over tea and sunshine, and your unfailing support and guidance. You continue to inspire me!

To Managing Editor Lisa Laing, Associate Development Editor Hillary Thompson, and Editorial Assistant Ross Weisman at Adams Media for making this project such a pleasure from start to finish.

And, finally, to all my wonderful family, friends, and clients—too many to name—you are the wind behind my artist's sail and an endless source of joy and love. Thank you all!

The Top 10 Ways Your Dreams Can Change Your Life

1. Discover what you truly believe and feel about your life, and use that knowledge to heal and prosper.
2. Get solutions in dreams to seemingly unsolvable problems.
3. Become inspired in dreams to help yourself and others to live better and happier lives.
4. Reconnect with loved ones who have crossed over, and heal from grief and loss.
5. Experience a deep connection with the Divine in your dreams, bringing peace, harmony, and balance to your life.
6. Set intentions for your dreams to help your career blossom and succeed.
7. Master the power of your subconscious mind and reset your vibration to attract all that you want in life.
8. Dream your way to greater creativity and self-expression.
9. Heal emotional wounds and use your dreams to draw into your life the perfect romantic partner.
10. Learn your own symbolic dream language and experience greater intuitive wisdom about what is truly right for you.

Introduction

YOU SPEND APPROXIMATELY ONE-THIRD of your life asleep. Although it may seem as if you are dormant when asleep, you are actually engaged in an exciting and revealing journey into your subconscious mind. It is a journey without bounds; a rollercoaster ride into a surreal world of the mind in which your own unique, symbolic language reveals your innermost desires, thoughts, and emotions. In your dreams, you can find your fears, anxieties, hopes, aspirations, and even self-healing. Most importantly, your dreams open a window into the workings of spirit—the reality of your inner and outer worlds.

The universality of the dream experience, coupled with spiritual law, raises the natural question of whether or not your dreams while asleep affect the waking dreams for your life. Does what you create on your vision board begin its manifesting journey at night as the conscious mind recedes and the true power, the subconscious, takes over? Or, do your nighttime dreams merely resolve issues of daily stress, while your conscious intentional self partners in a dance of co-creation with the universe? Could both be true?

In sleep, you reconnect with your very essence as a spiritual being. You have available to you a mystical power that, if harnessed, can have life-changing effects. The language of spirit is symbolic and, in the dream state, you are fully immersed in the world of symbolism. Learning to understand and interpret universal symbols as well as your own unique symbolic language is key to harnessing the energy of manifestation. The dream state tells you where you are ready to manifest your desires. It also shows where work still has to be done to clear your energy on the mental, emotional, physical, and spiritual levels in order to come into vibrational resonance with your deepest desires.

The truth is you are harnessing the power of the Law of Attraction all the time. In fact, you are an excellent manifestor. Yet in the waking state you may not realize why you are manifesting what you are. The secrets lie elsewhere—in the spiritual bridge of the subconscious—the universal translator of spiritual truth into conscious experience. In the dream state you can access the secrets of the subconscious as at no other time. You are the star of your own reality show, and the subconscious is the camera that is always on, capturing and recording every thought, feeling, and experience.

Your dreams can gently and sometimes powerfully move you along on your desired path. When you deeply desire something, your nighttime dreams will keep working on whatever you have set in motion, even if it is still on the mental or emotional level.

For example, Nancy wants to move on from her current career to writing mysteries for stage and screen. This is her deep and long-held love. Yet financial considerations seem to make it impossible. However, Nancy's dream world knows no such limitations. Often, she dreams of being in transit, endlessly commuting from where she is in her life now to where she wants to be. In her dream state, she frequently travels over water and many times encounters children on her journey. Whether Nancy is ready or not, her dreams are trying to remind her of her heart's desire. They also can help her reconnect with the child who first dreamt of how she wanted her life to be.

In this book you will learn to use your dreams to uncover and use the secrets of the Law of Attraction. You will learn how your dreams can help you come into alignment with your waking desires. You will be able to interpret any dream, using common universal symbolism while creating your own dictionary of shared and personal symbols. As part of the intentional process of working with the Law of Attraction, you will consciously focus your pre-sleep activities on preparing your subconscious mind to support the vision you have for your life.

With this book you will be empowered to unlock the mysteries of the Law of Attraction using the keys provided in your dreams.

PART I

Dream Interpretation and the Law of Attraction

CHAPTER 1

Spiritual Reality Explained

Nothing is more fascinating than the journey of discovery into the world within. Everything that exists in the outer world begins in innermost awareness. In dreams lie the seeds of who you truly are and your potential to create the life you want. Although your dreams reflect your unique life journey, the dream experience is universal, crossing borders of geography, culture, and consciousness. Like the dream experience, dream interpretation is both personal and universal. This chapter explores spiritual reality and universal laws that govern the experience of existence and why you dream.

Who Are You Really?

Your body needs to rest and restore itself through sleep, in particular what is called REM sleep. Identified by University of Chicago physiology professor Nathaniel Kleitman and his student, Eugene Aserinsky, in the 1950s, REM sleep is a normal stage of sleep characterized by rapid eye movements that signify active dream periods. In fact, it has been shown repeatedly that if you cannot regularly reach REM sleep, the level at which you dream, you will be stressed and anxious while awake.

ESSENTIAL

Your subconscious is a lot like reality TV. While you go about your daily life, the camera is always on, recording everything in your experiences, from thoughts to feelings to actions—your own as well as the impact of others' words, feelings, and actions on you. This is why recorded impressions from your childhood or past often surface in your dreams.

But your physical nature is only one part of the picture. When it comes to dreams, your spiritual nature is most significant. Your spiritual nature can be described as emanations of light waves of energy, vibrating and shifting constantly in a state of co-creation with the universe and each other. Your true existence is multidimensional and, when asleep, you effortlessly leave your waking physical reality to enter a multidimensional universe where all is possible. This nightly adventure is known as the dream state—a state of being in which you experience and explore your true nature through a language rich in symbolism.

What Is a Dream?

On the surface a dream consists of visual images, actions, characters, and emotional responses seemingly unrelated to daily life—your waking reality. When you go to sleep, another world surfaces—one in which you are unfettered by the constraints of physical, ethical, and moral law. In the dream state you can be anyone, go anywhere, do anything. Yet it is the dream state that reveals the truth of your daily experiences. In the dream world, your true beliefs, hopes, fears, and desires emerge.

While you go about your day, the subconscious busily records all your experiences and stores them alongside already-recorded experiences from childhood and even from past lifetimes. This inner aspect is the most real part of you. It is the part of you that constantly creates the outer reality of your day.

A dream is the true record of your life experience that awakens as the conscious mind rests, using the symbolic language of spirit to provide healing, insight, planning, connection, and spiritual growth. Simply put, a dream is a communication from the part of you that is always connected to spiritual truth.

Where Do Dreams Come From?

Read the following account of a dream and see what you can decipher about it.

> I'm sitting in a conference room at an oval table. I'm dressed in my normal business suit. As I look around the room, I see only cats—cats of all sizes and shapes—some smoking cigars. The cats are all screeching at each other. I can't stand it and just want to get out of there.

Did you guess that this dreamer was processing something about her work life? If you did you are on your way to understanding where dreams come from. The woman who reported this dream was the single woman executive in a management team otherwise made up of men. After several days of meetings, a power struggle was evident among several of her male colleagues. Processing her experience at night not only helped her release her feelings of frustration but also enabled her to begin to see that she didn't have to take their conflicts so seriously. Her colleagues showed up in her dream as cats, revealing how "catty" she thought their infighting was.

If you're like most people, your daily life experience is the main source of your dreams, but not the only one. You will explore many types of dreams in this book, as well as many sources of dream content and imagery. If you understand and correctly interpret the symbolic imagery of your dreams, you can successfully use the information to change your life to bring it into alignment with your waking dreams.

Why Do You Dream?

All dreams originate in the subconscious. A good model for understanding the subconscious is the computer. Behind the façade of your computer, software programs enable it to perform its functions. When you access your subconscious in the dream state, you access your own internal "software," which is often invisible to your waking consciousness. Your dream experience gives you the opportunity to discover your own internal programming.

FACT

Studies have shown that all humans dream, but so do all animals—including your pets. Although people's autonomous nervous systems usually shut down during the dream state, animals move while dreaming. If you've seen your dog seemingly running while asleep, he might be chasing a squirrel in his dreams.

Your subconscious is equipped with video, audio, and sensory capabilities. It stores your life experiences as images, sounds, smells, sensations, and feelings—not text—creating a symbolic bridge between the subconscious mind and your conscious waking state. When you dream you bring your conscious waking state and your subconscious mind into coherence and harmony. Dreaming balances, heals, and restores your psyche. The need to reconcile life experiences, thoughts, emotions, and events, whether past or present, is common to everyone.

Any dream can be of a particular type. It may contain a single theme or a combination of themes, but there are, in general, five main categories:

- Emotional release dreams
- Wish-fulfillment dreams
- Precognitive dreams
- Astral dreams (past-life dreams or spiritual visitation dreams)
- Problem-solving dreams

As you progress through this book, you'll learn more about the nature of dreams and where they come from. You'll discover how categorizing your dreams is one of the most important steps in the process of understanding them.

Emotional Release Dreams

In spiritual reality, emotions are energy. Without a permissible outlet for expression, your emotions can build up over time and become stuck in the physical body. At night, in the dream state, even long-held emotions can finally be experienced, expressed, and released. Your regrets, worries, and concerns—things you find too difficult to deal with consciously—get detoured to your subconscious and come through in what are known as "emotional release dreams." The most important aspect of this type of dream is the emotion you experience. Sometimes emotional release dreams can be frightening or disturbing as anger, fear, and anxieties surface.

Upon waking from a dream, note the main feelings in the dream. If fear, anxiety, and anger are the primary feelings, realize these emotions are coming up so you can finally process them and let them go. This release can restore harmony and balance to your psyche.

You can ask yourself where in your current life you are experiencing those same emotions and why. (This will be explained in later chapters.) Once you've obtained this understanding through your dreams, you can shift your reactions and find appropriate ways to honor and express your feelings.

Wish-Fulfillment Dreams

Many people confuse wish-fulfillment dreams with precognitive dreams because wish-fulfillment dreams seem to be showing you a part of your life that hasn't already happened. The purpose of a wish-fulfillment dream is to let you try on your fantasies without risk—very much like a waking daydream, in which you lose yourself in the visual and emotional fantasy. A wish-fulfillment dream is a projection of what you would like to happen. Often it involves other people and events over which you have no control. Here's an example.

Amy dreamt that her boyfriend presented her with an engagement ring. She was very excited and wanted to know if it was a precognitive dream of what would happen. In fact, while awake Amy fantasized a lot about becoming engaged to her boyfriend; the dream played out her fantasy at night as well. She was sure this was the man she wanted to marry, and her dreams were projections of the future she hoped would transpire.

For Amy, understanding this dream as wish-fulfillment helped her release the expectation she placed on her boyfriend. She was able to see it as a reflection of her deepening love and her desire to have that love returned in kind. The dream enabled her to take her relationship for what it was, not what she wished it would be, and allow it to grow and evolve at its own pace. Three years later, Amy did indeed receive that engagement ring, having used the power of her dreams to clarify her feelings and needs.

Wish-fulfillment dreams often fill a gap when actual knowledge isn't available. A good way to distinguish a wish-fulfillment dream from a precognitive dream is that precognitive dreams usually aren't imbued with emotion. If strong emotion shows up in a dream in which you have a vested stake in the outcome, most often the dream is one of wish-fulfillment.

ALERT

Pay close attention to your wish-fulfillment dreams. Wish-fulfillment dreams contain important information about your deepest desires and your longing to know if your desires will be met. Sometimes you may not even consciously know what you want. But your subconscious knows and can help you discover it in your dreams.

Precognitive Dreams

Precognitive dreams most often, but not always, unfold logically, showing events that happen in sequential order. Here's an interesting tidbit: You don't have to be psychic to have a precognitive dream. Many people who are incredibly intuitive in their waking hours never have precognitive dreams, whereas those who do have them are not necessarily psychic in waking life. Ann was engaged to a man who lived in a distant state; she saw him infrequently. While she was visiting him to plan their wedding, she had a disturbing dream. In her dream, she heard a key in the lock and saw her fiancé come into the bedroom to say hello to her. She noticed he was wearing a certain blue shirt she liked. In the dream, she suddenly blurted out "you're cheating on me!" He became angry and asked who had told her.

Ann woke up feeling unsettled. She realized her fiancé was already up and about. Just then she heard a key in the lock and her fiancé came into the bedroom to say hello. He was wearing the shirt she had seen in the dream. Ann knew immediately that her dream had been a warning. She asked if he was cheating on her. Her fiancé got angry and responded with the exact words from her dream.

Precognitive dreams are often warnings. In Ann's case she was given information that spared her the grief of marrying an unfaithful man. In many cases of precognitive dreams, no action is required. The information given may be only partially received or remembered. Be patient if this happens to you. Ask out loud for more assistance just before you go to sleep the next night, and the next, until you get what you need. Never dismiss your dreams. If you get a warning that something may happen to your brother in his car, for example, make sure you tell him to be careful driving. Even if he thinks you're nuts, you'll still feel better later.

ESSENTIAL

Although prophetic dreams are rare, innovative biologist and researcher Rupert Sheldrake cites reports of numbers of people having unusual, seemingly precognitive, dreams preceding the September 11, 2001 global tragedy. One suggested explanation might be that these dreams served to prepare the collective consciousness emotionally and mentally for the traumatic events to follow.

Astral Dreams

Regardless of whether you remember them, you have astral dreams, or "travels" as they're sometimes called. When Marie was a small child she and her family often planned trips to theme parks. Marie became so excited and curious about each trip that she literally traveled there in her dreams the night before an outing. When the family arrived at their destination the next day Marie ran around telling everyone where everything was located—she even described the inside of the funhouse in great detail.

Astral travel is very common in the dream state. Your astral body, the energetic equivalent of your physical body sometimes referred to as the "dreambody," detaches when you are asleep; its movement is unrestricted by time or space. Astral travel can be the cause of what we call déjà vu experiences. You really have been there before—in your dreams. Other astral travel dreams may involve past lives and visitations.

Past-Life Dreams

In the dream world there are no limits of time, space, or even the distance you can travel. Many people revisit their past lives in dreams without knowing they've done it. Whether or not you believe in reincarnation, dreams of past lives can feel startlingly real—and they may just be!

Mark dreamt a lot as a young child, remembering big sweeping dreams from as early as age three. He called his dreams "movies." He told his parents he was watching a movie during the night and described the movie to them. His "movies" were true epics with large casts of characters, a storyline, and events placed in particular periods in history. When he grew up Mark began to study spirituality in earnest and came to believe that his experiences in the dream state during his early childhood were, in fact, dreams of his past lives.

As an adult you may still experience past-life dreams. Like your regular dreams, past-life dreams surface so you can integrate that past life and heal any residual emotional issues from that life experience.

Spiritual Visitation Dreams

A visit from a deceased loved one, spirit guide, animal totem, or angelic messenger is another type of astral dream experience. When someone you love dies, the desire to reconnect is strong. Often that desire is met when you are asleep.

Just before waking one morning, Cathy had a dream about her long-deceased mother. In the dream her mother was young and vibrant. A feeling of joy and tremendous love enveloped Cathy in the dream state. It took Cathy more than one hour after she awoke to even remember her mother was deceased, so strong was the visit and the emotional connection. Not only did the dream give great comfort to Cathy, but she got to experience a part of her mother that she had never known in real life. Cathy often feels her mother's energy around her now in that same joyful, loving way she shared during her dream visit.

The hallmark of a spiritual visitation dream is the uniformly loving energy it contains. Your loved ones in spirit reach out to connect with you to offer love, forgiveness, reassurance, and comfort. If a deceased loved one in your dream is angry or upset, it is probably not a spiritual visitation. Rather your deceased loved one most likely represents a part of you that is experiencing the disturbing emotion during your waking state.

ALERT

An emotional release can occur when you have an astral visit from someone you love who has died. Out of fear, grief, or shock, you may push him away in your dream, even though he's trying to tell you he's okay. Spirits are generally happy beings. Dreamers are the ones who are afraid.

Problem-Solving Dreams

Did you ever go to sleep trying to figure something out and then wake up with an answer? The term "sleep on it" really does have significance. Sometimes your subconscious knows the solution to a problem and can dig it up more readily than your waking mind. But there's something else. Astral and problem-solving dreams can combine to give you information that never existed in your conscious mind in the first place. Whether or not you remember it, some information is given to you through outside sources—from astral visits. Countless geniuses throughout history simply "happened" upon their inspiration in nighttime dreams.

FACT

Did you know that the famous artist Paul Gauguin came up with the subjects in his paintings from his dreams, or that Albert Einstein formulated the theory of relativity from a vision he had while he slept? Thomas Edison's light bulb and Mendeleyev's periodic table were inspired by dreams as well. Coincidence? Not a chance!

One inventor wrestled for years with a small but vital detail he needed to complete a machine he was building. But the detail eluded him like a mirage that vanished when he got too near. One night he dreamt he had been taken captive by savages who attacked him with spears with eye-shaped holes at the ends. When the inventor awoke, he realized the nightmare had provided the solution to his problem: the eye of the needle belonged near the point. With the help of his dream, Elias Howe was then able to complete his invention: the sewing machine.

The Laws That Govern Spiritual Reality

Like the physical universe, the spiritual universe operates under a set of consistent, unchanging laws. These laws, often called universal laws, govern every aspect of creation and function all the time, without judgment, on the principle of vibration and alignment. The principle of vibration or resonance is the foundational basis of the universe, recognizing that all is energy or light.

ALERT

All dreams begin first in the unconscious, making their way into actual manifestation through desire, intention, and action. As the Law of Attraction operates, the dream state lets you know where you have old beliefs, emotional blocks, or ingrained habits that need to be cleared so your desires can come into being. Don't ignore this vital information!

Think for a moment of a satellite orbiting in space constantly broadcasting and receiving signals. To tune in to a particular set of signals, like TV programs, you might have a small receiver satellite dish mounted somewhere on your house. That receiver dish would be calibrated (attuned) to pick up the exact energy waves (signals) that you want to receive. In the same way as that satellite, you are broadcasting and receiving vibrations to and from the world around you on a constant basis. Your vibrational resonance isn't made up of video images and audio signals. Instead what you broadcast and receive are energetic vibrations formed by your thoughts, emotions, and life experiences. And that unique vibrational resonance attracts to you the people, events, and life experiences that match your calibrated energy field.

All other laws flow from this foundation. All spiritual or universal laws are designed to seek wholeness and harmony—true alignment on both the personal and collective levels, reflecting the fact that there is no duality in spiritual law. This understanding of the interconnectedness of all creation teaches that what you give, you receive. More simply, you attract the people, events, and experiences that match the vibration you are sending out into the universe.

In recent years, books such as Rhonda Byrne's *The Secret* and the Abraham series by Esther and Jerry Hicks have popularized the spiritual Law of Attraction. Even though modern spiritual seekers have called the Law of Attraction a recently discovered ancient secret teaching, it has never really been lost. Through the centuries, spiritual teachers, philosophers, and others have mentioned or discussed the Law of Attraction, although they used various other names in their teachings and writings. Today, renewed interest in the subject has catapulted the ages-old concept into mainstream popular culture.

What the Law of Attraction Is and Isn't

Simply put, the Law of Attraction asserts that, on a vibrational level, like attracts like. Your energy vibration is composed of your thoughts and feelings, creating a resonance that forms a unique imprint of you. Your imprint, or resonance, draws to it people, events, and experiences that match your vibration. The following true story illustrates one way the Law of Attraction works.

A man mentioned to his wife one day that he would really like to have a small charcoal grill to use on the outdoor deck at their summer home. Having worked with the Law of Attraction herself, his wife encouraged him to just visualize it coming to him and let the universe find just the right grill. Skeptical, the man nevertheless did as she suggested. He saw the grill in his mind, felt the anticipation of having it and using it, and then he forgot about it entirely. Two days later a neighbor stopped over to borrow a tool and asked the man if he knew anyone who wanted a small charcoal grill he was getting rid of. It was exactly the grill the man had envisioned.

Proponents of the Law of Attraction assert that the law brings you what you desire when you:

1. Are clear about what you want.
2. Energize your desire with thoughts, emotion, visual imagery, and a strong conviction that what you want is coming to you.
3. Let go of how and when things have to happen and stay in faith (belief) that your desire is being met, even if it has not yet come into your experience.
4. Express gratitude as if your desire were already granted.

How the Law of Attraction Works

The Law of Attraction works in response to thoughts that have become energized—and the law is working all the time. Thoughts can be energized in positive or negative ways. The Law of Attraction does not judge the thought or the energy behind it. It works consistently each and every time. That is why so much emphasis is placed on recognizing and working with your thoughts as a first step in learning to harness the power of the Law of Attraction in a conscious and intentional way.

If the man who wanted the grill, for example, had despaired of ever finding the right one or was worried he could not afford it, that energy would have formed part of the vibration sent out with his request for the grill. He would have received back confirmation of his belief that he would be unable to find or afford the grill he wanted.

When you have conflicting beliefs (thoughts) about what is possible, the Law of Attraction responds to each one, and you often end up canceling out the very intention you wanted to manifest.

Letting go of *how* something should come to you is an important part of working with the energy of the Law of Attraction. If you are fixated on only one way your desire can be met, you, in effect, limit the flow of energy. The divine universe will always come up with greater options than you can envision.

What Do You Believe?

Most likely you already have a way of understanding and working with your dreams. If you are like most people, you perhaps see your dream imagery as literal reflections of the people and events in your lives. If so, this book will broaden your understanding of dreams and provide new tools to use to correctly interpret your dreams.

You may not remember your dreams. If so, you will learn how to increase your dream memory through techniques such as journaling, intention-setting, and using the dream dictionary (Part II).

ESSENTIAL

Edgar Cayce said, "All dreams are given for the benefit of the individual, would he but interpret them correctly." As you learn to interpret your own language of symbolism, you will discover that your life has overarching themes or metaphors that show up in your dreams again and again.

Your journey into the magical world within is only just beginning. As you progress through this book, you will not only become better at remembering and interpreting your dreams, you will begin to harness the power of your dreams to bring yourself into alignment with universal law and attract what you want into your life.

CHAPTER 2

Dream Symbolism

You may be wondering why the subconscious speaks through symbolism in the dream state. Why doesn't it clearly articulate what it is you need to know? As the spiritual bridge between the conscious mind and universal spiritual understanding, the subconscious has the difficult job of translating imagery and experience into metaphoric messages. In spiritual reality, there is no language adequate to express what is infinite and inherently inexpressible. So learning the symbolic language of dreams not only enables greater understanding, it also opens a window into the workings of your very soul.

The Language of Symbolism

Hippocrates, the ancient Greek physician, believed that the body sensed the coming of disease and often warned the dreamer about it. He said the appearance of the sun, moon, or stars in a dream symbolized the dreamer's organic state. If the dream stars glowed brightly, it meant the body was functioning as it should. However, if the stars seemed dim or cloudy, or if some cosmic disaster occurred in the dream, it indicated that disease was forming somewhere in the body. Hippocrates also believed dreams were the one place where gods and humans could meet—for real. He said that if gods came to you in your dreams, they could alleviate suffering and heal illness.

ESSENTIAL

Hippocrates rightly believed in the power of symbolic information flowing through the dream state. Whether or not his interpretation was correct, he formulated a dictionary that worked for him. As you learn to understand your own symbolic language, you, too, will develop an internal library of dream images that your subconscious will reference again and again.

Once you begin working with your dreams, you become more attuned to yourself and to your environment. Even if you can't recall your dreams at first, or you only remember them in bits and pieces, you may find yourself remembering a particular image during the day. Sometimes a conversation or a situation may trigger your recall. When you start to recall symbols, try to associate them with something in your life. When you hit on something, associate that with something else, working your way back through your life until something clicks.

Freud was the first to popularize this method of association. Dreams and waking life are not so different. Dreams come from your subconscious, a part of you. Therefore, you can take the signs and coincidences from your dreams and apply them to your waking life. If you watch for synchronicities and heed your guides (spiritual, animal, and otherwise), you can change the way things are going and plan for your future. That's what dream interpretation is all about.

In essence, synchronicity is when universal forces become perfectly aligned with your mind or perception. Perhaps you think of a person and she calls, or you know something is about to happen and it does. Synchronicity usually involves a feeling that something was destined.

QUESTION

What exactly is a synchronicity?
A synchronicity is when something happens that strikes you as more than a mere random occurrence. It can be an event or just an observation you make. Noted psychologist Carl Jung, who coined the term, said that synchronicities reflect "a peculiar interdependence of objective events among themselves as well as with the subjective (psychic) states of the observer or observers."

The intent of this chapter is to look at everyday life from a new perspective—the dream perspective. Synchronicity is one reminder that a subtle dreamlike quality underlies your waking life. In fact, synchronicities are like road signs of the unconscious that guide you by pointing out certain patterns to you. As you become aware of them, you begin to notice them more often. You can eventually learn to read these signs and understand what William Brugh Joy calls "the pattern level of reality."

Universal Symbols

Close your eyes for a moment and picture fire. Can you see the red and yellow flames? Can you feel the warmth? Fire is a primal universal symbol. A symbol of rebirth, it contains within itself the power of consumption and regeneration. It is one of the transforming universal symbols deeply embedded in the consciousness of all living beings. Just think about all the ways you use the imagery of fire in your daily life. If someone "lights a fire" under you, he is trying to get you motivated to do something, but if someone "lights your fire" she is igniting your passion. When you dream of fire—even the flame of a candle—you are being asked to come alive in some area of your life. Your subconscious is trying to connect you to that vital, primal energy of inspiration, life force, and passion.

Water is another of the primal symbols deeply embedded in the collective consciousness. The symbol of water embodies movement, rhythm, life-giving nourishment, and the ebb and flow of your emotional nature. If you dream of water, most likely your subconscious is using that primal symbol to help you understand and process emotional issues. Emotional release dreams almost always involve water imagery. Think first of your emotional state when you have water symbols in your dreams.

FACT

Although fire warms us and provides heat for cooking food, you may tend to think of fire as destructive when it occurs in nature. However, there are certain seeds in trees that are only released in a fire. Without the cleansing energy of fire, the new life contained in those seeds would never be born.

Air, earth, stars, the sun, and the planets are some other universal symbols. So are the shapes, and qualities of masculine and feminine. Even colors and numbers are universal symbols. Color, such as the red seen in fire, resonates universally in the consciousness of human beings. Your response to color is instinctual and immediate, even though there may be differences culturally in how certain colors are perceived. You are responding to the particular vibration, or resonance, that color evokes in you. Pay attention to the colors in your dreams as they, too, carry important messages you need to understand. Just connecting with a universal symbol in your dream can start you down the road toward a good interpretation. Jenni was in the planning stages of renovating her home when she had this dream:

I was standing in the kitchen and saw my house starting to sink. I opened the refrigerator and inside saw three large round blocks of ice. Within each block was a chicken—frozen—wings, feathers, and all, and each chicken had a human face. Then I woke up.

Because of the ice in the dream, Jenni correctly assumed this dream involved her emotional response to a situation. When she realized that the house sinking might quite simply mean she had a "sinking" feeling about the planned renovations, she was able to correctly interpret the symbolism in her dream. It turned out Jenni was ambivalent about the renovations and felt she was committing herself and her family to staying in this particular house instead of being free to move to another area that might be better for all of them. In her dream, she and her family were represented by the chickens frozen in place—unable to fly free. Once she understood her dream, she was able to reach a decision she was comfortable with regarding renovating her home.

As Jenni's dream points out, dream symbolism can be bizarre and difficult to interpret. The universal symbol of water in the dream opened the door for Jenni to realize this was a dream about feelings. Once she had that piece of the puzzle, she was able to think about the house sinking and the rest began to fall into place.

Common and Shared Dream Imagery

Below the layer of universal symbols, there are many symbols that are common and shared. Whether you know it or not, as a child you often encountered symbols known as archetypes. In play you might sword-fight with villains, mother your dolls, put on your magician's cloak, or get up on stage and play the part of the captive princess. From your earliest days your psyche has been aware of archetypes and has processed them. An archetype is a symbol or theme that rises from a layer of the mind common to all people. Carl Jung called this layer the collective unconscious. He believed that each person gives these symbols and themes his own individual stamp. The hero is an archetype, as is the villain. There is the universal mother archetype with her ever-nurturing and loving nature. The child is also an archetype. These archetypes appear in the art, myths, and folklore of cultures around the world.

If you would like to understand archetypes and work with them, one source is the ancient system of divination known as the Tarot.

Most historians believe that the Tarot as we know it came into being in the early part of the seventeenth century. Hidden within a drawing room card game, the precursor to the regular deck of playing cards, were messages about various aspects of the human and spiritual experience. The standard Tarot deck contains seventy-eight cards divided into two parts: the major arcana and the minor arcana. Each of the twenty-two images of the major arcana represents an archetype. If you want to understand the archetype of the star, the part of you that seeks to reveal your talent on the world stage, you can use the Star card in the Tarot as a visual and meditative aid.

ESSENTIAL

In the dream state, your subconscious might present an archetype as a symbol in order to let you know an aspect of your life is crying out to be expressed. If you dream often of your childhood, perhaps your dreams are letting you know that you need to embrace more of the child's spontaneity and sense of play.

The Tarot is a good system for working with archetypes because the images on the major arcana cards are wholly symbolic. You relate to the Tarot on a symbolic level, the same way your subconscious relates to you in the dream state. That makes it a useful tool you can employ to stretch your intuitive muscles. It can also help you add new symbols to your internal databank.

Basic Symbols for Daily Life

Once you have become familiar with the technique of categorizing your dream type, you will most likely realize that most of your dreams will be reconciling emotions and events of your day-to-day life. The next level below universal and common symbols includes the traditional and familiar symbols of daily life.

Houses

Demi dreamt she was looking into the basement of her home. She could see through the windows and noticed her ex-husband inside. In the dream she was wondering what he was doing in her basement and how best to get him out when she awoke.

When you dream of a house you are dreaming of your life. The basement most often represents the unconscious or long-buried feelings, ideas, and issues in your life. In this dream Demi can see into her basement, indicating that this part of her life is waking up and becoming visible to her. When she thought about the qualities of her ex-husband, she described him as highly creative and successful in his creativity. The dream was telling her that she, too, is creative and desires to express her creativity successfully in the world. The ex-husband represented a part of herself that she had "divorced" herself from in order to attend to the daily necessities of life. However, that creative part of her was still there and longing to be set free, as her dream revealed.

ALERT

Always notice the location of your dream. Where are you? Who is with you? What are you doing? How are you acting and reacting to the conversations or situations in the dream? Jot down these impressions when you first wake up as they contain important clues for interpreting your dreams.

A house usually represents your life at the moment, and each room of the house relates to different aspects of your life. Most often the living room symbolizes the image you present to the world—the face you show to others—whereas the bedroom indicates who you are in private. The bathroom is your deeply private self that you are not willing to let others see. How you nurture and take care of yourself can be significant in a dream where you are in the kitchen, the place where you prepare food and socialize with family and friends.

Is the house in your dream one you have lived in before, either in childhood or the recent past? If so, you are dreaming about a former time in your life, reconciling emotions and issues still unresolved that are coming into your current life situations.

Vehicles and Transportation

Methods of transportation also serve as common dream symbols from daily life. Dreaming about driving your car, or traveling in a bus, train, or plane, usually symbolizes where you are going in your life.

Maureen, recently retired from a long career in the school system, dreams on a recurring basis that she is looking for her car or her car key. Often she cannot find it. If she does, she has to drive on a long, winding road that curves back on itself, and she cannot seem to reach her destination.

Major life transitions trigger dreams about the next stage of life. Maureen, for example, is not yet clear about what she will do now that she is retired. Her recurring dreams are allowing her to express and release the anxious feelings she has concerning her new life.

Notice the vehicles in your dreams. If you are driving the car in your dreams, you feel you are in control of whatever is happening. If you are a passenger, you don't feel in control of where you are heading or are not yet comfortable with the direction your life is taking.

Your Unique Symbolic Language

Much of dream symbolism is personal. You have your own unique symbolic language, distinct from that of anyone else. It is comprised of the associations your subconscious mind makes based on the record of your life experience and how you perceive what happens to you and around you. As you learn to work with your dreams, you will become adept at understanding your personal dream symbolism—your own inner symbolic glossary.

To begin understanding your personal symbols, use techniques of brainstorming and free association with the imagery that surfaces in your dreams. Each week review the dreams you've recorded from that week and note in a separate area of your journal certain symbols that recur. As you interpret your dreams you will be able to identify what specific symbols mean to you. You might group symbols under the following categories:

- **Setting:** Where is the dream set? In a house, office, restaurant, school, church? Note the specifics.
- **Time:** Note the time, if you are aware of it in the dream.
- **People:** Jot down who appears in the dream, including yourself.
- **Emotions:** Note your emotions in the dream as well as upon waking.
- **Animals:** Note any animals or animal imagery in the dream.
- **Colors:** Jot down any colors that stand out in the dream.

- **Numbers:** Note any numbers or combinations of numbers.
- **Major objects:** Cars, books, clothes, and so on.
- **Major actions:** Parking cars, entering a library, shopping for clothing, and so on.

For each symbol, write down your interpretation of what it means to you or your associations with the symbol. This lets you begin to create your own glossary of dream symbols. Usually your subconscious mind will bring forward the same or similar symbols for particular messages. If you work with your dreams in this way, you will soon become proficient in your own symbolic language, the final subset of dream symbolism. You will learn to recognize these symbols, not only in your dreams, but when they cross your path in your waking life as well.

Techniques for Creating a Personal Dream Dictionary

The best way to create a personal dream dictionary is to first remember your dreams, and the best way to do that is to record them right after they end. If you don't usually wake up after a dream, try giving yourself a suggestion before you go to sleep to awaken when a dream finishes. Using this technique it is possible to recall four or five dreams a night. Remembering dreams is something anyone can do. It just takes practice.

FACT

Many people claim that because they don't remember their dreams, they don't dream. But it's a proven fact: Everybody dreams! The truth is, you can remember your dreams if you really want to. The more you practice, and adhere to a consistent sleep routine, the more you'll succeed.

Take Note

Jot down your dreams on a pad, record them on tape, or keep a special dream journal next to your bed at night. Don't worry about your penmanship. Your scrawls may be virtually indecipherable at first, but with practice you'll learn to write clearly enough so you'll be able to transcribe the dream in the morning. The best time to remember a dream is in the morning when you first wake up. Experts agree that the way you wake up in the morning has a lot to do with your preliminary recall of dreams.

Don't Analyze, Just Record

Avoid making value judgments—just write down your dream as if it were someone else's story. Later, when you interpret it, you might find that what seemed silly or outrageous or insignificant has deeper meaning than you initially realized. At first, you may remember only bits and pieces—an image, a word, or a face. But with practice, large parts of your last dream of the night will come to you. These parts, in turn, may trigger a memory of the dream before it. Eventually, this process will become automatic and as fundamental as brushing your teeth.

ALERT

Think of dream recall as if you were pulling a thread on a sweater. If you follow the thread, you will find more of the shape and pattern and, eventually, the entire image. Before you wake up fully, let that thread take you back to the complete imagery of the dream.

Reference points can sometimes help you remember a dream. Quite often, your own thoughts and beliefs about your dreams are the biggest obstacles to recalling them. A dream may be so unusual, for example, that you wake up certain you'll remember it—only to forget it within minutes of opening your eyes.

Remembering Exercise

To begin to develop your personal dream dictionary, try brainstorming to define key elements of your life. Once you recognize them, you'll have a better idea about what to request from your dreaming self. Start by going over these areas:

- **Consider your relationships.** What are your most intimate relationships generally like? Do you feel good or bad about your relationship with your spouse, significant other, or the people who are important in your life? Can you identify any patterns in your relationships with your parents, siblings, other family members, or friends? What would you change, if you could? In a perfect world, what would your relationships be like?

- **Think about your work and career.** Is there anything you would like to change about your work? How much money would you like to earn? What is your ideal job? How do you feel about your boss and other coworkers?

- **Analyze your physical body.** Do you like the way you look and feel? If you could change anything about your appearance, what would it be? How is your health at present? Do you have any chronic problems? Have you been to doctors recently? What is your ideal version of yourself?

- **Reflect on your spiritual life.** What do you believe in? How do you feel about your spiritual life? How would you like to develop spiritually?

- **Explore other aspects of your life in general.** In six months, where would you like to be? What about in a year, or in five years? Is there anywhere you feel a need for guidance?

As you record your dream, include as many details as possible. The interrogatives—who, what, where, when, and how—act as excellent guidelines when collecting details. Were you alone? If not, who was with you? Friends? Family? Strangers? What activity, if any, were you or the others engaged in? Was it day or night? Summer or winter? Where were you? How did the dream "feel" to you? Was it familiar? Odd? Pleasant? Scary?

Make sure to describe how you feel when you wake up. What is your dominant emotion? Exhilaration? Fear? Sadness? Happiness? Sometimes, when you go over the dream later, you may remember more details. When attempting to recall dreams, also jot down whatever you were thinking about when you went to bed. It may provide a clue to the meaning of the dream.

Dreams impart guidance, even when you don't remember them. You might not always remember the specifics of a dream. You'll only remember that you have dreamed. Then, later that day or several days later, something in your waking environment will trigger your memory of the dream. When this happens, be sure to note the event or experience that prompted the recollection—it may provide vital clues about the dream's meaning or significance.

Using the Dream Dictionary to Understand the Messages in Your Dreams

The best time to suggest to yourself that you will remember your dreams is when you are in a slightly altered state, because your mind is more open at that time. As you drift into sleep, tell yourself you will recall the most important dream you have that night. If you have a specific question, tell yourself you'll remember the dream that answers your question. Repeat this intention several times as you fall asleep. Make sure your dream journal and a pen are within reach.

During quiet moments throughout the day, remind yourself that you're going to remember your dreams. If you have particular questions, phrase them to yourself. Experiment with different methods until you find the one that works best for you. It helps if you sincerely believe you can receive answers through your dreams.

ALERT

The biggest misconception about dreams is that the visual images that surface in the dream state are literal representations of the people and events in your life. Instead, the opposite is true. Each aspect of a dream is symbolic, not literal. And symbolism takes time to understand.

Use the dream dictionary you develop as a rich resource of spiritual truth, life experience, and messages to guide you in your waking life. Continue adding to your personal dream dictionary as common objects appear in your dreams. You want to avoid a static interpretation of your dreams and dream images because your symbolic language will change as you change. The joys and fears experienced by a person at age forty may be different from what pleases or concerns someone at a later stage of life. Be prepared to periodically update your dream dictionary—delete and add information as necessary.

You can become more than a passive observer in your dreams. You can request guidance from dreams, and receive answers. As you begin working regularly with your dreams, you'll discover ways to attract all that you want in life.

CHAPTER 3

Dreams and
the Law of Attraction

How much of what is in your life now (what you've manifested) is what you truly want? The Law of Attraction requires that you release and transform old energy, while becoming clear in your mind and heart about what you want to draw to you. Manifesting is a process of working with energy. It involves trial and error and a deepened understanding of self. This chapter will explain the process of manifestation, and how to use and work with the dream state to recognize and overcome blocks of self-doubt, old beliefs, and fear.

Where Manifestation Begins

To deliberately utilize the Law of Attraction, it's important to understand how the mind works and how to train it to be your tool. If you have practiced meditation, you have experienced the mind's restless nature. Thoughts keep jumping around because of word associations, direct linkage, or internal and external stimuli. With practice, you can train your mind to stay on a topic. When you wrap your thoughts around your desire, sharpen your focus, and feel expectancy, you more easily draw the desired object or situation to you.

Manifestation begins with desire. Your desire for something sets in motion the energetic resonance of attraction. Your thoughts about that desire intensify or weaken the resonance. Thoughts are energy forms, meaning that thoughts, in simple language, are things—they have an existence separate and distinct from the thinker. You may find this a strange idea—to believe that you are not the "thinker" of your thoughts. However, from the spiritual perspective, thoughts are energetic vibrations that exist outside the physical body. What you believe are your own thoughts most likely came from beliefs you were given in childhood—they were thought forms handed down like an old suitcase of ill-fitting clothes.

In spiritual understanding, all thoughts exist in the realm of collective consciousness, and everything (every thought) is present in the mystical concept of the now. So you might want to think of thoughts as items you peruse and consider as if you were in a large department store. It is up to you which thoughts you put in your shopping cart and which ones you leave on the shelves. You can either form an attachment to thoughts or let them go. Most importantly, you have the power (the empowerment) to choose the thoughts you allow in.

Understanding Energy

Atoms are the building blocks of matter. Energy has been called the workhorse of creation. In grade-school science, you may have learned that the energy of the universe can change from one form to another, seem to disappear, move about, or remain available as potential energy. You probably also learned about the two main categories of energy: kinetic (energy in motion) and potential (energy stored or in position to be released). Both energy types have relevance to the Law of Attraction.

FACT

When you eat a meal, your body receives and converts the food it has digested into energy the physical body needs to perform its functions. Excess calories are stored to be accessed later. When you exercise, you expend those stored calories through physical activity.

Energy enables the work of the entire universe to get done, whether the work is fueling creation or digesting food or thinking thoughts. Energy of one type can change or be converted into a different type. For example, electrical energy becomes magnetic when it is run through an electromagnet. But what kind of energy is associated with your thoughts? That's a difficult question to answer, although you can gain some insight by shifting your lens from empirical science to esoteric and metaphysical ideas.

Walking the Path of Manifestation

An easy way to understand the path of manifestation is to think about how a work of art comes into being. First someone desires to express himself through a creative medium, such as painting. The vibration of desire attracts all manner of ideas and options for the fulfillment of the desire. The artist begins to play with the creative process, refining his vision as he goes along, and gains experience in the nuances of his creation. Through this process the artist eventually creates the painting that best reflects his vision. Once the painting is complete, that particular desire has manifested and the artist no longer feels the creative impulse in that same way.

The path of manifestation is rarely a well-paved and oft-traveled road. Rather it is a meandering journey through a landscape, both inner and outer, that reflects your unique life experience, perspective, feelings, and most of all, thoughts. Learning to control your thoughts is one of the key criteria to becoming conscious in your manifestations.

One of the easiest ways to recognize whether or not your thoughts are aligned with your desires is to notice the emotion you feel at any given moment. Emotions are hooked to thoughts. First you have a thought, and then you feel an emotion produced by that thought. This process happens instantaneously, so you may not even be aware that a thought has crossed your mind before you experience an emotional reaction. If you are feeling anxious, for example, a fearful thought has preceded the emotional reaction of anxiety. If you are feeling resentful, thoughts are running through your mind about a person or situation; the resentment is the emotional response to those thoughts. If you feel happy, thoughts are floating in your consciousness that generate the emotional response of well-being or happiness. When you begin to truly understand the power of thoughts, you'll realize that becoming conscious of how you expend your mental energy is vital to creating the life you want.

ALERT

If you use the metaphor of your home for your mind and each room for an area of thought, then you don't want to rent space in your magnificent mind to thoughts that rob you of your zest for life and your ability to manifest your dreams. Be conscious of the thoughts you choose to entertain!

Getting Clear

After you experience desire, the next step in manifestation is to get clear about what your desire would produce. The more crystal-clear you are about the object of your desire, the greater the chance you will receive what you want. Close your eyes for a moment and think of something you either want or need, something that would make you incredibly happy. Set aside doubt and pretend for a moment that anything is possible. Start small. Choose something that does not involve a great deal of urgency, so you can practice working with the power of manifestation.

Do you want to manifest an object, such as a new couch, an updated computer, or perhaps a beautiful fountain for your garden? Would you like to bring about a situation, such as improving your health, getting a better job, or attracting a new love relationship? Is it something you want to do in the world, such as write a book, establish a business, or create a masterful work of art?

Whatever you want, it is best to develop a crystal-clear picture of your desire and commit to it. Indecisiveness may produce some variant of what you really want. The more precise and unambiguous you are, the better your chances of manifesting exactly what you desire.

Tom experienced the importance of clarity when he worked with the Law of Attraction to find an ideal job. "I wanted a job in advertising that would allow me to use my creative writing skills on projects that would benefit the green-consciousness of the planet," he explained. "I spent time visualizing myself working on ad copy for green businesses, and being congratulated for my excellent ideas and concepts. After my first interview with a company that worked with green businesses as clients, I realized I needed to incorporate details about the kind of physical working environment that mattered to me. After the second interview, I found I needed to include specific details about the culture of the company, including openness to collaboration rather than competition. By the fifth interview I had a much more organized and clear idea of what I wanted and found the perfect fit."

This experience taught Tom how to think more broadly about all the aspects around what he was trying to manifest, as well as the specific details that brought his desire into physical reality. Tom had discovered one of the secrets of working with energy. Like all skills you attempt to master, mastering the Law of Attraction is an iterative process of trial and error.

In fact, the best attitude with which to approach manifestation is one of play. Children can manifest quite easily because they are free of the adult constraints that limit what is possible. So, clearly define what you want. Consider all the details possible. If you are trying to manifest a new car, for example, spend some time on the manufacturer's website and build the exact model car you want, with all the bells and whistles. Include the price you want to pay and how financing will be handled. As you visualize yourself driving the new car, smell the new leather, feel the ease of steering—bring the driving experience to life on an emotional and sensory level in order to lock it in with your personal vibration. Then let it go, and allow the energy you have created to bring the exact car you've envisioned to you.

Setting Dream Intentions

What you fervently desire is sure to manifest when you give yourself permission to have it. Think about your intention often and with feeling. Open yourself to all options possible. These steps set in motion the acquisition of your heart's desire. As already discussed, clarity of intention brings more exact results, and faster. Hold in your mind the image of your desired object or situation. See the colors, the details, the size, the weight, the opacity or clarity, and even the time frame in which you want it to manifest in your life. See it in its totality. Think of how you will enjoy it and use it. Know with certainty that it is already in the universe and on its way to you.

ALERT

When your thoughts, emotions, and intention are aligned in achieving the optimal outcome, you will achieve greater success. Conversely, when you slide into a place of lowered expectations and dilute the intention to have the best, you may fail to achieve your desired result. Keep your intentions in high focus and give them plenty of energy and commitment!

If you aren't satisfied with what you are attracting to yourself—negative people, undesirable business situations, poor romantic partners, and the like—you need to change your energy. It's time to send out different vibrations, in order for the Law of Attraction to help you make the changes you seek. Thoughts become more powerful when you magnetize them with your emotions. Intent becomes energized when you clarify your thoughts and think them repeatedly. Examine your reasons for wanting something, too.

By allowing your thoughts to frequently visit your desire and by opening your heart to feel the positive emotion of joy, you support your intention and strengthen the pull of the Law of Attraction. You draw toward you that which is already in infinite potentiality. According to teachers of the Law of Attraction, when you form a strong intentional desire, you shake up the status quo.

Even if you aren't doing things to fulfill your desire, you have initiated a shift in your thinking. That, in turn, sets up a new vibration that opens the way for new objects, opportunities, and individuals to show up in your life.

FACT

In *The Fabric of Reality*, David Deutsch wrote that the veracity of the external reality of a dream within your mind cannot be disproved. Perhaps all humans are collectively dreaming this dream of existence, or are merely actors playing roles in the dream of Divine Mind that spun itself outward from the One into myriad forms and beings.

At night you can reinforce your desired vibration. Set intentions for your dreams to help you either bring your desires into form or alert you to subconscious thoughts or emotions that may block your manifestation. In your nighttime dreams your fears, anxieties, hopes, and true beliefs about who you are and what you deserve reveal themselves. You may not even be aware of conflicting thoughts and emotions that weaken your vibration. Your subconscious holds the truth of what you believe is the reality of the situation.

QUESTION

Why it is so important to uncover subconscious thoughts?
Dream researchers Jane Roberts and Robert Butts, in their book *The "Unknown" Reality*, reveal that dreams alter the chemical balances within your body. The same can be said of thoughts. Every thought creates a chain reaction, or vibratory experience, within the physical body. It is important to uncover subconscious thoughts because they directly affect your vibratory field of energy.

The steps outlined below will help you to set a dream intention that will aid the manifestation of your desire:

- Before you fall asleep, take a moment to visualize your desire.
- While visualizing, ask to be given dreams about your desire.
- In your mind, ask to be shown any unconscious blocks to your desire.

- Ask to be shown any interfering beliefs or feelings.
- Give yourself a suggestion that you will easily recall your dreams.
- Express gratitude for the help you are to receive that night.

If you consistently practice this method each night before you fall asleep, you will find it easier not only to remember your dreams but also to remember dreams that provide direct information about your desire. Make sure to jot down any images, feelings, or experiences you might have throughout the night.

Working with Your Dreams

Once you're adept at remembering and recording your dreams, you can hone your abilities at interpreting and working with dreams while you're awake. To reinforce the dream-recall process, remind yourself at quiet moments throughout the day that you're going to remember your dreams in the coming night. If you have particular questions to which you'd like answers, jot them down—you can incorporate them into your dream intentions at bedtime.

ESSENTIAL

Sometimes, you may think that a dream is too silly or embarrassing to write down, or that it's not worth remembering. Don't judge the importance of a dream or the dream imagery. Do yourself a favor and write down everything. Things you consider insignificant may make more sense later.

You may want to start your day by setting your alarm about fifteen to twenty-five minutes earlier than usual. Immediately press the snooze button when the alarm sounds and go back to sleep. Experts say you will have your most vivid dreams during this time, and you should be able to remember them easily. If you make this a morning habit, it will become second nature to you. If you can awaken naturally without an alarm, you will find there is a dream available to you at that precise moment.

When you awake, don't open your eyes. Just lie there for a few minutes, retrieving your dream images. If nothing comes to mind, move into your favorite sleep position. This might trigger some dream fragment you had.

"For some (as yet) unknown reason," writes Patricia Garfield in her book *Creative Dreaming*, "additional dream recall often comes when you move gently from one position and settle into another."

Weekly, try journaling about recent events in the main areas of your life in order to see patterns and repeated messages. When you have a strong desire, information can come in the dream state from unexpected places. If you take a few minutes each week to jot down significant issues that are going on, whether they seem related to your desire or not, you will be better prepared to work with your dreams. Key areas to consider are your relationships, your work and career, your spiritual development, your health, and overall life circumstances.

As you journal about the various areas of your life, you may find you get an immediate awareness related to your desire. If so, write it down so you can explore it further and develop it in future dreams. If, for example, you experience fear or anxiety in your dreams or notice fear appears as a theme across several nights, you are being given important information about unconscious blocks on your path of manifestation. Work with the Dream Dictionary in Part II to develop each dream as fully as possible. Once you have identified key dream themes or messages, you are ready to actively engage your dreaming self in order to manifest all that you desire.

Using Your Dreams to Inspire and Motivate

As you are learning, your emotions affect your ability to attract the results you desire. Mood is the best indicator of your emotional state. The happiness and passion you feel when you do work you love can quickly change into hurt and discouragement when someone criticizes you. And, as we've discussed, your emotions are tied to thoughts, some so fleeting that you may not even be aware of them.

When working with the Law of Attraction, it doesn't matter whether you simply imagine positive feelings or really feel them. The limits of your abilities, according to many psychologists, are based on your beliefs. The good news is you can replace those beliefs with more empowering ones.

As part of your bedtime routine, ask for inspiration regarding your desires. Deep within you lies the answer to every question you ask. You are connected not only to your own memories and experiences but, through the dream state, to the universal repository that some people call the akashic records. All that ever was or will be exists in the oneness of universal consciousness. Trust that your dreams can and will reveal exactly what you need at any time, if only you are willing to ask.

ESSENTIAL

The words emotion and motivation derive from the same Latin word *movere*, meaning "to move." You are capable of expressing a wide range of emotions, just as there are many shades and tints within a single color. Noticing the intensity of the emotion you are experiencing will yield information as to how entrenched a particular thought pattern is in your mind.

Use the following bedtime process to ask for inspiring and motivational dreams:

- Before falling asleep, set the intention in your mind that you will easily remember your dreams.
- Ask your guides in spirit to give you messages of inspiration that you can use to take actions to achieve your desires.
- Express gratitude, as if you've already received the inspiration.
- Ask your guides in spirit to show you how to best motivate yourself to make any changes needed, so your desires can manifest.
- Affirm mentally that you are open to receiving any and all guidance.
- Express gratitude for the motivational messages, as if you've already received them.
- Visualize and feel your desire as having been fulfilled already.

Believe, intend, imagine, and charge your visualization of yourself with as many positive emotions as you can muster. Philosopher William James said that the unconscious manifests any image held in the mind and backed by faith. Psychiatrist and author, Dr. Judith Orloff, writes, "Your dreams can reveal many truths about your life. They can provide extraordinary intuitive insights, and give you information that can help your health, love life, and career."

Using Your Dreams to Clear and Heal

Imagine a world where, if you were sick, you could cure your body by healing what's in your mind. It makes sense. In fact, holistic medicine believes that the mind and body are integrally linked, and that most diseases have mental and/or emotional components. Your healer would work with you personally to understand the source of your disease. He or she would intuitively probe your beliefs about yourself and help you to identify general and specific patterns in your unconscious. Herbs, bodywork, special foods, and visualization techniques would be recommended. The healer might also suggest intense dream work to galvanize the body's defenses.

Many people have healing dreams that offer aid for various illnesses. As you learned earlier, Hippocrates, known as the Father of Medicine, believed the body sensed the onset of disease and warned the patient in her dreams. The irony is you don't have to remember a healing dream to benefit from the effects. As William Brugh Joy, author of *Joy's Way*, writes, "If we recognize that we are much more than we understand at the outer levels of consciousness, then we can see that the forces experienced in dreams may reflect healing and balancing processes that never reach the outer levels of our awareness, yet are profoundly important to the overall Beingness."

ESSENTIAL

If you dream you are ill, it doesn't mean you actually are. In fact, illness can symbolize how you feel mentally or emotionally. Maybe you feel guilty or regret not doing something. Sometimes you feel sick in dreams when you don't feel good about what you're accomplishing in waking life.

In the pre-waking state, AnnMarie dreamt she was visited by two light beings who performed energetic healing on her body. In the dream, she was fully aware it was morning, that she was in her bed, and that she was in a pre-waking state. She remembered that she had been concerned about a particular health issue and had asked in prayer for healing the night before when she went to bed. During her "dream" healing, she experienced actual physical sensations in the areas being worked on. When she woke up, she reported feeling extremely peaceful, comforted, and grateful for what had taken place.

Sleep provides a wonderful opportunity for clearing and healing—physically, mentally, and emotionally. As you work with your dreams, you will discover that most of the subconscious or unconscious blocks you have that prevent your desires from manifesting come from contradictory beliefs, negative thoughts, or unresolved emotional issues.

ESSENTIAL

Your dreams reflect what's going on in your body, just as your body reflects the texture of your dreams. The inner is a reflection of the outer. This is just one important reason for paying attention to your dreams—your body may be communicating vital information in the dream state.

Ellen dreamt that she was sitting in a house and was not allowed to enter the kitchen where her mother was preparing food. Her mother just called out to her to look in the mirror and to shine light on the dark places. When analyzing the dream, she thought about how her long-deceased mother had been cold and unaffectionate and how she found it hard to nurture herself as an adult. She had a powerful "aha" moment as she realized that the symbolism of the dream was telling her that her experience with her mother was "mirroring" her own lack of self-care. The dream guidance to "shine light on the dark places" not only alerted her to this legacy from her family, but also let her know she had the power to heal and release this pattern.

The body is a powerful repository of memories—not only memories of physical experiences, but of emotional experiences as well. Emotions literally can get held in the body as unresolved energy until such time as you become aware of them and actively release the stored-up vibration. Until you become aware of unhealthy patterns of thought and emotions you cannot effectively clear them.

As you become aware of old thought patterns, limiting beliefs, and negative or unhealed emotions, you can use the dream state to ask for clearing and healing, so your path of manifestation becomes easier. To work with clearing and healing energy in your dreams, sit quietly and concentrate on the particular thought, belief, or feeling that you want healed or cleared in the dream. You can enhance your concentration by repeating a relevant word, affirmation, or phrase. If you choose an affirmation, keep it positive. Say, for example, "I am open to clearing and healing this (thought, belief, or emotion). I bless it and let it go."

Aligning the Conscious and Subconscious Minds

Dream recall becomes easier—and manifestation becomes more natural—as your conscious and subconscious minds align around your desire and your true reality of thought, belief, emotion, and experience. Meditation is a widely recommended and effective way to align the conscious and subconscious minds. Daily meditation can also help you to better understand your dreams and set clearer intentions for future dreams.

FACT

Before yoga and Pilates were popular in the West, trance medium and channel Edgar Cayce always said that he entered a meditative state through alternate nostril breathing: inhaling through one nostril, exhaling through the other, repeating, and then changing nostrils. This method of using the breath for meditation and reaching altered states of consciousness is still in widespread practice today.

You can begin by meditating for five minutes a day, preferably in the morning. Choose a spot where you won't be interrupted and the distractions are minimal. Sit in a comfortable position. Make sure your back is straight and that both feet are on the floor. Don't wear shoes or constrictive clothing.

Start by firmly stating your intent: to remember a dream or to expand on one that you recall only in fragments. Take several long, slow breaths through your nostrils. Watch your breath and let go of your thoughts. Inhale slowly through the nostrils, holding your breath—without tension—and count to seven. Slowly exhale with the tip of your tongue touching the roof of your mouth. Start over again and repeat this ten times.

Relax your body, starting either with the top of your head or the tips of your toes. Feel all the tension being released from each part. Quiet your mind by turning off all your internal dialogue. Whenever you start thinking about something, gently release your thoughts and return to a meditative state. Wait for an image or impression to come to mind. This will feel different than a thought. You may have a sense that it's a message from "elsewhere," a higher part of yourself. If this feels weird, try not to rationalize or analyze, and just go with it.

ALERT

You want to meditate at a time when you are not tired or distracted. If you are tired, you may fall asleep and not receive the guidance you seek. Also, try to meditate on an empty or nearly empty stomach. You'll have a clearer head and you won't feel as groggy. Meditation requires focus.

Once you can meditate for five minutes, increase the time to fifteen or twenty. However, don't feel as if you have to stick to a particular time limit. When meditating to recall a dream, you'll probably feel relaxed and centered, and you'll be able to remember dreams more easily. If you continue to have trouble, ask yourself before meditating why you're experiencing difficulty. The answer should come to you. You have an inner voice of wisdom that's always with you. Use it. As you deepen your practice of meditation, you will find yourself experiencing greater and greater success, not only at recalling your dreams, but also at manifesting what you want in life.

CHAPTER 4

Conscious Dreaming

All creation begins in the mind. To create what you want, you must first be able to imagine it, not just as a passing thought, but with belief and desire. Once you have established a clear desire, what's next? What is your role in consciously creating your desire and what part does Divine Source play? This chapter will show you how to use the dream state to align yourself with what you want while letting go of preconceptions of how things should happen. Using the dream state you will become open to all the possibilities the universe has to offer to fulfill your daytime dreams. You can harness the dream state to access the abundance of limitless potential waiting for you.

Defining the Goal

As you've seen in the previous chapter, getting clear about what you want to manifest is key to success in working with the vibration of the Law of Attraction. You may know what you want, but if you were asked to describe that item in detail, could you? The universe will bring you exactly what you ask for, so it is important to be specific. When you see something you want, you will perhaps remember only the general shape, maybe the color, and perhaps a detail or two. Use the following exercise to establish a clear statement of your intention for manifesting a particular object with as many details as possible.

1. Name the category of the material thing you most desire to manifest (for example, car, house, jewelry, or clothing).
2. Name the specific item, make, or style.
3. Name the color, size, and shape.
4. Does it have a taste? If you desire a wonderful meal at a particular restaurant, you can envision the exact foods and note the flavors.
5. Does it have a scent? If so, write down your thoughts about what the scent is like.
6. Does it have a sound? Sound may not have relevance for some objects, but for cars, musical instruments, TV or stereo equipment, sound is an important detail.
7. Mentally run your hands over the object of your desire. How does it feel? What is its texture?

Now that you have employed your senses of sight, taste, touch, smell, and hearing in order to better imagine the object you intend to manifest, write a simple declaration of your intention. Here's an example to get you started.

I am elated to know that the Law of Attraction is in the process of bringing into my life the _____ that I deeply desire. I can see it clearly in my mind now (mentally imagine it) and am grateful (feel the gratitude) that it already exists in the realm of pure potentiality. I deserve this, am ready to receive it, and know that it is on its way to me and in the right moment it will manifest in my life.

When you affirm and visualize your desire for something in positive language and images, your feeling creates a magnetic vibration that draws the desired object into your experience. Use the following three techniques to clarify and refine your goal.

Correct Your Declaration Language

Use breath work or meditation to move into a quiet, centered place in your mind where you can name and visualize the object, experience, or relationship you desire to manifest.

FACT

Neuroscience has shown that people who meditate are healthier than their nonmeditating counterparts. Those who meditate experience a mental shift of their brain waves away from the right frontal cortex, an area associated with stress, to the left frontal cortex, resulting in a decrease in stress and anxiety.

Tell the universe what it is you want. Notice whether you used any negative words in your statement, for example, "I don't want any more bills." Check in with your feelings. How does the word bills make you feel? Most likely, it conjures a negative feeling. Rephrase your statement to include positive terms and get rid of words such as don't, won't, and can't. Replace the negative statement with a positive one such as, "I desire financial prosperity and the means to easily meet my financial responsibilities." Now, how do you feel? Notice the difference?

Fix Visualization Problems

The mind/body connection ensures that you will experience feelings in response to your mental visualization. Let's say you choose to attract powerful and influential people into your career path. Consider the imagery you are using to depict them in your mind. Do you see powerful people as stern, harsh, and demanding? If you envision them bringing into your life more misery, stress, and unreasonable deadlines and responsibilities, you most likely will feel apprehension and dread. Instead, re-imagine them as warm, friendly, helpful, generous, and wise associates. You could view them as mentors with a vested interest in helping you advance in your chosen field of endeavor.

Remove Confusion

Eliminate any image that muddies or confuses your vision. Perhaps you dream of having a trim, flexible, and muscular body, but you can't get rid of the extra pounds you gained during a pregnancy. You started a walking program with neighborhood friends and are now eating a healthy, balanced diet, but still the weight clings. In your mind, you see yourself in the bikini you wore at eighteen and you are doing affirmations. Why isn't it working?

The problem is that deep down on a subconscious level, you know you can never be eighteen with that same body again. Try taking a picture of yourself as you look today. Adjust your body size using scissors or a computer tool such as Photoshop. Create an image your mind believes is possible to achieve. Psychological experts say that any time there is a struggle between the conscious and unconscious mind, the unconscious wins. You must convince yourself that a flexible and leaner body is possible for the person you are now. Start with a photo image and make it plausible. Paste that image on your refrigerator, bathroom mirror, and scale. Feel gratitude for each pound or inch lost. Find positive ways to reward yourself as the Law of Attraction works with you to create a beautiful, strong, healthy, and leaner body.

ESSENTIAL

If you want good health, affirm it by proclaiming that you choose it and that you like the way your body feels when it is healthy. Law of Attraction experts say that thinking such thoughts makes you feel good. And those thoughts, coupled with the good feelings, place you in tune with the law to attract good health.

Once you have clearly defined the goal, whether it's a new circumstance or object you intend to acquire, you are ready to chart your course to achieve what you desire.

Charting the Course

The most important thing you can do to chart a course of success for yourself is to clear blockages from your mind and heart that may be preventing the manifestation of your desires. If you are going through the steps of deliberately manifesting but aren't seeing results, then perhaps you are subconsciously blocking the outcome you seek. Try these six steps to clear blockages:

1. **Cultivate positive feelings.** Imagine you have just received whatever it was you hoped to manifest. Using that moment as a point of departure in a journal entry, write how you feel about having that object, situation, or relationship now. Remember, the Law of Attraction responds to feelings around specific thoughts, rather than the thoughts themselves.

2. **Feel worthy.** Redirect negative self-talk into positive statements. What are some of the reasons why other people love you? Make a list of all the lovable qualities and traits you have and why you are worthy to receive the gifts you seek from the universe. Love yourself and others the way you want to be loved and cultivate feelings of self-worth.

3. **Make every day a conscious one.** If something goes wrong in your day, consciously shift the energy of that moment as soon as possible. Don't go through an entire day with a negative attitude after some small misstep. Listen to beautiful music, take a walk, lie down for a quick power nap so the dream state can help you make the shift, or offer a prayer or thanks to the Divine. You have phenomenal power in every moment of your life to change that moment, to shift the negative into positive energy, and to regain forward impetus.

4. **Focus on what you want rather than what you don't have.** Perhaps you can easily recount all the reasons why you don't own your own home, but you deeply desire to own a house. Make a list of all the positive reasons why you deserve it, and how living there will change your life. As a point of departure for writing about your hopes and dreams, imagine a celebratory meal in your new home. Take a mental snapshot of how you feel after that writing exercise. Remember those positive feelings every time you experience feelings of lack.

5. **Fine-tune the direction and intention of your desires.** Be decisive when working with the law. It is always at work, bringing you the things you mentally focus on, both positive and negative. Think of your mind as

a canoe floating along the river of life, buffeted and buoyed by forces of energy (wind and currents) you can't see. For certain, that canoe is going somewhere, perhaps places you like or don't like. Instead of going with the flow, remember you can use the paddles of your feelings and thoughts to navigate wherever you choose to go.

6. **Create space in your life for what you desire to manifest.** Consider that the new love of your life might not appear until your current relationship has ended. If a lot of negative emotional baggage is associated with the relationship you are in, you have to clear those patterns of thought. Replace them with positive feelings of anticipatory excitement, hope, and expectation, knowing you are attracting the new love you desire and deserve.

Release what isn't working in your life. Open your heart and mind to allow in new energy, relationships, and surprises that the universe may be ready to give you.

When to Act, When to Wait

You will need to align with the energy of the Law of Attraction to know when to push forward toward your dreams and when to wait and allow the universe to do its part. This can be one of the most difficult aspects of working with manifesting energy. To work with manifesting energy, you must relinquish control of how your outcome will happen. However, there are many things you can do to support the process of manifestation without trying to do the work of the universe in bringing you what you want. Here are four ways to start the process.

Shift the Status Quo Before the Passion Dies

If you hate your job and want to find a new one or perhaps start your own business, tender your resignation. Bless and release the old work and get started manifesting your new dream vocation. Feel the excitement of embarking upon a new path to a new dream. Brainstorm, write a business plan, figure out marketing, find funding, and set your dream into forward motion. When you do, you'll see how the universe puts the wind into the sail of your ship and pushes you quickly onto your chosen course.

Clear the Clutter

Energy flow is impeded when you are surrounded by clutter. Get that energy moving again by tossing out things you no longer use, that don't work properly, or are broken. Also put away pictures and things throughout your house that remind you of the demise of relatives and friends. Establish a special designated area in your home to honor them (for placement, read books about Feng Shui). Nourish relationships with helpful people and you'll open yourself to the inflow of healing, vibrant, and beneficial energy.

Reprogram Your Thoughts

Your outer life is a manifestation of your thoughts and feelings. When you release old patterns of negative thinking and replace them with powerful positive thoughts and expectations that make you feel hopeful and happy, you can attract an abundance of good things to you. Do you desire love with a man who is trustworthy, capable, and emotionally healthy? Examine your thoughts to see why he is not already in your life. Maybe the pain and drama associated with a previous relationship caused you to fear a future one. But if you can't imagine the possibility of a wonderful new love, how will it ever come to you?

Know When to Let Go

Learn to rely on your emotional guidance system of intuition or sixth sense to know when to let go. If something is not right in your life, you may be overriding the signals from your emotional guidance system that warn you to steer clear or break away. The more you rely on your inner guidance, the more you will trust it when it warns you to shift direction.

Sometimes when the things you desire don't readily appear, you have to make space for them. For example, if a relationship has soured and counseling or other attempts at repairing it have not helped, it may be time to move on. If your career has hit an impasse or your job doesn't inspire you, bless and release it.

The Power of Visualization

Law of Attraction experts advocate using visualization when you are deliberately working with the law. Your body responds to the feelings created by positive mental images and thoughts.

ESSENTIAL

A vital step in getting the relationships, objects, circumstances, or life experiences you desire is to allow yourself to receive whatever you are intentionally creating. That is why the affirmations "I am open to receiving" and "I allow my highest good to come to me now" are so powerful and should be repeated often.

Choose one of the following topics and focus on it. Fantasize and visualize as though you had already achieved phenomenal success in that area. As you visualize (no negative feelings or thoughts allowed), focus on how you feel as you place yourself in your chosen scenario. Allow any/all details to unfold in your mind's eye. It's a little like daydreaming your way to success. Write down any insights or ideas for goals, timelines, and specific action steps for quicker attainment of your desires.

- Financial prosperity/wealth
- Romantic love or partner
- Birth of a child or pet project
- Robust health
- Peaceful life or exciting life of travel and new adventures
- Career advancement or establishing/running your own successful business
- Meaningful and passionate work/journey in life
- Spiritual advancement

Feel free to add your own special desire to the list. Reinforce your visualization work by writing a desire/intention declaration or vision statement. Using the techniques popularized as vision boards, create your own manifestation poster (use images, words, symbols, and statements clipped from magazines and glued to the poster) for what you want to create or manifest. Record in your journal all the positive feelings you experience whenever you visualize the desires in your life.

Developing a Gratitude Habit

Some experts on the Law of Attraction say gratitude is the most powerful tool at your disposal to aid in manifesting your goals, dreams, and desires. You can certainly use music, art, affirmations, visualizations, journaling, dream incubations, and other modalities to attract the things you want in your life, but you hasten the work of the law when your thoughts, feelings, and actions harmoniously align in an attitude of gratitude.

Listen to music to lift your spirits as you express gratitude for the price-less treasures already in your life (such as family, your spiritual traditions, your home, and so forth). Let sound draw you into a prayerful mood and guide your thoughts and feelings to create declarations of gratitude throughout your day. You can make music part of a daily devotional walk as you contemplate all the blessings you already possess.

FACT

The Secret author Rhonda Byrnes and the speakers who contributed to her mega-bestseller stressed the importance of gratitude in working with the Law of Attraction. In 2007, Byrnes wrote a follow-up book to *The Secret* titled simply *The Gratitude Book* in which she included affirmations and tools to transform your life.

Art can deepen your understanding and appreciation for the past, emphasize your compassion and awe for the highs and lows of the human condition, and trigger feelings of gratitude for the aesthetic gifts in nature that are all around you. As you make known to the universe your desires—to have increased confidence, heightened self-esteem, better health, a prof-itable new business, the perfect mate, a baby, or any of a thousand other things—remember to be thankful for the things you currently have. Express gratitude with your feelings and thoughts.

Asking for Specific Dream Experiences

Dream work can inspire and enlighten. The most important thing besides remembering your dreams is knowing how to incubate them for understanding, insight, and guidance. When you are working with the Law of Attraction, you will find incubating a dream helps to clarify whether you are on your path or are obstructing the manifestation of something you deeply desire. You can also ask for guidance on how to turbo-charge your intention to get what you want.

Incubating a dream requires a little preparation. Before going to sleep, do some breath work. As you breathe out, visualize dark negative energy that you've acquired during the day flowing out through the soles of your feet and down into Mother Earth for reclamation and transformation. As you breathe in, visualize white light or positive energy flowing in through your heart center and filling your body. Ask for the dream you desire. Be clearly focused and specific, for example, "I open my heart and mind to receiving a dream about _____."

Here are three techniques for dream incubation:

1. **Prepare and pray for the dream.** Ask your dreaming mind for exactly what you want. Don't try to incubate a dream after consuming heavy food or drink as your body will be processing your intake and trying to restore balance. Likewise, avoid incubating a dream when you are extremely tired, grumpy, or overstimulated by work or socializing. Take a hot shower or bath to wind down from your day. Make certain your bedroom is clean, with fresh linen on the bed. You should feel peaceful and ready to sleep. Place the necessary tools for recording your dream close by.

2. **Fantasize and explore every aspect of your dream topic until you can write a short one-sentence dream question or goal.** During a meditation or quiet period, think about every aspect of the type of information you require or desire to receive from the dream. Clarity is essential.

3. **Open your heart and mind to any and all possibilities for information your dream (or dreams) may bring you about the topic in question.** Sometimes your dreaming mind may offer the dream in different ways on different nights. In essence, your dreaming mind brings you the information you desire sequentially, as if it were a flower slowly unfolding and yielding its secrets.

Over time you will become more and more proficient at incubating your dreams. Be patient with the process and allow your subconscious to give you the information you seek.

Trusting Spirit

Perhaps your desire has many steps. Pondering everything that must happen in order for your desire or goal to manifest boggles your mind. Your job is not to figure out how the Law of Attraction works to manifest. Your job is to create the vibration around your desire and the intention, and to stay in harmonious alignment with the law. The Law of Attraction will do the rest.

The higher your level of emotion and belief, the higher your vibration. The higher your vibration, the more swiftly you'll attract into your life the ideal romantic relationship, abundance, spiritual understanding, vibrant health, financial prosperity, meaningful work, or other desires. Self-limiting thoughts and doubt slow or block the arrival of your goals. Keep your energy and emotions high, and use everything you have learned thus far to stay in alignment with the law.

ESSENTIAL

A yogic technique for ridding yourself of a bad habit, such as being judgmental or overly critical, is to close your eyes and focus your attention at the point between the eyebrows. Don't strain, but focus gently and affirm a good habit instead. Keep thinking about the good habit until it becomes ingrained. Use this practice to reinforce it daily.

Poet Jelalludin Rumi, who wrote in the thirteenth century in what is now Afghanistan, left behind a legacy of beautiful mystic poetry. In the following verses, he seems to be counseling people to wake up and not miss the opportunities to learn the great secrets of life. The vast majority of people "sleep" through their waking lives, unaware of the powers within them. Capable of attaining spiritual heights, they seem to prefer the great dream of life instead of awakening to the true reality of themselves as a spark of the Divine. Here Rumi is using the word "sleep" as a metaphor for moving through life without intentionality and focus.

Across the Doorsill

The breeze at dawn has secrets to tell you.
Don't go back to sleep.
You must ask for what you really want.
Don't go back to sleep.
People are going back and forth across the doorsill
where the two worlds touch. The door is round and open.
Don't go back to sleep.

—Rumi, Spring Goddess

When you are awake in your life, you can harness the power of the Law of Attraction. Then true sleep becomes a time to turn within for guidance, insight, restoration, and healing. For many people, the waking life is the unrealized dream and the sleep state the profound glimpse into true reality. Spiritually, you are asked to awaken to this realization: that which you seek, you already are. As a child of the Divine, all creation is your playground. You can do and have whatever you desire. As you attune yourself to the wisdom of your heart, be conscious that you are a spark of the light and let your love flow unimpeded from your heart center.

Reinforcing the Dream State When Awake

Thoughts repeated daily become the instructions for your subconscious to carry out. The subconscious, as you have learned, is also the site of your beliefs and habits. You can reinforce the instructions you set by writing your goals, repeating affirmations, and spending time in creative visualization. You can impress upon your subconscious the belief that positive thinking brings you the good things you desire in life. In this way, habitual positive thinking yields faster results and reinforces work done in the dream state throughout your day.

How much time each day should I devote to visualization?
When you think about how you spend your day, most likely you will realize it is filled with work, activities, chores, and social connections. Very little time is left for you to sit quietly, visualizing what you want to create. Try to consistently set aside fifteen to twenty minutes for creative visualization on a daily basis.

You are a child of the Divine, filled with light and intentionality. Your birthright is to have abundance in all areas of your life, not just enough, but all you desire. Grasping this with your mind and feeling the truth of it with all your heart enables you to manifest success consciously. Open yourself to receive the fruit of your dreams and deepest desires.

CHAPTER 5

Living the Dream

You have within you everything you need to create a life that is joyful, fulfilling, and abundant. Through opening to the spiritual messages of your dreams, you can clear the way to fully express the gifts and talents only you can bring to the world. You possess the power to make your dreams, in many areas of life, a reality. As you continue to develop your personal dream dictionary and devote thought, desire, and action toward your dreams, you build the energy of commitment. And the universe responds with greater and greater speed and frequency.

Taking Small Steps

As you begin to use the techniques learned so far to work with your dreams and the Law of Attraction, it is important that you retrain your patterns of negative thinking. Develop a daily practice of actively engaging your mind in order to heal self-limiting beliefs that block manifestation of your desires. Observe your thoughts to see how much of your inner dialogue is negative in response to thoughts or external stimuli. Statements such as "I don't have time," "I can't help it," or "I can't afford it" are self-limiting. You remember an old hurt, and bring the negative feelings into the present. You see a coat you want in the department store window, but it costs too much. You feel bad. Such instant, reflexive responses must be subdued and eventually replaced with positive responses.

QUESTION

What is the best way to structure a positive response?
Do what author Robert T. Kiyosaki, author of *Rich Dad, Poor Dad: What the Rich Teach Their Kids About Money—That the Poor and Middle Class Do Not*, advises in his books and lectures. Replace the negative, self-limiting phrase "I can't afford it" with the positive question "How can I afford it?" This is a good format to follow.

To create a positive statement for a desire declaration, focus on feeling. For example, "I feel excited that I have all the time I need" or "I am thrilled to know that my talents are in demand in the marketplace and I am attracting the perfect job" or "I am attracting into my life ideal friendships that are vibrant, healthy, nurturing, and stimulating" or "I love feeling abundant and knowing that money easily flows to me from myriad sources." These kinds of declarative statements establish desire linked with positive feelings in the present moment.

Identifying Self-Limiting Beliefs

Law of Attraction experts assert that self-limiting beliefs are responsible for your inability to work effectively with the Law of Attraction to creatively and deliberately manifest. The following exercise can help you identify limiting beliefs. You can then work on releasing them.

Fill in the blanks. Then make a list of other self-limiting beliefs you have. Reword the negative statements into positive declarations that are true and make you feel good.

- I'd like to start my own business but I can't because _____ _____.

- I would run the Boston Marathon but I can't because _____ _____.

- I would like to buy my own house but I can't because _____ _____.

- If I were just more _____ I could attract my perfect soul mate.

- I wish I could lose weight but I can't because _____ _____.

- Because I don't have a college degree, I'm prevented from _____ _____.

- I don't dare attempt to _____ because I'm too _____.

Years of self-limiting beliefs may be sabotaging you without you realizing it. These beliefs reveal themselves in patterns that keep coming up again and again in your life. For example, you attract the wrong kind of romantic partner: "I can't attract a good man because I always fall for losers, just like my Aunt Betty did." Limiting beliefs are often so ingrained that they may seem to be at the heart of who you are, the very core of your being.

Self-limiting beliefs hold you back from personal and spiritual growth. You may harbor a fear of failure, a fear of never finding your right romantic partner, or a fear of success. Perhaps you have engaged in self-sabotage, working hard to achieve something only to undermine your hard work with persistent, self-defeating inner criticism. Or perhaps you have always equated success with "no pain, no gain." With the Law of Attraction, you can have success and abundance—and you do not have to suffer to achieve it. You do have to recognize and release self-limiting beliefs, however.

If you feel stuck or trapped, set goals for various areas of your life—spiritual, health, family, work, and personal. List specific reasons that keep you from reaching your goals, and include what has stopped you in the past. Know that you have the power to release even the most ingrained beliefs and turn them around into affirmations of unlimited potential. Use your dream state and dream incubation techniques to bring these self-limiting beliefs to the surface, so they can be released. As you take these small steps each day, you build empowering energy toward your ability as a creative force in your own life.

The Energy of Commitment

Commitment is the energy of thought, heart, and action aligned and consistently applied. When you commit to your desire, you are telling the universe that you will work with the Law of Attraction to continue to reinforce your energy of belief, desire, and actions. Each day when you take the time to visualize and meditate on what it is you are trying to create, you demonstrate commitment to your process. Each day when you take the time to monitor and shift negative self-talk, and identify and transform limiting beliefs, you demonstrate commitment to your process. Each evening when you set dream intentions to help you realize your desires, you demonstrate commitment to your process.

The universe rewards commitment of time, energy, and action in like measure. When you make a commitment, you unleash a powerful energy—a force that immediately begins to work to bring what you desire to you. The universe and the Law of Attraction do not require that you know everything that has to happen to make your dreams manifest. However, they do require that you align your actions, thoughts, and feelings in a manner consistent with your desire having been already fulfilled.

If you are trying to become physically healthy, for example, your commitment to working with the Law of Attraction would involve setting some goals for yourself regarding exercise, healthy meals, sleep, and perhaps meditation. Your goals might also include regularly visiting your doctors and asking health professionals for their expertise and guidance. Each day you would also visualize your healthy state, feeling the joy of good energy, a flexible body, and a healthy, optimistic mind. Each night as you prepare for sleep, you would reinforce your dream intention for good health and well-being.

However, if you set your intention for physical health and vitality, and then do not practice the self-care that supports your intention, you demonstrate to the universe a lack of commitment. You are, in effect, telling the universe, "I don't really believe that my health is important or that I deserve the time it takes to cook healthy meals or stick to an exercise program." By making the time in your schedule for activities that are aligned with the vibrant health you want to create, you demonstrate persistence and perseverance toward your goals. Through daily actions of commitment you create a partnership with the universe, which enables the shifts you desire to occur.

QUESTION

Why does it take so long for changes to occur?
You are learning with each intention how to work with the universe to create the life you want. As with any learning you do in life, it takes practice, perseverance, and patience to master a skill. Don't get discouraged by the passage of time. You are creating shifts in energy, and at the right moment, you will succeed.

All the power is always in the present moment. When you tell yourself that you will begin something *tomorrow*, it is the same as sending out a vibration that you will never reach your goal. Tomorrow will always be tomorrow. There is only the present in which to create change. You only need do your part and the universe will more than match you. It will present you with opportunities to make your goals easier and easier to achieve. Soon you will start to see results you may never have believed possible.

Letting Go of the How

When you do spiritual work, you must surrender and listen to the voice within. Surrendering to that inner wisdom allows you to know with a kind of understanding that goes beyond logical thinking. Likewise, when you work with the Law of Attraction, you must set aside logic and reason. Cultivate trust and faith, and know with an inner certainty that the law works. When the law gives you even a little indication that it is working, you will feel excited and your belief will be reaffirmed. Your excitement increases your joyful vibration, which, in turn, increases your level of trust in the law.

Working with the Law of Attraction requires letting go of the need to control the time frame during which your desire manifests. Trust that the universe is doing what's necessary to bring about your intention. As the noted psychologist Carl Rogers once observed, "You can't push the river."

The Law of Attraction works with momentum. Things can manifest instantly or take a long time to unfold. Why? A lot has to do with the strength of your desire, the clarity of your vision, and the power of your intention. The universe is rearranging itself to bring you what you want. It also allows you to wrangle with your choice and all the different aspects, elements, and options your mind conceives.

ESSENTIAL

Use affirmations, visualizations, journal writing, and poster-making projects to intentionally reprogram your thoughts to accept that you have been already given what you desire. Your job is to hold the vision. Devote time in your day to aligning your energy, and take whatever actions you are guided to take that support your goals.

Find a symbol that represents everything you want to achieve. Use that symbol as a touchstone throughout the day to remember to visualize, affirm, feel the emotion of succeeding, and know that everything you have created in your vision is in the process of manifesting.

Opening to Opportunity

How good a receiver are you? Many people are wonderful at giving, but not so adept of receiving. You need to be a good receiver to work with the Law of Attraction to create what you want in life. Think about the messages you might have heard growing up about giving and receiving. "It's better to give than receive" is an often-quoted phrase from the Bible. The phrase was specific to tithing, to giving what was needed to those institutions that provided spiritual support and sustenance. As with all things, giving and receiving is an exchange of energies. In fact, giving and receiving are the same energy. Try this exercise.

Draw a straight line on a piece of paper. Place an arrow pointing away from the line at either end. At the right end, write the word giving, and at the left end, write the word receiving. Assume that the midpoint of the line would be the point of true reciprocity, where giving and receiving come into balance. Think about where you are on that line. Are you usually giving or is your giving-and-receiving scale balanced?

You can also think of giving and receiving as a circle. As you move along the rim of the circle you are giving out energy, yet energy from elsewhere is moving around the circle and being offered to you. Do you have your back to the energy being offered? Or are you aware of the cycle of giving and receiving? Are you receptive to what is coming your way?

ESSENTIAL

Your beliefs about giving and receiving may have a lot to do with child-hood teachings in your family. Many people hold the false belief that it is their role to give of themselves, rather than be given to by others. In truth, giving and receiving complete a wholeness of aspects that are meant to be in balance in your life.

Opening to receiving means you are learning to be open to the opportunities the universe has been waiting to give you. Once you initiate your co-creative energy through your intention and desire, the Law of Attraction begins to work. Opportunities to move you along the path of manifestation start to come your way in the form of people, new job prospects, unexpected gifts, and even new financial abundance.

Look at your patterns of giving. Are you giving your time, energy, resources, or material possessions for reasons other than a spontaneous impulse of generosity of spirit? If so, you might be tied into self-limiting beliefs about the need to please and conform. When you give for the wrong reasons (out of a sense of obligation, because it is expected, when you feel you cannot say no, or to manipulate how others feel about you) you may become resentful. It's important to figure out your primary motivation for giving. Are you always the one who raises her hand to volunteer? If you have learned that this is the way you manipulate other people to love you, you are struggling with limiting beliefs of unworthiness. If you give so you won't ever need anything from anyone else and can't be hurt by others, then you hold the self-limiting belief that vulnerability and openness equate with weakness. Think about what you are afraid to give, and you will uncover more limiting beliefs that need to be transformed.

When you understand patterns of giving you can truly receive the wonderful opportunities the universe has for you. When you over-give you under-receive. If you want to strengthen your capacity for receiving, try asking for help. Admit a mistake. Let others know you are emotionally vulnerable and need their support. Fear of rejection or hurt can block your ability to receive; so can fear of being obligated to another person.

If you are fixed on trying to control the outcome, you are not letting things come to you. Instead, you are busy figuring out the universe's job in addition to your own. When you are doing the universe's job, it is the same as saying "no, this is not what I expected," or "no, this is not how it should happen."

Feelings of unworthiness or fear of disappointment can also block your ability to receive. If you unconsciously expect disappointment, that expectation will be met. To become a good receiver, do not take things personally when aspects of what you want don't materialize. Instead, think of the universe as a giant playground where you are practicing and playing with energy—"Oh, look what happened in that case." Looking at the process in a playful way helps shift this pattern of unworthiness and disappointment.

Begin putting your wishes out there in a more playful way. Start with things that aren't emotionally loaded. See it as a process of refinement until your vibration matches what the universe is waiting to offer you. Desired results become just a matter of timing as you grow into heartfelt resonance. Trust yourself and trust the universe.

One way you can improve your vibration of receptivity is through self-care. Do nice things for yourself. Treat yourself with kindness and respect. When you do so, you give the universe a message that other people can also give to you, and that you deserve it. To better open to opportunity, practice these rules of giving and receiving.

- Only give what you can; don't deplete yourself.
- Give whatever makes you feel joyful to give, and when you feel spontaneously motivated to do so.
- Give without expectation of getting a response or something in return.
- Give with a loving heart.
- Practice asking others for help. When you are offered assistance, accept graciously and with gratitude.
- Receive without any sense of obligation. Just experience what it feels like to not have to respond in kind.
- If you are offered something and you really don't want it, decline with love. You will start to develop healthy boundaries and send a message to the universe that you are grateful but are refining your desire.
- Receive self-care by nurturing yourself, which lets the universe know you are worthy of all good things.

Express gratitude for all opportunities that come your way. As you do so, you open yourself to receive more and more opportunities, until you have exactly what you want. Expect opportunities to show up and be open to all types of opportunities. The universe can come up with infinitely better ways to fulfill your dreams than you ever could.

The Infinite Universe

At first it may seem impossible that a person could eliminate his debt, acquire wealth, and grow that wealth into a huge fortune. But the Law of Attraction says anything is possible. Some experts on the Law of Attraction have pointed out that as soon as someone begins focusing on the thing he really wants, the universe gets busy arranging or rearranging the necessary elements and circumstances to make manifestation of that thing possible. When you decide to accelerate the process and work out a plan to allow for that manifestation, myriad opportunities begin to present themselves.

You need only change your mindset and opportunities for manifesting your desire will become more commonplace. The universe is working with you, putting wind in the sail of your dream ship to take you anywhere you want to go and to give you the experiences, relationships, money, and health you desire.

Altered States of Consciousness

Through the dream state or through other methods such as meditation or deep hypnosis, you can experience altered states of consciousness. These are distinguished by the frequency of brain waves, eye movements, and muscle tension. The four phases are as follows:

- **Beta:** You're awake.
- **Alpha:** You're in a relaxed state, with eyes closed, on the boundary between waking and sleeping. You may enter the REM stage here.
- **Theta:** You are asleep, perhaps still in the REM stage.
- **Delta:** You're in the deepest level of sleep, beyond the REM stage and too deep for dreams.

The Beta Level

In this first stage of sleep, the rhythms of the brain are in the process of shifting from beta, your normal waking consciousness level, to the alpha stage, where brain waves oscillate between eight and twelve cycles per second. Your heart rate, blood pressure, and body temperature drop slightly. Your muscles begin to relax, and you experience drifting sensations. "Hypnogogic" images—surreal scenes that usually concern your last thoughts before turning out the light—may flit through your mind. These hypnogogic images are often vivid and psychedelic. Though brief, the images can be as meaningful and significant as longer dreams in deeper stages of sleep. The hypnogogic state—the state between waking and sleeping—also refers to the time when you just start waking up from your dreams. You have the best chances for dream recall in this period.

The Alpha Level

In the second stage, called alpha, you experience a deepening of the drifting sensation as you fall into a light slumber. Theta waves are now included in your brain-wave pattern, characterized by rapid bursts of brain activity. On an electroencephalogram (EEG), these waves appear as spindles and are believed to signify true sleep. Yet people who are awakened during this phase report they weren't asleep, but were "thinking."

Most of your dreams occur during the alpha stage. If you watch someone while he's dreaming, you can see his eyes move back and forth beneath his eyelids. This period of rapid eye movement, or REM, usually lasts for several minutes. Twenty to forty-five minutes after the sleep cycle begins, the spindle pattern of brain waves is replaced by large, slow delta waves. Delta waves indicate the plunge into deeper stages of slumber.

The Theta Level

In the theta stage, the EEG shows twenty to fifty percent delta waves, as compared with the fourth stage, called the delta stage, in which the EEG registers more than fifty percent delta waves. People who are wakened during this phase are usually disoriented and incoherent and only want to go back to sleep.

FACT

In the fourth stage of sleeping, the delta level, there are no eye movements at all. Strangely enough, this stage—when you're in the deepest level of sleep—is when sleepwalking can occur. Because it is such a deep state, most people who sleepwalk don't remember the experience.

The Delta Level

In the delta stage, the high rate of delta waves can go on for periods ranging from a few seconds to an hour. Once this first delta stage is complete, the cycle begins again but in reverse—from delta, you revisit theta, then alpha.

When you enter the alpha stage while already asleep, your reactions are different. Your blood pressure rises, your pulse quickens, and your brain waves are similar to those during the waking state. Except for REM and twitches in your fingers and toes, your body becomes virtually paralyzed. If you are awakened during the REM period, you'll probably remember most of whatever you were dreaming.

In practical terms, this means that if you sleep seven hours, then half your dreaming time will occur during the last two hours. If you sleep an additional hour, that eighth hour will consist almost entirely of dreaming. This, however, is only an average. People who need fewer than eight hours of sleep may simply be more efficient sleepers.

Awakening Powerful Energy Centers

Your body contains powerful energy centers, called chakras, an ancient Sanskrit term meaning "spinning wheel." You have many thousands of chakras that serve to receive, transform, and release energy between the physical and nonphysical bodies. Seven major chakras align along the spine of the human body. Each has specific attributes, functions, color associations, sound associations, and challenges. The main seven chakras are:

- **The root or first chakra**—the spiritual center of your connection to the physical world and to nature.
- **The sacral or second chakra**—the place of your emotions, childhood experiences, and sensuality.
- **The solar plexus or third chakra**—the place of your sense of self, your self-esteem, and your will.
- **The heart or fourth chakra**—the integrating or balancing point in the chakra system.
- **The throat or fifth chakra**—the place of self-expression.
- **The third eye or sixth chakra**—the place of intuition and mysticism.
- **The crown or seventh chakra**—the place of divine connection.

In working with the Law of Attraction, two of the most powerful energy centers engaged are the heart and the crown chakras. Desire arises out of the heart chakra. If your heart is not connected to the thoughts and visualizations of your dreams, then the emotional energy needed to create the resonance around your desire will be missing. Equally important is the crown chakra. The crown chakra connects you to divine source. It is where you find the faith needed to work with the Law of Attraction.

Your destiny, and that of everyone, some say, is to be transformed into spiritually evolved beings. That happens through the awakening and ascent of the kundalini energy up through the spinal channel. Kundalini is the divine transformational energy that can bestow knowledge of the past and future, the mysteries of the universe, and the secrets of all creation when it is activated or awakened.

ESSENTIAL

The Sanskrit meaning of kundalini is "coiled up." Usually depicted in imagery as a coiled serpent, it is wrapped around itself three and one-half times. You may find yourself dreaming of snakes as you work with these centers, a symbol in the dream state that kundalini is moving.

The Law of Attraction will bring you what you deeply desire and need. Your greatest benefit of an awakened kundalini is the culmination of the process of spiritual maturation. Kundalini arousal can bring about self-realization, the recognition and knowledge of the true self.

You can awaken kundalini energy through meditation, yoga, and other spiritual practices. Such awakening confers powers from all the energy centers of the body and brings about divine consciousness. When your heart is open and your mind is beyond duality thinking, you can truly live in the present moment and manifest your deepest desires.

Living Your Dreams

There is no greater feeling than seeing your cherished, long-held desires and dreams manifest. As you work with the dream state and reinforce that work in your waking life, you will find within you a creative power that is always connected to the infinite source. When you work with your dreams and the Law of Attraction together you amplify the energy. You can more easily clear unconscious blocks or self-limiting beliefs this way. You will find it easier to trust in a universe more loving and abundant than you ever imagined. And magical things may begin to happen. Wendy Woods, speaker, trainer, and coach of Principal Watershed Training Solutions, shares the following dream experience:

When I found out that Oprah was going to be at this year's Toronto International Film Festival, I said out loud and with determination and commitment, "I want to meet Oprah when she is in town for the Toronto

Film Festival." I then made plans with my girlfriend, Claire, to go to the festival area, Yorkville, on the weekend. We had both been joking for months that we were going to be on Oprah. That night I had a dream that I met Oprah and hugged her. A few days later we went to Yorkville and I couldn't imagine how I could meet Oprah, but felt it was possible because of my dream.

In the elevator at one of the festival hotels I thought I recognized Oprah's makeup artist and noted the floor where he got on. Later Claire and I went to that floor and, to our amazement, we heard Oprah's voice. When we saw her at the elevator, I gushed, "Oprah we love you. Thanks for coming to Toronto." She walked around her security to come over to us. Both Claire and I said a few more things and then I asked for a hug. Now I never would have done that if it wasn't for my dream, but now it seemed like a natural request. She said "yes"! Who would have thought it would have come true? It was wonderful. Meeting Oprah had been a long-held dream and it was exciting to have it come to life.

Wendy's dream intention allowed her subconscious and higher consciousness to work together to not only manifest her desire, but to describe precognitively how it was going to happen. When she was at the actual event Wendy trusted she was going to have the experience she dreamt about. Her desire to meet Oprah and her dream incubation came together to create the exact vibration needed for the experience to happen.

Like Wendy, you, too, can work with your dreams and the Law of Attraction to live the life you want. As you become proficient at setting dream intentions and developing your dream dictionary, you will find that you can bring your dreams into action. You can weave together your dream symbols with your waking reality to create the unique tapestry of thoughts, feelings, and experiences that express your vibration in the world. Instead of merely reacting to the events of your life, you can now choose to live a different way. By harnessing the power of your dreams, you can live your life from the inside out. As you become more present in your life, you will find greater joy, happiness, and peace.

PART II

Your Dream Dictionary

Two Dream Glossaries

Understanding the symbolism in your dreams is key to successfully interpreting what your subconscious mind is trying to tell you. Regardless of the type of dream, the language will be symbolic, and, as mentioned earlier, symbols can mean different things to different people. As you write down your dreams, keep track of colors, numbers, the setting, your feelings, and other elements.

This dream dictionary is organized in two ways—by symbolic grouping and alphabetically. Going first to the groupings of dream symbols will help you identify some broad aspects or let you look up many common dream experiences. Read the given interpretations, and then decide if the meanings make sense for you. Specific symbols described in each category are repeated in the alphabetical glossary so you can look up a specific symbol directly.

Add your own interpretations and associations as you go along. Write notes in the margins or add your own definitions to your dream journal. As you recognize and record patterns in your dreams, you'll be able to personalize this dictionary to fit your dream life. Happy dreaming!

Common Dream Experiences

Some dream themes seem to be more common than others. It makes sense, considering most people have similar experiences during the course of their lives. Sometimes these classic dream themes express fears or anxieties; other times, they depict joy or triumph. In all cases, though, they tell you what's on your mind and in your heart. Some of the most common dream experiences involve flying, falling, taking tests, nudity, lost wallets, and dreams of sex.

Falling

Dreams of falling may be metaphors for feeling you have "fallen down on the job," or that some aspect of your life is taking a downward spiral. It can also represent a fallen woman or man, a fall from grace, or even the fall season. The interpretation depends, to a large extent, on what is going on in your life. It can even refer to what happened to you within the twenty-four hours preceding the dream. Most often the genesis will lie in your daily life and experiences.

Dream therapist Gayle Delaney suggests that you ask yourself how you feel in your dream as you're falling. Do you feel terrified? Helpless? Out of control? Or is the sensation pleasant? If so, how? These responses can be clues to what the falling means for you. If you have a recurring falling dream, note what was going on in your life at the time of the dream. Had you just reached a crossroads in a relationship? Was an important partnership in the throes of change? Had your children recently left home? Did you, previously, have a drug or an alcohol habit? Interpret the dream. Note if a decision was made as a result of this dream. Let the dream speak to you.

Flying

If you find yourself flying in a dream, it could be an astral dream or an out-of-body dream. But flying can also occur in a dream of emotional release. Carl Jung saw flying dreams as the desire to break free of restrictions, and to gain a new perspective about some aspect of life. As with other dreams, it's best to look at flying dreams as individual experiences. To that end, ask yourself whether the sensation of flying is pleasurable or stressful. Why are you flying? Are you escaping pursuers? Are you showing off? Do you feel elated? Explore your feelings about the dream. Where does the action take place? Does it seem familiar, as if it's somewhere you've been flying before?

Make sure to take note of where you're headed in a flying dream. Your destination can clue you in to where you want to go or where you're afraid of going in your waking life.

Test-Taking and Classrooms

If you dream you are hurrying to get to a class and can't find the classroom, your locker, your books, or other materials that you need to take a test, then you are having an emotional release dream. Your dream is helping you release anxiety about feeling unprepared for some situation in your waking life. It's interesting to note what age you are in the dream. Are you the age you were when you were in school or the age you are now? If you're the age you are now, the test-taking dream is a metaphor for something you're currently experiencing.

In *The Dream Game*, Ann Faraday explains that most of these dreams occur when you feel you're being tested or examined by someone, as in a job interview, for example. Everyone feels unprepared at one time or another. The examination dream is often a reflection of an uneasy sensation of not being ready for something coming into your life.

When interpreting this type of dream, make note of whether you have an important deadline or are under extreme pressure in your waking life. If you're not, then ask yourself whether there is something in your life with which you feel unprepared to cope. In your dream journal, record the dream in detail.

Nudity

In *The Dream Game*, Ann Faraday writes of a young man's dream of being naked in front of a cheering crowd. In the dream, he was exhilarated. What were the circumstances going on in his waking life? Well, he'd recently had his first experience of sexual intercourse, and for him the dream meant that he had shed his moral prohibitions. "Had the onlookers in the dream been disapproving, this would have indicated guilt feelings; for in the objective world, his fellow students would certainly have approved," Faraday wrote.

Dreams in which you're naked can indicate a need to express yourself. Fears, inhibitions, and classic "exposing yourself" issues come up in an instant. The key is to examine how you feel in the dream about your nudity. Do you feel good? Free? Scared? Nude dreams don't always refer to actually being naked. Sometimes you have problems in which you feel vulnerable, and your fears translate into and liberate themselves as nude dreams.

Nude dreams in which you feel exposed are often the result of feeling inadequate or insecure about your position in life.

Lost Purse, Wallet, Keys, or Briefcase

Purses and wallets usually contain credit cards, money, and identification—these are important. In fact, they're society's evidence of who you are. Keys open your door, start your car, and allow you entrance to your home and office. Briefcases typically contain papers related to work. In some ways, these things define you. They're your personal possessions— yours, alone. People in transition from one way of life or mode of thought to another often report dreams of losing personal items. This has to do with a shift in perceived identity. Pay close attention to these dreams.

If you're constantly losing things or if you are usually late for appointments, chances are you know full well that you need to get your priorities in order. Sometimes, if you don't want to deal with these matters head-on, they might come into your dreams. Losing personal objects in dreams indicates a lack of dedication to your responsibilities. When you don't feel you have control over the things that are important, it shows up in your dreams as the loss of personal possessions.

Perhaps, in your waking life, you feel you're not taking care of your financial obligations. The loss of a purse or a wallet in a dream sometimes indicates how you feel about your monetary situation. Closely examine what you're taking care of and what you're not. Most likely, you'll come up with the solution quickly.

Sex Dreams

Sex dreams may not have anything to do with sex, but they can be immensely helpful in recognizing and overcoming inhibitions. Pay close attention to how you feel about sex. Chances are that if you think something is "dirty" or "wrong," it will come up in your dreams—your mind will liberate what your body won't, to give you a chance to deal with your issues. Pay attention to other people's reactions to your actions in your dream. Though these reactions seem to be coming from other people, they actually signify how you feel about yourself. Change your behavior accordingly, and you'll stop having anxiety dreams of this nature.

Many sexual dreams are a commentary on your past and present relationships. These dreams often feature past lovers. The function of such dreams is to help you analyze past involvements that continue to impact current relationships. It's important to look for patterns that mark your relationships, so you can use the information in your dreams to create a fulfilling intimate life for yourself.

You're Not Alone!

If you're having some of the popular release dreams, involving nudity, traveling, losing personal possessions, or taking a test, don't worry. Everyone has them. What's interesting is that common dream themes, like society itself, change over time. For the children of today, new topics may include computer system crashes or being unable to text or get on the latest social media networking site. Still, the same message holds true. These common anxiety-release dreams are asking you to understand your own feelings and to meet and conquer your fears.

Symbolic Groupings

Through the various exercises in this book, you may already have built an impressive glossary of personal definitions. If some symbols still puzzle you, however, this section and the following glossary may trigger ideas that "click." Use them as much or as little as you deem necessary. When you begin interpreting symbols and themes in your dreams, work with your own dream symbols first.

ALERT

Notice details in your dreams—colors, vividness, sounds, action—and anything unusual that stands out. Follow the guidelines given earlier to keep as complete a record as possible of your dreams. The more details you can remember, the more complete your interpretation will be.

Because most dreams are attempting to provide the psyche with information about daily events, your interpretation should always begin there. However, if your interpretation doesn't seem to be relevant to daily events, look for more mystical meanings. When it comes to interpreting your dream symbols, there are no universal rules or meanings.

Use a technique developed by dream therapist Gayle Delaney and her partner, Loma Flowers, directors of the Delaney and Flowers Center for the Study of Dreams. In your dream journal, for each dream, list the following:

- **Setting:** What is the main location of the dream? Where do the events take place?
- **Time:** Note the time of day or night in the dream situation.
- **People:** Jot down the people in the dream, including yourself.
- **Emotions:** Describe your feelings in the dream and/or upon waking. Be specific.
- **Animals:** Notice any animals or other creatures in the dream and describe them.
- **Major objects or symbols:** Note such items as vehicles, furniture, jewelry, or clothing that stand out in the dream. Also pay attention to universal symbols or imagery such as fire, water, sun, moon, and so on.
- **Major actions:** Describe the dream story and the major actions in it.

Have fun with your dreams. Explore them thoroughly, and learn from them.

Animals

Animals you encounter in your dreams can be symbolic or actual guides. Psychic Sylvia Browne calls them totems. She says that before a soul is reborn into this world again, it picks its protectors: a spirit guide, a totem (or animal guide), and angels who will help it through both dreaming and waking life. Browne also says that if you have an extreme affinity for one particular animal, chances are good this is your animal guide. Animal symbolism can be very strong and meaningful.

Animals that appear in dreams may be frightening, charming, or puzzling. But they can also be revealing. The meaning is related to your own thoughts about the particular creature. To one person, a frog might represent luck; to another, the creature might represent transformation. Do some free association with the animal you dream about. It will clue you in to whether or not that animal is your totem.

To work with animal symbols in your dreams, write down the answers to these questions:

- What animal do you feel closest to?
- Has this animal appeared in any of your dreams?
- What were the dreams with the animal concerning?

- Were there other symbols in the dream?
- What did the animal do in the dream?
- How can you apply what the animal did in your dream to your waking life?

As you go about creating your personal dream dictionary, you can add to your knowledge of animal symbols by using a resource such as Ted Andrew's book Animal Speak. If the animal in your dream is a baby, then you might be receiving a dream message about a part of yourself that feels small and vulnerable. Some common animal symbols that occur often in dreams include:

Dog(s)

Dogs are beloved around the world. When you dream of a dog, notice what you are doing with the dog. Is it friendly, threatening, or wary? What color and breed is the dog? How do you feel with the dog? In your companion animals you may see qualities that reflect ones you would like to have yourself. Most often, unless you are afraid of dogs, they symbolize friendship, unconditional love, and loyalty. If you dream of dogs, you might see these qualities in yourself or another person, or you might desire a romantic partner who has these qualities.

Cat(s)

Cats have had many mystical and superstitious connotations throughout history. Cats have been reviled as evil and bad luck and revered as gods. When a cat shows up in your dream, it often indicates you are wishing for more independence in some area of your life. Or you could be receiving a message to be more curious and adventurous. Cats are hunters, so you may be in the process of trying to hunt down an important piece of information or lost object. If the cat in the dream is purring, you may be feeling particularly content in a relationship or situation.

Bird(s)

The appearance of a bird in a dream could relate to a wish to be free, to fly away, or to flee from something. Because birds fly through the air, when you dream of a bird you may be receiving messages about detaching from a situation so you can see it from another angle or perspective. As with all animals, you have your own personal associations to birds. In many cultures, birds can also be spiritual symbols. Among certain Native American tribes, an eagle symbolizes spiritual knowledge. If the bird you dream about is very colorful and has beautiful plumage, you might be feeling particularly attractive. If you dream of a peacock, you may have pride of accomplishment or feel someone you know is stuck up. Dreaming of a mythical bird, such as a phoenix, may portend a rebirth in your life.

Snake(s)

According to *Medicine Cards: The Discovery of Power Through the Ways of Animals* by Jamie Sams and certain Native American teachings, snakes represent transmutation. Snakes do not always have a negative connotation; they also symbolize healing. A snake coiled around a staff is a symbol of health and medical practitioners. It also matters whether or not you are afraid in the dream. What associations do you have with snakes in your waking life? Because many symbols have more than one meaning, it's important to consider them all before making a final interpretation. Analyze your dream and what's going on in your life, and then see what makes sense for you.

Colors

Whether they realize it or not, most people dream in color. Only about 12 percent of people dream regularly in black and white. So, whether you notice the colors in your dream or not, most likely you do dream in color. Like numbers, colors are vibrational symbols carrying important messages for you to understand. You immediately respond to color at a deep, visceral level. Color is one of the universal symbols that crosses borders, cultures, and traditions. While associations with certain colors may vary depending on regional tradition, colors remain symbols shared in collective and universal consciousness. All nuances of color flow from the seven colors of the rainbow. In eastern spiritual systems, these colors correspond to the seven energy centers of the human body. Colors in your dreams may indicate that a specific message is being sent, so pay attention to color to better understand what your dreams are trying to tell you.

Mary often dreamt she was wearing a light blue scarf around her throat. The dream situation would change, but Mary noted the repetitive appearance of the light blue color. Most times it turned up in the form of a scarf, but sometimes it would be a piece of jewelry around her neck or even a high-necked blouse she was wearing in the dream. In each dream, Mary was being given a message about expressing herself. Light blue is the color of the throat chakra, the place from which you speak your truth and express yourself. In her waking life, Mary had trouble speaking up for herself. The dreams of light blue objects around her neck were encouraging her to find her own voice.

By considering the seven colors of the rainbow in connection with the seven chakras, you may be better able to interpret what a color might mean. If the interpretation does not seem to fit, think about the associations you have personally with a particular color or shade of color, and add those associations to your personal dream dictionary.

Red

Red is the most intense color in the spectrum of the rainbow. It has the longest wavelength and is associated with the root chakra, the spiritual center that connects you to the physical world and to nature. Red represents vitality, energy, and physical stamina. It can also correspond to anger as in "seeing red." Because it is the color of blood, it can symbolize the life force. If you dream, for example, that you are bleeding, look to see what situation in your life is literally sapping your energy and vitality. If you are wearing red in your dream you are feeling vital and alive in that situation. Red is also the color of passionate love and sexuality, so when you dream of red you may be dreaming of the passion you have for someone or something in your life.

Orange

Orange is a joyful color. It is the color linked with the second chakra, the place of your emotions, childhood experiences, and sensuality. The second chakra is associated with your emotional nature, water, and propensity toward addictions. Orange connotes creativity. It is a color of warmth, connection, and affection. If you dream of orange, you may be revisiting issues from childhood or opening up your creativity. Because it is connected with childhood, orange can be encouraging you to be playful in the way of the child, especially in creative pursuits. When the second chakra is healed you are in balance; therefore, orange is also the color of balance and harmony.

Yellow

Yellow is the color of the sun and the third chakra. The third chakra is the place of your sense of self, your self-esteem, and your will. The sun is the life-giving force for our planet. Therefore, yellow is often associated with an active mind, happiness, warmth, and vitality. If you dream of yellow, your mind may be particularly active right now, or you could be trying to empower yourself in your work and your life. Yellow is also connected with cowardice, the opposite of empowered will in action. If you dream that something treasured in your life is "yellowing," you may be afraid that some aspect of yourself or your life is fading away.

Green

Green is the color of nature and is associated with the heart chakra. It is the integrating or balancing point in the rainbow of colors. It is the color of money in many nations, so green is often related to abundance on the material plane. If you dream of green, you might be experiencing feelings of jealousy toward another person or situation—the "green-eyed monster" may be present. With the expanding consciousness toward green living, your dream may signify a desire to be more in harmony with nature and her resources.

Blue

Blue is the first of the cool colors in the rainbow and is associated with the fifth or throat chakra, the place of self-expression. If you dream of blue, you may feel a need to express yourself or to communicate with someone. Blue is often associated with spirituality and teaching. A soothing color, it is the color of the oceans and the sky. When blue shows up in your dreams, you may be feeling calm and relaxed. Or you might be feeling "blue" and experiencing sadness about some situation in your life. In some areas blue is associated with improper speech, e.g., "the comic's jokes were blue."

Indigo

Indigo is the dark blue-black color of the night sky and corresponds to the sixth chakra, the place of intuition and mysticism. It is the color associated with the subconscious, the bridge between spiritual and physical reality. Indigo speaks of deep mystery, the unknown, and psychic energy. When indigo shows up in your dreams, you may be opening to intuitive wisdom or experiencing psychic or precognitive dreams. Pay attention when indigo appears, as it could be alerting you to hidden information not obvious in your waking life. If you dream of someone wearing indigo, you may need to be wary as there may be hidden aspects not yet revealed.

Violet

Violet has the shortest wavelength and is associated with the seventh (or crown) chakra, the place of divine connection. A delicate, ethereal color, violet reminds you that the physical world is transitory. If you dream of violet, you may be in the process of having a spiritual awakening or desire to open more to spiritual concepts in your daily life. Violet is also one of the colors of wisdom. If violet shows up in your dreams, you may wish to withdraw from the world and retreat within. You may be a "shrinking violet" and in need of alone time, or experiencing fear about being center-stage in your life.

Directions

The four directions—north, east, south, and west—hold special meaning in many native cultures. When you dream about traveling west, for example, you might symbolically be experiencing the completion of something in your life. You could be literally "riding off into the sunset" or closing a particular chapter or ending a relationship. The four seasons are also linked to the four directions, at least in the Northern Hemisphere. Each of the directions holds universal, cultural, and individual associations.

East

We associate east with dawn, the place of new beginnings. It symbolizes spring. If you are heading east in your dream, you may be about to embark on a new project or a new beginning in some area of life. In many South American shamanic traditions, east is considered the place of the visionary, home to the eagle. It signifies a new point of view or a spiritual vision for yourself and the world. The sun rises in the east so perhaps your "sun" is about to rise. This could mean a promotion or other positive development is on the horizon for you.

South

Daylight is longest and brightest in the south. It is summer here. South is also a metaphor for declining fortunes. If you are "heading south" in a dream, you might be experiencing a reversal in your plans. In astrology the south represents the past and your origins. If you dream of returning to the south, you may be revisiting your past or past lives. South American shamanic traditions connect the south with shedding the old and the past, so the present can come into being.

West

In many traditions west is the place of the adult. It is associated with the season of autumn. New life, born in the east, has moved through the ties of the past (south) and come into full expression in the west. In the history of the United States, the west signifies a place of adventure, exploration, and the courage to move into the unknown. In Peruvian shamanic traditions, west is the path of the warrior who has moved beyond fear and stands in harmony, balance, and peace. Because the sun sets in the west, a dream of moving in a westerly direction may indicate something is coming to an end in your life. Or, you may be experiencing a peak in your professional or personal life as west also represents the place of attainment.

North

North is the place of dormancy, winter, and hibernation. The compass point north also shows direction in life. You follow the North Star. It is the reference point for finding your way in the world, and has been for centuries. If you are searching for "true north" in your dreams, you might be trying to find your own core of integrity. If you are heading north, it might be time to lay fallow, to withdraw and turn inward so you can rest and regenerate. In Native American traditions, north is the place of the elder or ancestor, the direction of wisdom, retreat, and healing.

House

Houses appear frequently in many people's dreams. You might find yourself dreaming you are in your house, perhaps in a particular room with people and events from daily life symbolically unfolding there. Overall you can think of a house in your dream as representing you or your life in the larger context. If you dream you are in your childhood home, perhaps your subconscious is letting you know that whatever is happening in your current life has its roots in your childhood experiences. If you dream you are in a hotel, you might feel you are not "at home" in some part of your life. Consider recent events and situations where you might have felt out of place or not totally comfortable with what was happening. If you dream you are in an office, most likely you are processing experiences and emotions about your work life and career. The various rooms in a dream house represent different facets of your life; their meanings correspond to their uses in your waking life. Here are some common interpretations for the rooms in a house:

Living Room

The living room is the main room in most houses where you greet your guests and socialize. Most often when you dream you are in your living room you are dreaming about the image you project in the world. Your dream might be concerned with how you want other people to see you. Depending on the emotions and actions in the dream, you may feel you are being judged unfairly, or that who you truly are and the image you want people to have of you are inconsistent. The people in the dream as well as what transpires during the dream scenario will reveal specifics about how others see you.

Kitchen

For most people, the kitchen connotes the "heart" of the home. This is the place where you were nurtured with food and sustenance in childhood and where you still nourish yourself and your loved ones. The kitchen is connected with family and friendship, and how well you feed and care for yourself. If your dream is set in the kitchen, think about how you are nourishing yourself. Do you feel nourished by the events of your life? The kitchen is also the place where you might chat with neighbors, family, and friends; therefore, kitchens in dreams can also signal intimate conversations you might have had or want to have with others—or even with yourself. When you dream you are in a kitchen, think about what you were "fed" (thoughts, beliefs, feelings, events) growing up and what you feed yourself today. Usually the kitchen represents nourishment of an intangible kind. This symbol lets you know where you need to better care for yourself or where you feel uncared for in some part of your life.

Bedroom

In the bedroom you dream, rest, restore, and experience romantic, physical, and emotional intimacy. When your dream is set in the bedroom, most likely you are processing something about your intimate relationships and/ or your physical and emotional needs. Sometimes noticing you are in your bedroom in a dream can trigger a lucid dream—a dream in which you realize you are dreaming even though you don't wake up. Think about the emotional and romantic relationships in your life when your dream is set in your bedroom. Consider whether or not your needs for intimacy and connection are being satisfied. Even dreams of sex are often about unexpressed desire for greater intimacy with someone rather than the physical act of sexual intercourse.

Bathroom

The bathroom is the most personal of dream locations, where your most private self comes to your attention. In the bathroom you hide yourself from the eyes of others to perform intimate personal functions. If your dream is set in the bathroom, you may be processing old feelings of shame and embarrassment. Your dream may also be letting you know where you have feelings of inadequacy about your self-image or body-image. What is it about yourself that you want to keep private from others? Because the bathroom is where you eliminate bodily wastes, dreaming you are in your bathroom can mean you want to release or get rid of emotional or mental "waste" in your mind, heart, or life. If you dream you are trying to go to the bathroom, you might need to. Your physical body sensations will intrude into the dream state to let you know when you need to wake up.

Basement

Even if you don't have a basement in the house you live in you may dream you are in the basement. The basement most often represents the unconscious or long-buried feelings, ideas, and plans for your life. When you dream of being in a basement you are connecting with your subconscious mind, the source of that long-buried information. You could also be unearthing something hidden in your past that you need to examine.

Attic

Whether or not you have a real attic in your home or grew up in a house with an attic, you might find yourself dreaming you are in an attic. Usually, the attic is the place of memories and family legacies. If you dream you are in the attic, you may be feeling nostalgic about the past, or you may be processing family patterns that cause distress in your waking life. The attic can also be the place of rediscovered treasures you didn't know you had. If you dream you find some precious heirloom in the attic, your subconscious is alerting you to gifts within you that you need to rediscover and express.

Nature

The natural world surfaces in the dream state to reveal more about your inner world. Like animals and other dream symbols, nature symbols can have multiple layers of meaning. They depend on the universality of the natural element, such as a mountain or a waterfall, as well as your unique associations with nature. A nature element in a dream may represent the quality of that element—or it might even represent you. Consider the other factors already discussed, such as location, feelings, and actions, in connection with the particular nature symbol to better understand what your subconscious is trying to communicate.

Tree(s)

When you dream about a tree it may represent a desire to be out in nature. Trees can also symbolize a part of your life, your body, or even your home. In dreams trees may indicate whether or not you feel securely rooted in your life. Notice whether or not the tree has leaves or flowers. Is it in the process of shedding leaves or in the dormancy of winter? Dreaming about a tree whose leaves are falling may be a message that some part of you or your life is in transition. Perhaps you are losing something that once was an important part of you. A tree in winter, bare of leaves, may mean you feel exposed in some way at the present time. Dreaming of a tree whose roots are exposed may mean you are being uprooted and worry whether or not you will be safe. Trees can represent your foundation and sense of security—even your heritage and ancestry (i.e., your family tree). When a tree shows up prominently in your dream, think about all the associations and the dream content to determine what makes the most sense. Notice the type of tree as well. In some traditions, different types of trees represent various qualities, characteristics, and even magical properties.

Kathy dreamt she was outside in her front yard. There was a big tree with several branches in the yard. She wanted to cut off one of the branches but felt she wasn't ready yet to do that. She woke up.

In this dream, the tree represented the dreamer herself and her current life. After working through what was going on in her life at the time, Kathy was able to see that the branch she wanted to cut off represented a significant change she wanted to make in her life. She was not confident that the change would work out. Her dream helped her understand the importance of this change. When asked what associations she had to trees, Kathy talked about growth, death and rebirth, shelter, and deep roots. The change she was contemplating shook her own "roots"; she feared she would be losing an important part of herself in the process. Once she had interpreted the dream, Kathy was able to work through her feelings around the change and the pending decision, which enabled her to move ahead with greater confidence.

Stone(s)

Stones, rocks, and boulders in dreams can have several meanings depending on the circumstances and your feelings in the dreams. A stone can represent a person in your life whom you feel you cannot reach on an emotional level. Someone could be "stone cold" to what you want, need, and desire. You may have withdrawn emotionally from a relationship and your dream imagery is letting you know that your feelings have gone cold for that person. If in your dream you are dodging stones, consider whether you are feeling attacked on some level in your day-to-day life. Because stone is hard, dense, and enduring, it can also represent qualities of strength, endurance, and solidity. You may feel that someone in your life is a solid person or that you yourself possess these qualities. If someone is being stoned in a dream, you may actually be receiving an intuitive message that either someone you know is addicted to drugs or feels victimized. Examine issues in your current life, as well as your own associations and connotations about stones, to come up with the interpretation that works best for you.

Dirt

When you dream about earth or dirt, you may feel "dirty" about some recent action. Or, you may be trying to bury feelings that make you uncomfortable. If you are experiencing stress at work or in your life in general, your dreams about the ground may symbolize your desire to "ground" yourself and your anxious feelings.

Grass

Dreams set in meadows or tall grass have a mystical, fluid quality to them. You may be in a period of new growth in your life and in the process of discovering different aspects of yourself. If you are barefoot, you feel part of whatever is happening. If you dream you are lying in a meadow in an idyllic setting, you feel in the flow of events, secure with the natural and instinctual side of yourself. Dreams about awakening sensuality often involve tactile imagery like soft grasses, wildflowers, and color and light. Think about where in your life you may need to reconnect with your natural sensuality.

Flowers

Flowers have universal connotations of celebration, love, and ceremony. If you dream of dead flowers, however, you are dreaming about a part of yourself or your life that is in the past. If you dream of flower buds, you are opening to new experiences or aspects of yourself. If the flowers are in full bloom, you feel confident and fulfilled at this time in your life. Flowers represent your own unfolding, so think about what in your life may be just beginning, flowering, blooming, or past the peak. The type of flower will also have particular associations. Roses, for instance, symbolize love, whereas lilies are linked with purity, death, and resurrection. Think about the color and type of flower in your dream and the connotations you have to decipher your dream's message.

Numbers

Numbers are among the oldest symbols. In many spiritual traditions numbers possess mystical significances and hidden meanings. Think for a moment about the singular vibration of the number one. It conveys independence, solitude, beginnings, wholeness—all at the same time. When numbers show up in your dreams, they always bring a message.

When Cathy was planning to move out of the city, she was drawn to a new housing development being built along a river. The night before she planned to go and select her building lot she dreamt she could see the mailbox outside her house. On it was the number eleven. Cathy took this to mean she was supposed to purchase building lot eleven. However, when she arrived at the sales office the following day, lot number eleven was already in contract. Disappointed, she contracted for the next best lot, which was number fifteen. Many months of construction followed. Finally moving day came. When Cathy arrived at her new home, the mailboxes were just going up. The post office had numbered the street and on her new mailbox she saw the number eleven. While Cathy had interpreted her dream to mean she was supposed to purchase lot eleven, instead she now understood her dream had been telling her the address of her new home.

Numbers will show up in dreams singly or in groups. Look at them both as individual numbers and in combination to understand what they are trying to tell you. If the number is easily understandable, your date of birth for instance, then the numbers represent your vibration in the world and in the situation. The following are some common interpretations. Many more can be found in spiritual texts from around the world. Expand these definitions with your own affinity for numbers and your numerical symbolic language will become rich and clear.

FACT

The mystical study of numbers is called numerology. According to its tenets, you have a "life path number" derived from your birthday. Your birth number is your particular vibration in the world. Numerology can help you understand your individual gifts and challenges. Your birth numbers may show up often in dreams and in waking life as messages from spirit.

Zero

Zero is the empty space, the void, the unknown. When zero shows up in your dream, the answers you seek may not yet be known. You could also be experiencing emptiness in some area of life. On the positive level, you are ready to receive new gifts from the universe once you have allowed yourself to create open space in your life.

One

The number one is almost always linked to new beginnings, whether it shows up alone or in combination with other numbers. One is the initiator, usually a very positive indicator of moving in a new direction in life. It is also the divine unity. You become one with another. In some cases it can indicate a time period such as one month or one year.

Two

The number two is the number of relationship and partnership. When it shows up in your dreams it may refer to your personal relationships, the opportunities and the challenges. It is also the number of harmony and balance as well as the number of duality—of opposites. You may be asked to make a choice between two options.

Three

Three is the number of the universal triangle, the trinity, and the mysteries of body, mind, and spirit. Three almost always represents creative self-expression. It may also refer to the nurturing mother energy. If three shows up in your dreams, perhaps you are being prompted to begin or continue a creative project. If you are dreaming about a relationship and three shows up, beware of a triangle; however, the portent of a pregnancy is also possible.

Four

Four represents the masculine, father energy in numerical symbols. It is the number of stability, structure, and foundation. Even the appearance of the number with its square 90-degree angles suggests firmness and support. When four shows up in a dream, look to issues of fatherhood or with your father. Your dream might also be bringing messages concerning your own stability and security in life, financial or otherwise.

Five

Five is the connecting number—the swing number between the four basic symbols and the higher numerical vibrations. It reflects the shift from the more purely personal numbers of 1, 2, 3, and 4 (self, duality, mother, and father) toward the transpersonal experiences reflected in 6, 7, 8, and 9 (others, spirituality, eternity, and cycles). As such it usually represents change when it shows up in a dream. Change is unpredictable and can bode good or ill, so notice the situation when five comes into your dreams. Five can also represent the struggle between freedom and discipline, and can give you important messages about how you approach goals and tasks. If you are giving someone "high fives" in your dream, you are celebrating an accomplishment or shared success.

Six

Six is usually associated with career, so notice what is happening with your work life when six shows up in your dreams. According to the Bible it took six days to create the world, so some spiritual texts associate it with worldly pleasures and the imperfection of humankind. Six also symbolizes romantic love relationships—the sensual lover aspect—whereas the number two depicts all types of relationships. If in your dream you are at "sixes and sevens," it suggests you are scattered and need to organize your thinking regarding a particular situation.

Seven

Seven is the number of spiritual attainment, connection to the Divine, and luck. There are seven days in the week, seven sacraments in the Roman Catholic faith, seven main chakras in the body according to Hindu and Buddhist traditions, seven notes in the musical scale, and seven colors in the rainbow. Even in mythology and folklore, the number seven shows up repeatedly (think about Snow White and the seven dwarves). If seven appears in your dreams, expect good luck with a spiritual foundation. Meditate on the number seven to understand how you can best develop and work with spiritual energy in your own life.

Eight

Eight is the number of infinity, eternity, and also universal abundance. A visually beautiful number, eight depicts balance and symmetry. When eight appears in a dream, you may be about to make a major romantic commitment or celebrate an anniversary. It may also signify that opportunities for financial growth are on the horizon. Like seven, eight is a "luck number," so good fortune could be on the way if eights show up in your dreams. If you dream you are "behind the eight ball," however, you have missed out on a lucky opportunity or have been blocked from success somehow.

Nine

Nine is the number of completion and endings. It also celebrates accomplishment. You may have attained a goal. If so, celebrate and acknowledge yourself and your accomplishments. You may be experiencing an end to a career, lifestyle, relationship, or even an outdated way of thinking. Nine encourages you to let go of what no longer serves you. When nine shows up in a dream, ask for support in releasing what is meant to move out of your life. If you are "dressed to the nines" in your dream, you have reached the pinnacle of elegance and opulence.

Physical Body

Often the physical body is represented in the dream state through symbols other than the literal body. However, when you go to sleep, any distress you are feeling in the physical body, such as heartburn or muscular aches, may express itself symbolically in the dream state. Pay attention to dreams about your physical body—there may be a literal problem you need to address. If you have a pain in your lower back while sleeping, your dream state will bring that pain into a dream situation to get your attention—it might even awaken you so you can shift position. It is not uncommon to dream of the physical body in detail; however, those parts of the body that you most closely associate with your identity are the ones that will have the greatest symbolic meaning.

Hand(s)

George Gurdjieff, a nineteenth-century Russian mystic and teacher, believed you could train yourself to look for your hands when you were dreaming in order to become lucid in the dream, stop the dream, and carefully examine your surroundings. In that way, seeing your hands was a trigger to remember you were dreaming. When you dream of your hands, notice what action your hands are performing. If you are shaking someone's hand in a dream, you might be anticipating a successful partnership, concluding an agreement you are satisfied with, or saying hello or goodbye to a person or situation. If you are grasping or trying to grasp something and having difficulty, this is a form of anxiety dream. Think about what you are trying to obtain or achieve that keeps eluding you. If you dream of clapping your hands, it suggests you feel joyful and appreciated about some accomplishment in your life.

Face(s)

If you see your own face in a dream, this is a symbol for the face you show to others and the world. Your face is your identity in the public arena. It represents the most public aspect of your persona. Other people or elements in the dream may represent various facets of your persona. In the dream notice the expression on your face, as well as the feelings and situation in the dream. The dream most assuredly will be trying to reveal something about you that hides beneath your public "face." If the face is the main element of the dream and you dream you are turning away, you may be having difficulty facing some situation or behavior in yourself or other people.

Teeth

Dreaming of teeth is one of the more common and shared dream experiences. Interpretations can range widely, depending on what is happening to your teeth in the dream. On the most basic level, you show your teeth when you smile or feel comfortable enough with another person to relax. Teeth are part of your appearance to the outer world, so if you dream of losing your teeth or that your teeth are dirty or damaged, you are having an anxiety dream in which you are worried about how you appear to others. Teeth also are instrumental in the process of taking in nourishment. Therefore, a dream about teeth may indicate you are receiving information about your ability to nourish yourself or to digest something in your life. If you dream you are biting something, you might desire to "sink your teeth into" a project or undertaking. A dream about your teeth falling out expresses anxiety. What's going on in your life that is causing anxious feelings? Where do you fear you might be seen as inadequate?

Feet

You get around in the world on your feet. Your feet enable you to move forward in life. When you dream about your feet, notice whether they are bare or shod. Bare feet may signify that you feel comfortable, relaxed, and free about a situation in your life. If you have difficulty moving your feet in the dream, consider where you may be fearful of moving forward. If your feet are firmly placed in the dream, you feel confident of your ability to get where you need to go in life.

Shapes

Geometric shapes are ancient universal symbols that often surface in dreams. Notice shapes that appear in your dreams, and when you remember them jot them down. By examining shapes and your corresponding feelings and actions in the dreams, you can interpret another layer of meaning in the dream's content. The basic shapes and their meanings are as follows.

Circle

A circle in Jungian terms represents the self and wholeness. It can also symbolize protection or social connections, as in a circle of friends. If you're "circling around something," caution is indicated. If you dream you are "going in circles," you are confused about how to proceed in an area of life or feel frustrated that you are not accomplishing what you set out to do. Dreaming of a circle can also portend a desire to marry, as a ring's circular shape might indicate dreams of partnership. If someone gives you a ring in a dream, it may represent your desire to marry or move your relationship to the next level. In many cultures, artists paint or create mandalas, large circles representing the spiritual nature of life. Notice the colors and designs of your circle as many layers of meaning may be present. If you dream you are inside a circle looking out, you may feel trapped by a situation or feel a need to protect yourself from some person or situation.

Square

A square represents solidity and a strong foundation. If you dream of square shapes, you may need to be more precise in your work or life. Squares may also indicate you are building a strong foundation in some area, or are trying to "square things" with someone else if there has been a misunderstanding or dispute. If you are called "square" in your dream, you may feel left out of a group or that you don't fit in somehow. If you are hiding in the corners of a square structure in your dream, you could feel "cornered" and want to protect yourself. A square can also represent equality and balance, as no side of a square is longer than another. If you dream of a town square, you may be feeling the need to get together with others for companionship and common activities.

Triangle

Triangles have many spiritual and mystical meanings. A triangle in a dream could represent the Holy Trinity or body, mind, and spirit. In relationships, triangles signify unfaithfulness or betrayal. Perhaps you feel you are caught in the middle between two people. If you are dreaming of triangles, you may have three projects or concerns with which you are dealing and each may feel equally important. Triangles in dreams can also indicate you need to look at a situation from more than one angle to see the whole picture. A triangle has beautiful symmetry and harmony—you may be in a period in life where you feel balanced and peaceful. If you dream of a pyramid, you may be remembering past lives or desire greater mystical knowledge.

Transportation

One of the most common dream experiences involves transportation of some kind. In dreams, almost all modes of transportation are symbols for where you are trying to go in your waking life. The type of vehicle has more specific meanings. Whether or not you are in control of the vehicle indicates whether or not your feel in control in your daily life or the transition you are experiencing. You may find that transportation symbols surface in your dreams during times of change or when you are striving to accomplish a goal. When you are trying to create something new or are in the midst of a transition, transportation symbols show you the truth of the situation and reveal whether you are in control of your destiny. Here are some of the most common transportation symbols.

Car

When you dream you are in a car, notice everything you can about the car. Is it going forward or in reverse? Is it a shiny new model or an old clunker? Are you the driver or a passenger? Are you in the front seat or the back? Are you traveling on a straight or winding road? Is the car going too slow or too fast? Is the car broken down or are you having trouble starting it? These questions will give you clues as to how you feel about your capability to get where you want to go in life. The car symbol can also tell you a lot about what you feel you deserve in life or how you see your station in life as compared to others'. If you are sitting in the back seat, perhaps you are depending on another person to get where you want to go in life (the ultimate back-seat driver). If you are a passenger, you don't feel you really are in charge of what is happening.

When Jim was laid off from his job during a corporate downsizing, he had recurring dreams of being a passenger in a car. He felt frustrated that he couldn't control where the car was going or how fast. The dreams were helping him express his frustration at the life change that had been forced upon him by decisions that were not his own. His sense of helplessness surfaced at night in his inability to control where the car of his dreams was taking him.

If you are driving the car, you may feel you have power in connection with the change taking place. However, even if you feel in control, the car may have fits, or stop, or circle back around. Perhaps it must climb a particularly steep hill. All these events indicate the level of difficulty you feel you must face to move forward in your life and get where you want to go. If the car is going backwards, you may feel you are slipping backwards in some area of life or work.

Bus

Dreaming you are on a bus is similar to a car dream, except that you are with other people on a vehicle that makes stops along the way. What is different about riding in a bus instead of a car is that a bus has a predetermined route and destination. When you dream you are on a bus, you know you will eventually reach your destination, even though you may be impatient with the stops and starts along the way and your inability to control the length of time it takes to reach your destination. Buses usually have fairly frequent schedules—you always can catch the next bus if you miss the one you wanted. The bus, in that way, speaks to the mundane, predictable nature of daily life.

Train

Like a bus, a train in a dream means you are on this journey with others having a similar experience. Also, like a bus, you are collectively subject to a schedule and route that is predetermined by those in authority. You might dream you are on a train when you feel conflicted about decisions authorities are making that affect a group of people. Trains can also indicate that you feel you have a long way to go to reach your destination as trains often travel over longer distances than cars or buses. If you commute to work by train, you might reconcile events from your workday by dreaming you are on a train trying to get from one place to the other. Trains also contain wonderful connotations from childhood. If you dream of a toy train set, you may be revisiting childhood memories of adventure and travel. Your subconscious may be asking you to again embrace those childhood dreams and plans.

Bicycle, Unicycle, Motorcycle, Tricycle

If you dream you are riding on a bicycle you believe you can accomplish what you want under your own power. Your own hard work will get you where you want to go. Notice the number of wheels on your cycle and whether or not you are comfortable riding it. Riding on a unicycle requires balance and skill. If you dream you are on a unicycle and fear falling, you may be experiencing similar emotions in your daily life. Perhaps you're engaged in a project or situation that requires a great deal of finesse and skill that you are not confident you possess. A tricycle indicates you feel you require support to get where you want to go, or perhaps you need additional training to be successful. A motorcycle is like a car in that you should notice the model, make, size, and any other pertinent details. Motorcycles are associated with rebels so you might feel the need to rebel against some part of your life that seems restrictive. A motorcycle can also symbolize the need for freedom. Do you feel burdened with responsibility in your daily life? At night your desire for independence and a carefree life emerges.

Boats

Like cars, boats in dreams can come in all sizes, shapes, and degrees of power. If you are rowing or sailing your own boat, you feel in control of a situation in your waking life. If you are a passenger on a ferry or other boat, you probably don't feel you can control what happens. The important thing about a boat as a symbol is that boats traverse water, and in dreams water relates to your emotional life. Anytime you dream you are on a boat you are trying to move through an emotional situation, either a current one or one from the past. If the boat is trying to break through ice, your feelings around the issues are old, frozen, and hard to access. If the boat is navigating through rough seas, you are experiencing emotional ups and downs about something in your life. If you are in a small boat and cannot get to shore, you are feeling out of control with regard to an emotional issue in your daily life.

Planes

The most important distinction about planes in dreams is that planes traverse the medium of air. This clue signifies that plane dreams represent your thoughts or even spiritual matters, because the air element is associated with the mind. If you dream you are flying a plane, you may be making a shift in how you think about your life. Perhaps you are gaining new perspective on a situation or experience. If you are a passenger on a plane, you are being guided, perhaps by divine energy, to change how you think about things, or to change beliefs that no longer support who you are. If you are in a plane experiencing turbulence, your dream suggests you are struggling in your waking life with changing thoughts and beliefs; you are not yet reconciled to a new point of view. If you dream the plane is going to crash, you are releasing fear in the dream state that you won't be safe or survive if you let go of your old way of seeing things.

Universal Symbols

The four elements we discussed earlier are universal symbols stored in the consciousness of everyone. Each element is associated with a particular aspect of being and has practical as well as mystical meanings. The element is often the dream milieu. It is the stage on which the dream drama is played. If you correctly identify and interpret the meaning of one of the elements in your dreams, you will have gathered a great deal of information about the dream.

Air

Air is universally symbolic of the realm of the mind and, in some cases, the realm of spirit. When you are moving through air in your dream you are almost certainly dealing with how you think about something. Your dreams suggest where you need to get a fresh perspective or advise you to watch your thoughts concerning a particular person or situation. Your subconscious can also be letting you know what you truly think and believe, regardless of what it is you have told others. Air signifies the breath of life; if you dream you are in need of air or trying to catch your breath you may be feeling pressured in some way. If someone is cutting off your air in your dream, you may feel suffocated by a personal relationship. If you dream you need to "get out in the air," you seek freedom and space.

Earth

The earth is the ground underneath your feet, the soil in which all things grow. To dream of the earth signifies an awareness of the interconnectedness of all things. It also may indicate your need to be more grounded and stable in your relationships or financial matters. If you dream you are digging in the earth, you may be searching for stability and a strong foundation in some situation. If you dream about seeing the earth from space, you may long to return home and to be nurtured by a familiar setting. A dream about gardening or farming the earth suggests you are growing as a person and planting seeds you want to blossom. If you dream of someone as being "earthy," you might want to connect with your physical nature. Someone who is "down to earth" in your dreams may represent an aspect of yourself that is real, honest, and trustworthy. Dreaming of the earth is usually a positive, healthy sign.

Fire

Fire is a primal universal symbol. It represents rebirth, containing within itself the power of consumption and regeneration. It is one of the transforming universal symbols deeply embedded in the consciousness of all living beings. Just think about all the ways you use the imagery of fire in your daily life. If someone "lights a fire" under you, he is trying to get you going in some way, but if someone "lights your fire" he ignites your passion. When you dream of fire—even the flame of a candle—you are being asked to come alive in some area of your life. Your subconscious is trying to connect you to that vital, primal energy of inspiration, life force, and passion.

Water

Water is another primal symbol deeply embedded in our collective consciousness. Water represents movement, rhythm, life-giving nourishment, and the ebb and flow of your emotional nature. If you dream of water, most likely your subconscious is trying to help you understand and process emotional issues. Emotional release dreams almost always involve water imagery. Think first of your emotional state when water symbols appear in your dreams. If you dream you are drowning, you are feeling overwhelmed emotionally at this time in your life. If you dream you are trapped in ice or snow, your emotions have hardened and you are having difficulty identifying and releasing them. If the water in your dream is warm, pleasant, and cleansing, you feel emotionally balanced at this time.

A dream of water can also relate to the unconscious. From the Freudian perspective, water relates to sexual matters, usually the female genitalia (see *lake*, *ocean*, *river*, and *waves*). A dream of muddy water means your emotions are not clear about a certain person or situation. If the water in your dream is clear, you know what your heart desires. Rough water may connote problems communicating with a loved one.

Alphabetical Glossary

A

abandonment

Dreams of being abandoned by a lover, friend, or family member suggest that this is something you fear in waking life. Childhood feelings of being left out often translate into abandonment dreams. In this case, you need to work on strengthening your self-esteem. You may have not spoken up for yourself in a difficult situation. In that case the dream might indicate that you have abandoned yourself, your principles, or values.

abdomen

Seeing your abdomen in a dream suggests the gestation or digestion of a new idea or phase of your life. If your abdomen is swollen, the birth of a new project may be imminent. If you have pain in your abdomen in the dream, you may be having difficulty digesting something that has happened in your waking life. The body also speaks in the dream state, so if you are feeling sick you may dream of an upset stomach.

abduction

If you're abducted or kidnapped in your dream, it means you're feeling pressured to do or say something you don't believe in and don't want to do in waking life. Abduction dreams often stem from guilt concerning things you've done or are about to do that aren't typically in your character. If you witness someone else being abducted, it means you're not acting on the opportunities you've been given. Abduction dreams can also indicate you feel someone else is unfairly receiving credit for your work.

abnormality

If strangely formed things appear in your dream—a crooked mirror, a misshapen arm—don't be alarmed. One interpretation is that your mind might be open to new and unusual things. However, the dream could also be telling you something that appears "normal" is not what it seems. If you dream someone you know has an abnormality, your intuition could be cautioning you that the person is not who he appears to be.

abortion

Dreaming of abortion is not usually literal. Many times, an abortion dream reflects the guilt you feel about doing something you shouldn't. The abortion in the dream is a warning to "abort" your actions and stop. The dream can indicate fears about a direction you are taking in your life. It may warn you that you have a tendency to stop out of fear and miss opportunities the new direction presents. Dreaming of an abortion might indicate a relationship has suddenly gone off course, or that your behavior or the other person's is killing some aspect of the relationship.

abroad

Dreaming of going abroad may predict positive new situations you'll soon encounter. It can also represent a desire for a change from your day-to-day life. Notice how you feel in the dream. If fear or anxiety is present, you might feel you are in foreign territory when dealing with something or someone in your waking life. If you are happy or excited in the dream, you may be expanding in new and positive ways.

absence

If you dream someone is absent in your dream, you may be looking within yourself for something or some quality that person possesses. This is a form of an anxiety dream, where you are searching for important items in your life. What are you missing, either in your work situation, a relationship, or within yourself, that you need to be happy?

abuse

If you dream of being abused, it's a sign you feel you're being taken advantage of in some way in your waking life. You feel powerless or helpless to protect yourself in a situation or relationship. You may also be receiving information from your subconscious that you are abusing some responsibility or gift you have been given.

abyss

Dreaming of falling into an abyss signifies that some part of your life is out of control. It could be you're not working hard enough or not taking care of yourself. Maybe you're due for a move—in your career or elsewhere. You could also be feeling that you are losing yourself in a situation. Looking into an abyss means you'll soon be challenged to go deeply within. An abyss dream can also encourage you to trust the void within, even though you can't see your way to the bottom.

accelerator

This could be a release dream if you feel out-of-control in some area of your waking life. If the accelerator on your car is pushed down and you can't stop it, you feel things are moving too fast and you don't know how to manage the rapid change going on.

accent

Hearing or speaking with a foreign accent indicates you may feel like a "foreigner" in a situation or relationship in your waking life. Your dream may be encouraging you to gain insight into an irksome problem from a different (foreign) perspective. It may also signify that you will be traveling soon.

accident

A car crash in a dream can be a literal warning—be careful in the coming weeks or months. However, vehicles in dreams often symbolize transitions in life. A car accident, particularly if you are driving in the dream, may indicate you feel the changes you are making in your life won't succeed. A skiing accident or crash while going very fast is an out-of-control release dream. It advises you to take hold of your life before things get more complicated. A plane crash usually indicates worrisome thoughts. Where are you experiencing worry or anxiety? Accidents at sea relate to your emotional nature—perhaps you feel your emotions have gone dangerously off course or you are on a collision course with someone important in your life. Most crash dreams are not precognitive, so first try to see what information the dream might be giving you about where you are going in your life, not just in everyday matters but on many levels.

accordion

Accordion music often signifies a longing for the past. The sound of an accordion has a melancholy quality, so you may be feeling nostalgic or melancholy about an earlier time in your life. What are you missing about your earlier life? Try to integrate those experiences into your current life.

accusation

Accusations in a dream may be literal. Do you believe you've done something wrong? If you're accused, you may feel you're being judged or unfairly treated. The person judging you in these dreams is usually you. This dream could also reflect worries about how other people perceive you.

ace

An ace in your dream is always a good omen of things to come. Aces and the number one stand for positive beginnings. Perhaps a new business opportunity is coming your way, or a new friendship or love interest.

ache

Aches or pains in your dreams can be literal sensations coming from the physical body while you are sleeping. If the ache or pain seems severe in the dream, it might be time to get a checkup. If you actually feel the pain in the dream, you're probably half-lucid and feel the pain in waking life, as well. If the ache is imaginary, it could mean you are hurting emotionally in your waking life at this time. Often the body sends a message during a dream to alert you to something you may not be aware of in your waking life.

acid

To dream of acid being poured on you signifies your anxiety levels are high right now. It may be time to take a break. If you dream of drinking acid, the dream is a metaphor that something is "eating you up." Figure out what's bothering you and fix it.

acorn

A dream about an acorn is usually an abundance dream—you want something you don't have. Acorns signify the ability to be patient while your desires manifest. Squirrels often hide acorns for times in the future when they will need them. Consider small steps you can take toward your goals—the harvest will be there when you are ready.

acrobatics

Performing acrobatics in your dream is a good sign that you feel vital and healthy. It could also mean you're able to overcome emotional difficulties now because luck is on your side. Perhaps you feel someone is making you perform complex maneuvers to get what you want. If you are anxious in the dream, it could be time to stop jumping through hoops to please others.

actor or actress

Perhaps you're only seeing your own or someone else's persona—the side that person wants to show to the world. Seeing yourself as an actor in the spotlight suggests a desire for publicity or a more public life. Such a dream can also suggest you're acting out a role or putting on an act for someone. Another interpretation is that you admire the qualities of the actor you are dreaming about. If so, those qualities exist within you—your dream wants you to recognize and develop them.

addict/addiction

If you dream someone is an addict or has an addiction, your dream may be alerting you to something that has not been revealed about someone you know. If you are the addict or addicted in the dream, your subconscious is letting you know you are obsessing about something to your detriment. You don't feel in control of whatever is happening in your life and seem helpless to control your need for the situation to continue.

address

If you dream of the numbers of your house you are being given a message from spirit about your current living situation. You feel at home where you are right now. If you see the address of your childhood home in a dream, the dream is asking you to relate experiences from that time in your life to a current situation in which there are similarities.

admiration

If someone is admiring you in the dream, it's a sure sign you're feeling good about yourself. If you're admiring someone else in the dream, it signifies your insecurities may be your downfall with your current problem. The other person could have qualities you wish you had. Your dream is telling you that those qualities exist within you. You have only to seek them out.

adoption

If you dream of adopting a child, it could be a literal dream; perhaps you'd like to do so in the future. This dream can also indicate you are ready to adopt new ways of being or a new start in life.

adultery

If you're committing adultery in a dream, it could mean you worry you could fall into it or that you're contemplating doing it. If you dream your partner is committing adultery, chances are you worry he could. But it doesn't necessarily mean he is unfaithful. In this case, use the dream as a jumping-off point to explore possible problems in the relationship. Adultery can just signify you are not being honest about your needs and feelings in a relationship. Make sure you communicate with your partner often to maintain closeness. If you are not in a relationship, think about where in your life you may be betraying your values.

affliction

Dreaming that you have an affliction of some kind can mean you feel some part of you is unable to do what you want. Figure out what it is that is holding you back. This dream rarely signifies an actual physical affliction.

afternoon

Dreams that take place in the afternoon suggest clarity and lengthiness, as daylight is at its strongest and longest in the afternoon. Are you with friends in the afternoon? If so, the dream describes positive and lasting associations that exist now or may soon be formed. Notice the events and people in your dream to further understand the dream's meaning.

age

A dream of old people who are strangers might indicate a fear of aging. However, it can also signify reason or wisdom coming from your unconscious. Do the old people in the dream give you advice? Take it. Your inner sage is telling you what to do. This is also true if you dream of yourself as an aged person. If you dream of an older relative who has already passed on, you may be receiving a visit from the Other Side.

aggression

Aggression in a dream could be an emotional release dream of pent-up frustration or anger at a person or situation in your waking life—even at yourself. If you are not the aggressor in the dream, you might feel someone has control over you. Perhaps you feel weak and vulnerable. Think about where you are being pressured and by whom. If you're the aggressive one, you may harbor resentment against yourself or the person you're attacking. Usually, this type of dream signifies an emotional release of stresses built up during the day.

air

Air symbolizes the realm of the mind and, in some cases, the realm of spirit. When you are moving through air in your dream, you are almost certainly dealing with your thoughts about something. Your dreams are suggesting you need a fresh perspective or should watch your thoughts concerning a particular person or situation. Your subconscious can also be letting you know what you truly think and believe, regardless of what you have told others. Air also represents the breath of life, so if you dream you need air or are trying to catch your breath you may feel pressured in some way. If someone is cutting off your air in your dream, you might feel suffocated by a personal relationship. If you dream you need to "get out in the air," you are seeking freedom and space.

airplane

Airplanes not only fly, they traverse the medium of air. This clue signifies that plane dreams represent your thoughts or even spiritual matters. If you are flying a plane, you are making a shift in how you think about your life. Perhaps you are gaining new perspective on a situation or experience. If you are a passenger on a plane, you are being guided, perhaps by divine energy, to change how you think about things or to change beliefs that no longer support who you are. If you dream you are in a plane experiencing turbulence, you are struggling in your waking life with changing thoughts and beliefs and have not yet become reconciled to a new point of view. If you dream the plane is going to crash, you are releasing fear in the dream state that you won't be safe or survive if you let go of your old way of seeing things. You may be soaring to new heights in some facet of your life or taking a metaphorical journey into the unconscious realm. An airplane dream can also mean career advancement or refer to an upcoming journey. A flying dream can be used as a launching pad to a lucid dream. If you miss your airplane, it refers to a missed opportunity you need to look into.

alarm

An alarm ringing in warning in your dream indicates you have worries about some aspect of your life. Try to figure out what the problem is, and do something about it. In some cases, an alarm in a dream may be literal. It's time for you to wake up.

alien

To dream of one or more space aliens indicates you feel you don't fit in some situation in your life, or something about the situation feels "alien" to you. You may fear trying something you have not yet mastered, or you feel incapable of handling a situation that has come up. If you dream someone you know is an alien, something about what that person believes or how he behaves may be foreign to your nature. This person could also represent qualities you have rejected about yourself or feel are not part of who you are.

alligator

This symbol may suggest you're being thick-skinned or insensitive to someone else. It may also signify danger. An alligator that guides you or talks to you may be your totem. Notice your emotion in the dream. If you're not afraid, think about what an alligator represents—perhaps you need to be more thick-skinned yourself and less sensitive to the remarks of others.

altitude

In your dream, you're looking down from great heights. What are you standing on? Is it something steady or is it shaky? If it's a big mountain, for example, you might feel on top of things at this time in your life. Looking down from a high place enables you to get a fresh perspective on things. Notice where in your life you need to change your thinking about a situation and gain a new view. If you are fearful in the dream, you may worry that you have taken on more than you can handle or you may be feeling overwhelmed.

ambulance

Being in an ambulance most often indicates a release of anxiety and a desire to heal your emotional imbalance. You may be worrying over things that are out of your control. If you have a medical problem in the dream, though, it might be time to get a checkup. If you see someone else in an ambulance, you may have hidden guilt about hurting that person in some way. If you have been dealing with one crisis after another at home or work, everything can feel like an emergency! In that case, learn to ask for help.

amusement park

Dreaming of an amusement park may suggest you need a vacation from your concerns over a troubling issue. To dream of being on a ride denotes enjoying life and letting go of inhibitions. You are being reminded to play and to make time for the carefree, spontaneous activities of childhood.

ancestor

To see an ancestor in your dream could represent a part of you that this person portrayed in life. What it is about your ancestor that you want to find in yourself? If she appears to you in a loving, vivid way, it may be an actual visitation. Enjoy it and feel blessed. You could be looking to the past for answers. Usually, this suggests you are releasing your worries in a dream.

anchor

An anchor grounds you. It acts as your foundation. It also holds you in place, which can be either beneficial or detrimental. If you need to let go of a situation, this dream advises you to do it now. If you've been contemplating making some kind of commitment, it's a good time to do so. An anchor also predicts stability and security. If you dream of having problems with the anchor, however, it means you're currently dealing with a difficult situation that needs to be resolved.

angels

Angels represent help from your higher self or from a guardian. The appearance of an angel may suggest a growing spiritual awareness. If you encounter an angel with a human face, it is most likely your personal spirit guide. Listen to what he or she has to say.

animals

Animals can represent your instinctual nature, wisdom, innocence, predatory tendencies, or sexuality, depending on the perceived nature of the animal. An animal can also symbolize the physical body, or appear as a metaphor for an astrological sign (such as a lion for Leo). It could be letting you know about a pain within your physical body. If you're not scared of the animal in your dream—especially if you're intrigued by it—this may be your totem, your personal animal guide or guardian spirit. Your dream may encourage you to discover what qualities of the animal you possess and need to develop or express.

anniversary

To dream of an anniversary signifies current and/or future happiness and many festive occasions. It also indicates good health. Note your feeling about the anniversary. Are you happy? Envious? Interpret the meaning as it applies to you.

ant

This signifies difficulties that can be overcome with a little bit of work. Normally, they're small problems you may be making into a big deal. Look within yourself to find the source of the negativity. Ants suggest restlessness ("feeling antsy"). They also indicate small annoyances and irritations. Alternately, they may represent feelings of insignificance. Consider the number of ants in the dream. A single ant? A colony? A huge, swollen anthill? One ant suggests loneliness. Many ants suggest trivial problems are "bugging" you.

anxiety

Anxiety is one of the most common dream experiences. Normally, anxieties in your waking life translate into your dreams in strange ways. Anxiety dreams do not need deep analysis. Let your subconscious work it out for you while you sleep on it. Just know you have released some of the anxiety that has built up during your day.

apparition

An apparition can signify a message or warning. It can be seen as communication with the dead. Alternately, you might feel that another person in a relationship is like an apparition—he's there, but not truly present. If you are the apparition, you may feel you are losing yourself in the relationship.

applause

Applause in dreams signifies you are seeking a reward for genuine efforts. This is a healthy dream that means you feel good about what you've done, and you're looking for the respect and appreciation you deserve.

apples

An apple in a dream is usually a good sign. Apples stand for wholeness and for knowledge. Ripe apples on a tree may mean your hopes and hard work have borne fruit. Apples also stand for long life and achievement. To dream of eating an apple suggests you're currently in good physical health.

appointment

A missed appointment signifies the same thing as a missed train, bus, or airplane. You've missed an opportunity or will miss one if you don't act soon. Figure out what that opportunity is, and put your best foot forward. If you have an appointment coming up and you dream you've missed it, you are just releasing anxiety about something that is important to you.

April

April is the time of spring in the Northern Hemisphere. When you dream of April or your dream is set in the month of April, you may be experiencing the flowering of aspects of yourself. April can signify new beginnings or long-held efforts beginning to blossom. April is also associated with the warming of the sun and time to be outdoors, as well as spring weddings and new beginnings in love. Look to what is happening in your life to understand what April means to you. April in dreams can also refer to someone born during the month, so look to see what aspects of yourself might be reflected in friends or family having April birthdays.

arch

Passing under an arch in a dream may symbolize a transition in your life—a move from one phase or stage to another. If you avoid walking under the arch, you could be resisting transition or change. Note the characteristics of the arch, whether it's adorned in any way, and whether other people are also passing through it. This will flesh out the symbol's meaning for you. An arch can also suggest you are opening up to new experiences.

argument

If you have a dream in which you're arguing with someone, it could mean you fear intimacy with this person in waking life. On the other hand, it may also be that you've had an argument or sense an argument is soon to come. If you see two people arguing in your dream, it indicates you feel there is too much confusion around you right now. Lighten your load.

arm

Arms allow you to manipulate things in your environment. The same might be true in a dream. Seeing an arm suggests you can maneuver or manipulate things in your dream environment. If the arm is pressing against you in some way, you may be feeling "strong-armed" by someone.

arrow

An arrow often signifies a precise message—look where the arrow points. If you're defending yourself from a foe, this dream means you'll have the strength to triumph in whatever situation you're soon to face. Arrows indicate directions, so notice the direction in which the arrow is going. In a precognitive dream it can signify a path you are to follow.

artist

To dream of yourself as an artist suggests a great need to express your emotions and creativity on a bigger scale. It doesn't necessarily mean you want to paint. Try to integrate some of your creative ideas into your work or personal relationships. You are the artist of your own life.

ashes

Are they the ashes of a person or from a fire? If you dream of ashes from someone you know who is alive, you may fear losing that person. If the ashes are from someone who has passed away, maybe that person is actually giving you a message from the Other Side. If the ashes remain from a fire, you may fear an endeavor that is important to you might not come to fruition.

atlas

Dreaming of an atlas may suggest you are considering moving or taking a trip, or that you should. It can also mean the world is yours for the taking. Big things could be on the way.

attack

If you're being attacked in a dream, physically or otherwise, you believe you are under emotional attack in real life. Chances are you're feeling very vulnerable. Who's attacking you? If you dream you're attacking another person, it means you have strong feelings of resentment toward someone.

attic

Whether or not you have a real attic in your home or grew up in a house with an attic, you might find yourself dreaming you are in an attic. Usually, the attic is the place of memories and family legacies. If you dream you are in the attic, you may be feeling nostalgic about times past, or you may be processing family patterns that are causing distress in your waking life. The attic can also be the place of rediscovered treasures you didn't know you had. If you dream you find a precious heirloom in the attic, your subconscious is alerting you to gifts you have within yourself that you need to rediscover and express. Perhaps you should take some part of yourself out of "storage" or dispose of things you are clinging to from your past. You may be exploring the realm of the higher self or seeking knowledge from a higher source in your dream.

August

August represents summertime and relaxation for most people. You may be working hard and looking forward to time off. A dream about August could carry a message about a particular person, including you, whose birthday falls in August. Look at what you are doing in the dream to interpret its meaning.

authority

A dream of being in a position of authority can be a release dream or a wish dream. However, you are the authority in your own life, so your dream may be bringing that part of you to the fore. Usually, you work out responsibilities from waking life in your dreams. This is simply a matter of figuring things out during the nighttime, when your choices make you less vulnerable than they would in waking life.

avalanche

During an avalanche an extreme amount of snow buries all in its path. This anxiety dream suggests you feel overwhelmed emotionally. The dream is helping you release your fears at night. Examine the jumble of emotions you experience. If you can change your daily situation to reduce stress, do so.

award

If you've won an award in your dream, it may mean you secretly desire more recognition for your achievements or that you are actually being recognized for your work. You have positive feelings about your capabilities and what you are worth. Create some momentum. It could be time to ask for a raise or promotion.

ax

How is the ax used in your dream? If you're wielding it, it means that you are trying to chop a problem or situation down into manageable pieces. If the ax is aimed at you, you may fear someone is trying to take away important parts of who you are.

B

baby

A baby in a dream almost always represents new life or a new beginning. Your dream may have nothing to do with a physical pregnancy; instead it may represent an idea that is gestating or growing. It could also relate to the pending birth of a child or a desire for a family if that is on your mind. Alternatively, a baby could indicate dependent behavior or infantile longings you are demonstrating in a particular situation. Notice how you feel toward the baby in the dream to see if you are joyful or afraid about moving into a new part of your life.

babysitter

If you dream you are a babysitter or need a babysitter, the "caretaker" part of you is being called forth to nurture and care for yourself. Do some inner child work to connect with the small, helpless, vulnerable part of yourself so you can feel confident and secure in your waking life.

bachelor

A dream of being a bachelor indicates unwillingness to shoulder responsibilities in your waking life. You feel weighed down with responsibilities and desire freedom or escape. If you are afraid in the dream, it could signify that you fear being alone and not having someone with whom to share your life.

back

Your back is a source of strength and support. If you turn your back to someone in a dream, you might be turning your back on an opportunity or rejecting a part of yourself. If someone in your dream turns her back to you, you are experiencing rejection on some level. You may be asked to take on a lot of responsibility, which will require effort and strength. If you have been trying to see all sides of an issue, your dream may be revealing what is hidden from view.

backpack

If you are carrying a backpack in your dream, you may be feeling weighed down or that you have taken on too much in some area of your life. If you are carrying someone else's backpack in the dream, you are assuming responsibility for problems that are not yours. If the backpack is light and easy to carry in the dream, you feel you can easily handle your responsibilities.

backward

If you dream you are walking. moving, or traveling backward in your dream—or slipping backwards—you feel you are covering old ground in some situation in your life. You may be slipping into old patterns of behavior, thinking, or emotional response.

backyard

If you are in the backyard in your dream you may be feeling relaxed and at ease. Notice who is there with you and what you are feeling. The backyard is where you entertain, relax, and have fun, so most likely you are feeling good about an upcoming event in your life. In the front yard you are visible to your neighbors, so you may dream of being in the backyard because you want to hide something in your life from prying eyes.

bacon

A dream of bacon may relate to your financial situation. Notice if you are worried in the dream—are you able to "bring home the bacon"? You could be experiencing worries about your continued employment and ability to support yourself. If you are enjoying cooking and feeding others the bacon, you feel you are a good provider.

bad

Dreams in which you are being told you are bad relate to inner judgments you make about your own behavior or value. If you dream someone else is bad, you see in that person an aspect or quality of yourself that you feel is not healthy for you. If you feel bad in the dream, you might be feeling guilty or sorrowful about an action you have taken or failed to take that has, in some way, let you or others down.

badge

Seeing a policeman's badge in a dream may mean you believe you have done something wrong and are worried you will be found out. If it is a merit badge of some sort, you are feeling a sense of accomplishment and recognition.

badger

If you dream of a badger, think about the qualities you associate with this animal. In nature a badger is a resourceful creature whose adaptability helps it to survive. These qualities may represent aspects you need to cultivate or express at this time in your life or in a particular situation you are currently facing. The animal can also represent the literal word—you may feel pressured or "badgered" by someone or you are pressuring someone else.

bag/baggage

Like the backpack, a bag in a dream can symbolize the "baggage" you are carrying in your life and in your relationships with others. Notice whether the bag is heavy or light, and whether or not it impedes your movement in the dream. You may be trying to "bag" something in the dream, in which case the dream portends an opportunity you hope will materialize.

bail

If you dream you are in jail and hope to be bailed out, you feel you need help in some area of your life and that this help has to come from someone else. You don't feel you can be successful on your own in the situation, so it is time to ask for the help you need.

baking

A dream of baking could be literal—you're thinking about upcoming events. It may also signify that you crave more self-nourishing activities. Baking in a dream is a sign that your creative juices are flowing and you want to make something that will also nourish others.

balcony

If you are on a balcony in your dream you are being seen by others in an elevated state. Consider the condition of the balcony. If it's clean and polished, the dream may indicate that others hold you in high regard. If the balcony is crumbling or tarnished, the dream may suggest you need to repair your public image.

baldness

For a woman to dream of being bald indicates her fear of getting older or losing her femininity and appeal. For a man to dream he is bald signifies his fear of loss or a desire to come completely clean in a situation.

ball

Because a ball is round, it connotes wholeness and completion. If you are playing with a ball, you are being asked to embrace your inner child and make time for play. If you are competing in a game such as ping pong, you are experiencing life's ups and downs but holding your own. If you dream of attending a ball or big event in a ballroom, you desire more socialization and prestige.

balloon

Seeing a balloon in the air indicates a wish to fulfill some desire or fantasy. You'd like to be more creative and rise to new heights. It also may refer to a longing for childhood. If you dream of a child carrying a balloon and it blows away, it signifies your sadness at the loss of the child-part of you.

band

If you are part of a band in your dream, you long for creative expression and want to feel you belong. If you are watching or listening to a band, you are expressing desire to have that experience of togetherness and collective purpose in some area of your life.

bandage

A bandage indicates you feel wounded in some aspect in your emotional life, but you have the resources to comfort and heal yourself. If you dream of putting a bandage on someone else, you are trying to heal something in your relationship with that person that you see as unhealthy or detrimental to the success of the relationship.

bank

Generally, a bank is a symbol of security and power—a foundation— but the meaning depends on what you're doing in the bank. If you are receiving or depositing money, it's usually an auspicious sign, an indication that you are financially secure. If you are waiting in line, it may mean you are literally waiting for a check or money to arrive. If you're holding up a bank, it may symbolize that money you're expecting is being "held up" or delayed.

bankruptcy

You may dream about being bankrupt even if you have no financial problems. Though the dream could be literal, more often it suggests you feel you've missed an opportunity that was foolish to pass up. You might also be expressing worries about your finances.

banquet

If you dream you are at a banquet this may be a time in your life when you are feeling well-nourished emotionally. It could also mean that you want more opportunities in your life or that you want to "have it all."

baptism

Baptism is a rite of initiation into a spiritual life. If you dream you are being baptized, you are undergoing a spiritual initiation or embarking on a new part of life. If you dream of a baby being baptized, you may be inaugurating a new project or venture.

barbs/barbed wire

Barbed wire in a dream may indicate you feel confined or restricted in some area of your life. If you are trying to go somewhere and have to cross barbed wire, you might be in a life transition that you fear will be painful. If you cut yourself on a barb or barbed wire, you fear being emotionally hurt in a situation, possibly by someone's "barbed" tongue.

bargain

If you dream you are searching for a bargain you may feel something you have agreed to do in your life is exacting too high a price. If you are excited about getting a bargain, the dream is telling you that you feel you got something of high value with little effort on your part.

bark/barking

If you hear the sound of a dog barking in your dream, it is most likely a warning to alert you to something going on in your waking life from which you need protection. Notice the action in the dream to understand fully the message the barking is meant to convey.

barrier

If barriers in your dream are keeping you from getting where you are trying to go, you are experiencing the same feelings in your day-to-day life. If you are the one in the dream putting up barriers, you may feel vulnerable in a relationship, situation, or undertaking, and fear you won't succeed.

basement

The basement most often represents long-buried dreams, fears, and hopes for your life. When you dream of being in a basement you are connecting with your subconscious mind, the repository of that long-buried information. You could also be unearthing something hidden in your past that you need to examine (see *underground*).

basket

A dream of holding or trying to fill a basket can represent what you feel you have and still need in order to make your life complete. If you are carrying a basket to someone else, you are offering what you have to another.

bath

In a bath you wash away dirt and grime, and feel refreshed and clean again. When you dream you are taking a bath you are cleansing yourself—mentally, physically, emotionally, and/or spiritually. It represents a desire to restore yourself to a pure state in some area of your life and wash away what is no longer needed. If you are watching someone else bathe, you may feel that person needs to "come clean" with you about something, or that you need to do the same with her.

bathroom

The bathroom is the most personal of dream locations. It is where your most private self comes to your attention. In the bathroom you hide yourself from the eyes of others to perform intimate personal functions. If your dream is set in the bathroom, you may be processing old feelings of shame and embarrassment. Your dream may also be letting you know where you have feelings of inadequacy about your self-image or body-image. What it is about yourself that you want to keep private from others? Because the bathroom is also the place where you perform bodily functions, dreaming you are in your bathroom can mean you want to release or get rid of emotional or mental "waste" in your mind, heart, or life. If you dream you are trying to go to the bathroom, you might need to. Your physical body sensations will intrude into the dream state to let you know when you need to wake up. Dreaming of being in a bathroom could simply mean that your bladder is full. If the bathroom is crowded, the dream could mean you lack privacy. If you find yourself in a bathroom for the opposite sex, it may suggest you are crossing boundaries.

battery

A battery provides energy. If you dream you are charging the battery in your car, your dream is telling you that your own energy needs refueling. If the battery in the dream is dead, you feel depleted and need to rest and restore yourself.

beach

To dream of being on a beach is, most likely, a wish or release dream. You'd like to find some time in your life to take off, go on vacation, and leave your responsibilities behind. If you're on the beach with someone, notice what he or she is doing and examine the symbolism related to it. If you are lying on the beach looking at the horizon, you are anticipating an unknown future that has deep emotional significance.

bear

Like all animal symbolism in dreams, a bear can have many meanings, depending on the feelings and actions in the dream as well as your own associations with the animal. Consider the bear's characteristics and how it behaves. In Native American cultures a bear represents strength, so if you have a bear in your dreams you may be facing a situation in your waking life that requires strength. You also may be being asked to "bear" a certain responsibility, condition, or development.

beard

If you dream of someone with a beard, you may feel that person in real life is hiding some part of himself. If you dream of yourself with a beard, you may be trying to conceal some aspect of yourself that doesn't fit with your public persona.

beating

Being assaulted in a dream is most often a dream in which you are releasing the emotion of fear. You fear something in your life is going to hurt you emotionally or hurt your opportunities. Think about the people connected with the situation in your life and whether or not you feel they would hurt you to get ahead. You may also feel "beaten down" about something that has heartfelt meaning to you. Your dream is expressing the depths of your discouragement so you can find your power in the situation. If you are beating someone else in the dream, you have unexpressed anger or frustration about a particular person or situation. Or, you dislike the qualities in yourself that the person in the dream represents.

beaver

A beaver is a hardworking animal, known for building dams in water. If you dream of a beaver, think about where in your life you feel you need to "dam" up your emotions for your own safety and protection. You might also possess the hardworking qualities of the beaver and feel at home in your emotional life right now. The beaver can also represent someone close to you whom you admire for his beaver-like qualities.

bed

Your bed is your place of retreat and rest, and where you engage in physical and emotional intimacy with another person. If you dream you are in your bed, this is a dream about intimacy. Notice if you are alone or with another. What you are doing in the dream? Think about where in your life you are longing for greater intimacy.

bedroom

In the bedroom you dream, rest, and restore yourself, and experience romantic, physical, and emotional intimacy. When your dream is set in the bedroom, most likely you are processing something about your intimate relationships and/or your physical and emotional needs. Sometimes noticing you are in your bedroom in a dream can trigger a lucid dream—a dream in which you realize you are dreaming even though you don't wake up. Think about the emotional and romantic relationships in your life when you dream of being in your bedroom. Your dream may be letting you know whether or not your needs for intimacy and connection are being satisfied. Even dreams of sex are often dreams about unexpressed desire for greater intimacy with someone rather than the physical act of sexual intercourse.

bee

Bees are industrious creatures who live in colonies and have common goals. If you dream of bees, you may desire to have a greater common purpose with others in your life. Or, you may recognize qualities you associate with bees in yourself or another person. If the bees are stinging you, your subconscious is asking you to wake up to something in your life that needs to change.

beggar

If you dream of a beggar, notice how you treat this person. Your dream shows how you feel about your weak side. Are you kind to him? If so, it most likely means you are good to yourself. If you're nasty to him, you need to be less hard on yourself.

beheading

If you dream about a beheading, notice who the victim is. If it's you, think about where in your life or your relationships you are "losing" your head and not thinking clearly. If another person is being beheaded, you are trying to get rid of some qualities you associate with the other person that you see in yourself as well. Beheading dreams can also be past-life dreams.

bell

Hearing the sound of a bell in a dream may mean unexpected good news is on its way. If you're ringing a bell, it means you may soon need to call upon trusted friends. They'll help you in your current situation. If you hear bells at a distance, you may hear from someone far away or from your past. If you dream of a joyous bell ringing, expect happy communication.

bench

If you dream you are sitting on a bench, there may be a situation in your life where you feel you are sidelined and out of the action. Perhaps you've been working to create something and are waiting to see results. Think about where you are procrastinating in your life and not getting into the action—make the necessary changes.

bicycle

If you dream you are riding on a bicycle you believe you can accomplish what you want under your own power. Your own hard work will get you where you want to go. A bicycle also requires balance, so you may be feeling balanced in your life now.

big

Often in dreams you see things bigger than they are in normal, waking life. When something or someone is big in a dream, it indicates that this person or situation looms large in your thoughts, emotions, or actions. If you are bigger in your dreams than in your waking life, you may be growing as a person. Your dream is using the symbol of size to acknowledge that development.

birds

The appearance of a bird in a dream could indicate you wish to be free, to fly away, or to flee from something. Because birds fly through air, when you dream of a bird you may be receiving messages about detaching from a situation so you can see it from another angle or perspective. As with all animals, you have your own personal connotations to birds. In many cultures, birds can be spiritual symbols. Among certain Native American tribes, an eagle symbolizes spiritual knowledge. If the bird you dream about is very colorful and has beautiful plumage, you might be feeling particularly attractive. If you dream of a bird such as a peacock, you may have pride of accomplishment or think someone you know is stuck up. Dreaming of a mythical bird such as a phoenix may portend a rebirth in your life.

birthday

Birthday dreams can have contrary meanings depending on the context. To dream of receiving birthday presents may mean happy surprises are coming, or advancement is in order. If you are in your childhood home in the dream, you may be receiving messages about events from your past at a particular age in your childhood that are causing you distress in your adult life. Notice your feelings around the birthday: whether you are alone or at a celebration; whether you are happy or sad; whether you get what you wanted or are disappointed. All these clues will help you correctly interpret what the birthday symbol means in your dream.

black

The color black in a dream may indicate transformation and canceling out negative energy. It can be a good sign, depending on how you feel toward the black object. The color black can also signify boredom, but the former translation is usually correct. In some cultures, black represents the void (think "black hole"), and in others it signifies wholeness and unity.

bleeding

Blood is vital to life. To dream of bleeding suggests a loss of power or a change in matters of the heart. If you dream of having your blood sucked by a vampire or other entity, a partner or friend may be draining you emotionally. End contact with this person.

blue

Blue is a cool color and is associated with the fifth or throat chakra, the place of self-expression. If you dream of blue, you may feel the need to communicate with someone about a particular event or situation. A calming and relaxing color, blue makes you think of the oceans and the sky. It is often associated with spirituality and teaching. When blue shows up in your dreams, you may be feeling calm and relaxed, or you may be feeling "blue" and experiencing sadness about some situation in your life. In some areas blue is associated with improper speech, e.g., "the comic's jokes were blue."

boat

Like cars, boats in dreams can come in all sizes, shapes, and degrees of power. If you are rowing or sailing your own boat, you feel in control of a situation or transition. If you are a passenger on a ferry or other boat, you don't feel you can control what happens. Boats traverse water and water in dreams relates to your emotional life. Anytime you dream you are on a boat you are trying to move through an emotional situation, either in your current life or from the past. If the boat is trying to break through ice, your feelings around the issues are old, frozen, and hard to access. If the boat is navigating through rough seas, you are experiencing emotional ups and downs in your life. If you are in a small boat and cannot get to shore, you feel out of control regarding an emotional issue in your daily life.

bomb

A bomb in your dream suggests you worry that your emotions will get out of control and you will "blow up" at someone. If you are trying to defuse a bomb, it means you are attempting to get control of your emotional reactions.

bombshell

Dreaming of a bombshell may mean you are feeling particularly attractive at this point in your life or aspire to that kind of recognition from others. You could also be processing unexpected and surprising news that has upset you.

bones

Bones in a dream signify the bottom line—bones are the raw material of a dream. Are the bones scattered? Maybe you're torn in waking life over a decision you have to make. Notice the condition of the bones. That's how you feel about a current nagging issue.

book

A book in your dream can signify new beginnings or a new chapter in your life. Books also represent inherent wisdom and listening to your gut. An old or worn book means that you should leave the past behind you and look happily toward your future.

boss

A dream of your boss suggests she has qualities that you either like in yourself or that trouble you. It may also advise you to become the authority in your own life or embrace your innate leadership abilities.

bottle

A bottle holds liquid, which in a dream equates with emotions. Think about where in life or with whom you are "bottling" up your feelings.

Your dream is encouraging you to deal with your emotions in a more healthy way.

breakdown

To dream of having a mental breakdown indicates you feel completely overwhelmed and out of control in waking life. Talk to someone and ask for help with the responsibilities on your plate. If you dream your car breaks down on the road, you don't feel ready for a transition occurring in your life, or you worry that you don't have everything in place that you need to be successful.

break-in

Dreaming of someone breaking into your house means you fear people changing your ideals or getting involved where they shouldn't in your waking life. If you hear noises, it could also be a literal dream and you should investigate. Is the security for your home adequate?

breasts

Women's breasts may relate to sexual desire. They can also symbolize nurturing and motherhood. Are the breasts exposed? If so your dream could reveal a concern about exposure. Are they diseased or injured? This can be an indication of how you feel personally.

bride

To dream of a bride, whether it's you or another person, indicates you are about to join your fortunes to another in some way. It may also indicate a deep desire for marriage if you are unmarried. A bride is also about to embark on a new stage of life, so think about where in your life you are ready for a new beginning, a fresh start.

bridge

A bridge connects one place to another, and in dreams it may represent crossing from one state of mind to another. Because bridges most often span bodies of water, you may be trying to move from one emotional state to another. Consider the other elements in the dream. What's waiting for you on the other side of the bridge? What did you leave behind?

You may be trying to connect two experiences in your life that share a common emotional response.

broom

If you dream of a broom, you may be trying to sweep something under the rug, hiding some action or issue you don't feel good about. This dream can also suggest you are in the process of cleaning up a part of your life.

bubble

Bubbles in dreams stand for rebirth or a completely different way of looking at things. Bubbles floating in the air indicate excessively lofty ideas. You need to be more practical about the matter at hand. Bubbles can also be fun and joyful; you may be feeling particularly playful about a situation in your life.

bugs

Seeing bugs in a dream usually means that something is "bugging" you in your day-to-day life. Think about what is going on in your waking life—what or who is causing you distress? Something you need to complete could be weighing on your mind and may need to be resolved.

bull

A bull is a powerful, dangerous, and stubborn animal. Think about where you or another person is evidencing those qualities in a particular situation in your life. Perhaps you feel out of place like a "bull in a china shop." Someone might be bullying you, or you may be exerting inappropriate power over another person.

bus

Dreaming you are on a bus is similar to a car dream, except that you are with other people on a vehicle that makes stops along the way. A bus has a predetermined route and destination. When you dream you are on a bus, you know you will eventually reach your destination. However, you may be impatient with the stops and starts along the way and your inability to control the amount of time it takes to reach your destination. Buses also have fairly frequent schedules, so you always can catch the next bus if you miss the one you wanted. In that way, a bus speaks to the mundane, predictable nature of daily life. Notice other aspects of the dream, such as the luggage you're carrying, your destination, and what you're leaving behind.

butterfly

Butterflies are magical creatures of transformation and beauty. When you dream of butterflies you are undergoing transformation on a very deep level. Ask for support from your angels and guides as you become who you are meant to be.

buttons

Buttons in a dream signify social change and how the public perceives you. Are the buttons fancy? Do you have problems buttoning your clothing? If they're very tight, it could mean you are being too rigid in your ideals or behavior.

buy/buying

If you dream you are buying something it suggests you are open to allowing new thoughts, feelings, or perhaps people into your life. If you dream you have overpaid, you feel a new situation in your life does not have the value you'd hoped it would.

C

cabbage

Cabbage represents simple and inexpensive food to which everyone has access. When you dream of cabbage, it may signify a longing for simpler, easier times.

cafeteria

A cafeteria in a dream can signify social times in your life that offer no real connection. You may yearn for more emotional nourishment. Is the cafeteria nice and clean or dirty and depressing? Its condition shows how you feel about your social life.

cage

A cage represents possession or control, and what you see in the cage is the key to interpreting this sign. A cage full of birds may signify abundance, whereas a single bird may indicate you are narrowly focused at this time. An empty cage may mean the loss of something or someone important to you. A cage full of wild animals may signify you have control over a particular aspect of your life and you will triumph over your emotional ups and downs.

cake

A dream about a cake may mean a celebration is at hand. It can also indicate there's something to celebrate that has been overlooked. Maybe you should push for something you desire, such as a promotion at work.

camp

Dreaming of camp depends on how you feel there. If you're having fun, it signifies longing for youth, fun, freedom, and a release from the constraints of everyday life. If you're not, it means that you feel someone is trying to steal your thunder and take away your simple pleasures.

canal

Canals represent a journey through the unconscious. Pay attention to other details in the dream. Is the water muddy or clear? Are you traveling with friends or family? A dirty canal suggests you have hidden emotional issues you need to work out as soon as possible.

cancer

Dreaming of cancer doesn't mean you have the disease or are going to get it. To be successfully treated for cancer in a dream signals a change for the better. Dreaming of cancer may symbolize a desperate or foreboding situation, or a draining of resources.

candles

Usually the appearance of candles indicates spirituality. A candle provides light in the darkness, or guidance through dark matters or the unknown. If a candle burns down to nothingness, it might indicate a fear or concern. A candle being put out could mean you feel overworked. A steadily burning candle may signify a steadfast character and constancy in friends and family.

cannibalism

To dream of cannibalism shows that your unconscious feels a need to consume someone else's energy. Are you emotionally draining the people around you? If you dream of someone eating you, be careful of the people with whom you surround yourself. They're not good for your self-esteem.

canoe

Canoes suggest a short journey that requires some effort, but that journey is often pleasantly tranquil. Pay attention to other elements in the dream, such as the state of the water and how hard you are paddling. A dream of paddling on a calm stream symbolizes confidence in your own abilities. If the river is shallow and quick, the dream may indicate concern over a hasty decision in a recent matter. To dream of paddling with your lover may indicate you are on the same page in the relationship; but if the waters are rough, there are some issues that need to be smoothed out.

car

When you dream you are in a car, notice what you can about the car. Is it going forward or in reverse? Is it a shiny new model or an old clunker? Are you the driver or a passenger? Are you in the front seat or the back? Is the road the car is traveling on straight or winding? Is the car going too slow or too fast? Is the car broken down or unable to get going? These questions will give you clues as to how you feel about your capability to get where you want to go in life. The car symbol can also tell you a lot about what you feel you deserve in life, or how you regard your station in life compared to others'. A moving car may mean you are headed toward a goal or moving ahead. Being in the driver's seat symbolizes taking charge of your life. Is there a back-seat driver in the vehicle? Or are you taking the backseat in some situation in your life? A stolen or lost car could indicate you are losing control of your life. Cars sometimes represent the physical body, so take note of the car's condition. Even if you feel in control the car may have fits and stops. Maybe it circles back around or has to climb a particularly steep hill. All these events may indicate the level of difficulty you feel you must face to move forward in your life and get where you want to go. If the car is going backwards, you may feel you are slipping backwards in some area of your personal life or work.

carousel

To dream of riding a carousel suggests that you are going around in circles and not making any progress in your endeavors.

carrot

Carrots, in dreams, could mean you're a solid, earthy person with great inherent value, in the same way that a carrot has great nutritional value. If you are upset in the dream, someone may be enticing you with a promise that doesn't materialize. You need to be true to yourself.

castle

Seeing one of these majestic structures in a dream might suggest power and strength, security and protection. Castles in the sky are fantasies and illusions—you may wish to escape from your present circumstances. Help will come soon if you need it.

castration

Dreaming of castration refers to feelings of inadequacy or impotence in life. You fear the unknown. Think about situations in your life where you feel powerless, helpless, or at the mercy of outside forces.

cat

Cats have had many mystical and superstitious connotations throughout history. Cats have been reviled as evil and bad luck, and revered as gods. Most often, when a cat shows up in your dream, you might be wishing for more independence in some area of your life. Or you could be receiving a message to be more curious and adventurous. Cats are hunters, so you may be in the process of trying to hunt down some important piece of information or lost object. If the cat in the dream is purring, you may feel particularly content in a relationship or situation. Cats can represent independence, the feminine spirit, or sexual prowess. They can also stand for evil or bad luck, or represent a catty or cunning person.

cattle

To dream of healthy, content cattle grazing in a green pasture suggests prosperity and happiness. Conversely, dreaming of weak, poorly fed cattle warns you are wasting your energy on the wrong things. Stampeding cattle imply that something in your life is out of control.

cave

A cave represents the hidden you—the person you truly are. How did you feel inside the cave? Were you frightened? Was it cozy? Caves also refer to rebirth and changing old ideas.

cedar

Cedar represents strength of conviction and health. It can also signify earthiness. Do you need to get back to basics? Cedar chips can refer to scattered thoughts. Get your ideas together and focus on your priorities.

celebrities

Celebrities in your dreams can signify a yearning to be more involved in the social scene. This dream also represents a part of you that craves recognition for past efforts. Dreams about having sex with celebrities are merely wish-fulfillment dreams or indicate a desire to embrace some quality in yourself that you associate with a celebrity.

ceremony

Dreams about ceremonies indicate you're entering a new phase of your life. Do you feel comfortable with the changes? Are you enjoying the ceremony in your dream? Dreaming about a ceremony is usually a positive sign of good things to come.

chain

Seeing a chain in a dream means you are in the process of connecting different experiences, thoughts, or emotions together to make a whole. If you are chained up in the dream, you feel restricted or trapped in some area of your life. If you dream you are chained to other people, you feel your own ability to do what you want is tied to the fortunes or actions of others, whether you like it or not. You need to find your own power to chart your course.

chair

If you dream of a chair, perhaps you need to sit down and reflect on a situation in your waking life, or you just need to take a break. It is time to rest and just be with yourself.

chanting

Hearing chanting in your dream can refer to two things. If the chanting is loud, it means you're ignoring a problem in your life. If the chanting is soft and meditative, it means that there is too much confusion around you—your subconscious is telling you to slow down and take a break.

chariot

Riding in a chariot in a dream suggests you want to speed up whatever is happening in your life. You are determined to take the reins and beat out the competition. In rare cases this could be a past-life dream.

cheese

Food in dreams almost always shows how you nurture yourself. Think of your associations with cheese and whether or not you like cheese. You may need to adopt some self-care habits. If you dream of Swiss cheese, there may be some aspect of you or your life that feels incomplete (holes). Alternatively, you may feel something or someone in your life is cheapening you (cheesy).

chemistry

The mixing of potions in a dream refers to intensity of life, alchemy, and purification. What things do you need to simplify in your life in order to make it work? Are you balancing your life well? This dream also indicates you need to take responsibility for your actions. You have the formula to make your life work.

cherry

A cherry can signify lust, female desire, and forbidden fruit. It also represents wholeness, as a circle does. Who in the dream is eating the cherries? Are they in a bowl? Are they beyond your grasp?

childbearing

Dreaming of childbearing signifies you are giving birth to new ideas, to a new part of yourself, or to a new stage of life. If the childbirth is difficult, it means you'll have some serious struggles along the way, but your efforts will eventually come to fruition.

children

Dreaming of children may mean you yearn to return to a simpler, less complicated life. Such dreams might also relate to a desire to return to the past to recapture good times or to satisfy unfulfilled hopes. Children in dreams can also represent creative projects that are heartfelt and need to be nurtured.

chimney

To dream of a chimney signifies a spiritual ascension and approach to life. Your dreams are becoming more defined, and you need to follow your instincts. If smoke is going up the chimney, you are sending your wishes up for divine support. Alternatively, you may be worried that long-cherished plans will go "up in smoke."

chocolate

Chocolate suggests a need or a desire to indulge in something. Or, conversely, it can indicate a need to limit your indulgences. Chocolate speaks to your sensuality and shows you want to sweeten a situation or relationship in your life.

cigarette

If you are a smoker, this dream could be a literal warning to quit. If you are a nonsmoker, dreaming of cigarettes could indicate you feel the words you are speaking could be harmful to yourself or others. If another person is smoking in the dream, the same may be true of someone you know. Cigarettes could simply indicate an unhealthy habit of thinking, or that you are addicted to certain patterns of thought or speech.

circle

A circle in Jungian terms represents the self and wholeness. It can also be a symbol of protection or social connections, as in a circle of friends. If you're "circling around something," caution is indicated. If you dream you are "going in circles," you feel confused about how to proceed in an area of life or frustrated that you are not accomplishing what you set out to do. Dreaming of a circle can also reveal a desire to marry, as a ring shape might indicate hopes of partnership. If someone gives you a ring in a dream, it may represent your desire to marry or move your relationship to the next level. In many cultures, artists paint or create mandalas, large circles representing the spiritual nature of life. Notice the colors and designs of your circle, as many layers of meaning may be present. If you dream you are inside a circle looking out, you may feel trapped by a situation or sense a need to protect yourself from some person or situation.

circling

Circling around and around can mean that you feel you're going in circles without getting anywhere. Pick and choose your battles. Analyze your goals.

city

Cities represent challenges, fun, and new enterprises. Are you starting something that can directly affect your financial situation? If so, examine how you feel about being in the city. That's how you feel about the way the tides are turning in terms of your career.

climbing

Climbing up in dreams represents a longing for more knowledge. It can also signify that you want more challenges, yet emotionally you may feel drained. You're searching for a belief system that matches your ideals.

cloak

A cloak hides your true intentions. It protects your secrets. Are you feeling guilty about something you've done? If someone else is wearing the cloak in your dream, chances are you feel left out of the loop.

clock

A clock can mean you are worrying about having enough time for something in your life. This dream symbol can also refer to a past event you wish you could change. Don't be so hard on yourself.

closet

Closets are places where things are stored or hidden. If you are hiding something in your life, your dream may indicate that it is time to release this secret.

clothing

The clothing you wear in your dreams represents how you currently feel about yourself and your accomplishments. Is your clothing regal and expensive? Or is it tattered and torn? The clothing you wear refers directly to your self-esteem.

clouds

Dark, stormy clouds rolling in at a low altitude and flashing lightning may represent your anger regarding a situation. A slate-gray cloudy sky might indicate that your views on a subject are clouded. What in your life needs clarity? Dreaming of white, billowing clouds floating in a blue sky suggests matters are clearing up.

clover

This is a good sign that happiness is coming your way. A clover always signifies luck. If the cloverleaf is any color but green, it will take a bit of perseverance on your part to make the good things happen.

clown

Clowns can represent fear of the unknown and the dark, insecure side you feel within. If your reaction toward the clown is one of happiness and joy, it can also mean you long for happier, simpler times.

club

If the club in your dreams is a weapon of some sort, it might symbolize hidden aggression from your past. Because clubs were used long ago, it can refer to an old hurt that something current has unearthed. If someone is shaking the club, it could be a warning to deal with current emotional issues. If you dream about a group of people who form a club, your dream could be indicating you feel part of something, connected to like-minded people. Or perhaps you want to "join the club" but don't feel you fit in.

cockroach

Dreaming of a cockroach can be a literal dream—you saw one while you were awake and it filtered into your dreams. Think about what you associate with cockroaches. Do you believe they are dirty or carry disease? If so, think about recent events—some situation in your waking life may have made you feel unclean in mind or heart. Roaches are incredible survivors, so depending on your association with them, you might be receiving a message about your own resiliency. Perhaps something in your life that you thought was over has reappeared, and you don't welcome it. Were the dream cockroaches in your house? Because a house represents your life, consider what has been going on in your current life that might be "bugging" you.

cocoon

A cocoon represents safety, warmth, and protection with family and friends. It also signifies rebirth, a new stage in your life that's soon to come or has already begun. This dream advises you to accept the new factors in your life. This is a positive change.

coffee

Drinking coffee is a pleasurable morning ritual for most people, so if you dream of drinking coffee, you might be feeling content at this time in your life. If you are making coffee in the dream, you want to start your day off right, or you might be nurturing yourself, family, or friends. If you dream you have spilled coffee, you are worrying that you have lost something you hold dear.

coffeehouse

People gather in a coffeehouse to talk and share ideas with each other. Where in your life would you like more social interaction and the chance to relax with like-minded people? Make time for such activities and personal connections.

coffin

A coffin may symbolize a feeling of confinement. Coffins also relate to death, so ask yourself what might be causing you to feel "dead" on an emotional level.

coin

A coin in a dream indicates a change in resources. A dream of many coins signifies money and prosperity. If the coin is heads-up, it means things are going in your favor. Tails-up on a coin indicates the tides are about to turn.

collar

A collar refers to possessiveness. Who is wearing the collar in your dream? If you dream you're wearing the collar, it signifies oppression you feel from others. Are you looking for your dog's collar? Many people dream of a dog's collar if the dog is sick or after the dog has passed away. It indicates true love and affection for your animal.

college

College represents distinction and the attainment of your hopes through hard work. To dream of a college may suggest you will advance to a long-sought position. Dreaming you are back in college could mean you are working to achieve distinction in an area of your life. Rewards will follow a period of hard work.

columns

To dream of a building with columns suggests higher wisdom, intelligence, and authority. Are you standing near the columns? If you are, it means you long for more mental stimulation. Columns also stand for sexual prowess and virility. Incidentally, the akashic records—on the Other Side, where your soul's purpose is written down—are said to be located in a building with huge columns.

contamination

This dream can be a warning about your health. If you feel you're contaminated in the dream, it may be your body senses something is not right. This dream can also refer to obsessive tendencies or worries that someone else's viewpoint is contaminating your own belief system.

contract

Seeing a contract in a dream means you are making a choice that involves a significant commitment on your part. It may refer to your finances, a relationship, or even commitments to yourself about lifestyle changes you intend to make. If you sign the contract, it means you are comfortable with moving ahead. If you don't sign the contract, this could indicate you don't feel ready to commit to something at this time.

corn

Corn refers to fertility, health, and rebirth. Usually corn in a dream is a positive sign of good things to come—think cornucopia. It can also mean you have thoughts that are now outdated (corny) about your life, others, or yourself.

corpse

To dream of yourself as a corpse or to experience your own death usually signifies a major change in your life, such as a divorce or the ending of a long-held job. If you dream of killing yourself, it could mean you are going through a traumatic personal transformation and want to leave your old life behind. If you dream of someone you know as a corpse, then the dream is telling you that an aspect of yourself represented by that person has died. Think about the qualities possessed by the person who is the corpse in the dream, and then reflect on whether or not you have failed to nurture those qualities in yourself. Often the message is an alert that a critical aspect of self has died through neglect or unawareness. Once you know what it is, you can take steps to revive that aspect of yourself if it is vital to your personal happiness.

costume

Are you wearing a costume in your dream? If so, this is how you may see yourself. A costume represents a disguise you wear and show to others. Is someone else wearing the costume? This may be how you see him or her.

couch

A couch in dreams represents analysis of the self. Are you comfortable on the couch? If so, you're probably comfortable with who you are and how things are going in your life. Is the couch tattered or torn? If so, it's time to do some self-examination and reorganize your priorities.

court

A dream of going to court can reflect a literal situation. Is a legal matter pending in your life? Dreaming of being in court also indicates a fear of being judged. Who is the presiding judge in your dream, and why do you feel he or she disapproves of you?

courtyard

A courtyard in a dream represents tranquil, peaceful times. It can also refer to family. What are you doing in the courtyard? If there is a lot of greenery, the dream can be a positive omen of prosperous financial times ahead.

cow

A cow can represent fertility, sustenance, or even prosperity. Because cows give milk, this might be a dream about your need to be nurtured or to nurture others.

coyote

A coyote is considered a slick, sly creature. Is there someone in your life whom you feel is sneaky or taking advantage of you? In your dream, are you scared of the coyote? If you're not, the coyote could be your totem.

crab

Crabs live in water and walk sideways in a funny pattern rather than straight ahead. Dreaming of a crab may indicate your moods are unstable right now, or that you are having trouble finding a clear direction in a problem or relationship. It can also indicate pesky annoyances or fear of being brought down by trivial matters. If a crab bites you, it means your emotions are getting the best of you. The crab also refers to the month of July and the zodiac sign of Cancer.

cradle

A cradle in a dream can have a literal association if you have a baby. It can also symbolize yearning for one. Cradles signify protection and comfort. Who is in the cradle? Is the cradle secure? If the cradle is faulty, you might feel you're not providing a stable life for yourself or a loved one.

creek

A creek represents a short journey or a new experience. Are you exploring a creek with a friend? What is the condition of the water in the creek? Water in a dream symbolizes emotions, so the creek's characteristics will describe your feelings about your journey. Note the other aspects of the dream to discover more about the journey or experience you are undergoing.

crevice

A crevice signifies the unknown. Be wary of upcoming situations in which you may be placed. Is there something inside the crevice, or is it simply dark? This also refers to hidden desires in your unconscious mind.

crocodile

If the crocodile in your dream is immersed in water, it means you may be looking for the key to unlocking hidden emotions. Something is blocking you. If the crocodile is on land, it may signify you're not being truthful with yourself.

crow

Crows are messengers. What is the crow in your dream trying to tell you? If someone is crowing in the dream, you may see that person (or yourself) as boastful and arrogant. If you fear crows, the crow in your dream might represent some aspect of your personality that you consider dark or negative.

crowd

Being lost in a crowd can signify a loss of individuality. You may feel the need to stand out from others. This dream can also describe confusion around you, or even boredom. Maybe it's time to break away or travel.

crown

The obvious definition is wealth, position, power, and authority. But is the crown something desired or feared in the dream? Is it within reach or escaping your grasp? A crown may also indicate good advice from an older, wiser person or mentor.

crutches

If you have a dream about crutches, you may feel you're relying too heavily on something or someone. It can also signify fear of being more independent and venturing out on your own.

crying

To dream of crying indicates repressed sadness, usually referring to problems of the heart. It can also signify a release from problems. Try not to analyze this dream. Let your unconscious work it out for you.

cup

Notice the other influences in the dream. A cup indicates that the answer to a current situation or problem is right under your nose. Is the cup full or empty? Cup symbolism can show you how you view situations in life—is your cup half full or half empty? If you dream of a full cup, then you are feeling satisfied and satiated in the situation. If empty, then you don't yet know how to resolve the situation. A cup can also be a gift coming to you, so pay attention to signs and synchronicities in the days following the dream.

cursing

If you dream that someone is shouting curses at you, it could mean you are upset with yourself for something you've thought or done and feel a need to be punished. If you are the one cursing at others, you are releasing built-up frustration and irritation through the dream.

cypress

A cypress tree may indicate the desire to travel to a Mediterranean destination. It also signifies the mystical qualities of wholeness, immortality, security, and wisdom.

D

dagger

If you dream of a dagger, you may be feeling threatened emotionally by a situation in your life. If you see daggers in someone's eyes, you feel disapproval from him. If you are the one shooting daggers, you disapprove of something in yourself or in another person but are not directly communicating or trying to clear up the situation.

daisy

Daisies are light, happy flowers that bloom in the summer. Dreaming of daisies indicates you feel good about your life right now and are hopeful about the future.

dancing

A dream about dancing represents movement, freedom, joy, and a time of happiness. It also indicates liberation from constraints and a deep connection with your current emotional state.

darkness

Darkness is a symbol of the unconscious, the hidden, and the unknown. Darkness can also stand for lower impulses, death, and fear. To dream of being overtaken by darkness suggests fear or trepidation about a matter at hand. To dream that you lose a friend or child in the darkness indicates you may be unaware of certain behaviors you have that are driving others away. You may also be losing aspects of yourself mirrored in relationships with others that you are not paying attention to and illuminating in your daily life. Darkness speaks to the hidden, shadow-side of our psyche. It is the ultimate unknown, and in the dream state our psyche reaches out to let us know where darkness is obscuring important information about our thoughts, emotions, behaviors, relationships, and actions.

dawn

Dawn signifies rebirth or embarking on a new direction in your life. Translation of this symbol depends on how you feel about the dawn. If you're afraid, it could mean you feel turmoil about moving forward with new projects, ideas, or undertakings.

daybreak

Daybreak indicates the outlook on a matter is brightening. A gloomy or cloudy day suggests you feel discouraged about something you are doing, whereas sunlight represents clarity and hope.

dead

If you dream of someone who has crossed over, most likely you are reconciling unfinished emotions (grief, anger) concerning that person. You may also see qualities in yourself that were qualities the deceased exhibited when she was alive. In that case the dream is pointing out similar attitudes, beliefs, and patterns of behavior, so you can learn and grow from the experience. If you dream of a loved one who has passed away, and the dream is vivid and deeply loving, it may be an actual visitation from that person.

death

A death dream usually isn't a premonition of death, but it may indicate a death of some part of yourself or an area of your life. If you feel no sense of fear in the death, the dream can mean you're letting go of something. On the other hand, a corpse can indicate you feel stuck in a lifeless routine.

decapitation

A dream about decapitation can happen when you feel a sense of disconnect from your body. You may want to stop certain thought patterns, or wish to reconcile certain ways of thinking with your physical day-to-day life. You may also fear "losing your head" over a situation in your waking life.

decay

Decay, in a dream, can indicate you are ready to get rid of the old to make room for the new. It can also signify you're neglecting your body or mind. Notice what is decaying in your dream.

December

December is traditionally a time of giving and receiving gifts. To dream of this month can suggest anticipation of good things to come. Because December is a winter month, you might be worrying about a time of dormancy or loss.

deer

Deer are graceful and gentle creatures that are easily frightened. In folklore, deer are the messengers of fairies and therefore could be messengers of the unconscious. Are you feeling fearful in some area of your own life? If you dream of hunting deer, and are not a hunter, this might indicate you are trying to capture the gentle, graceful nature of the deer for yourself.

dentist

Going to the dentist in a dream could be literal reminder. Do you have an upcoming appointment or do you need a checkup? If not, dentists in dreams can refer to worries that something is wrong. Your dream might also indicate a need to rely on an authority figure. (See *teeth* for more associations.)

desert

A desert is usually thought of as a barren place, where little grows. It can symbolize a fear of death, or of being infertile. But dreaming of a desert can also alert you to hidden beauty and hidden life that is camouflaged by ordinary perceptions.

dessert

Desserts represent enjoyment, forbidden pleasures, and hidden guilt. How do you feel about eating the dessert?

devil

The devil is an archetype for your hidden, nonconforming side. Dreaming of the devil might mean you feel you are acting in a way that is harmful to yourself or others. Perhaps you believe someone close to you is acting in a malicious way. Are you scared of the devil in your dream? If you're married or in a committed relationship, the devil can represent your partner. Pay close attention to how you feel toward him. If you are "bedeviled," you are being asked to have a sense of humor about a situation that is frustrating you.

dew

Dew represents tiny treasures or small pleasures. To dream of sparkling dew may portend a coming blessing.

diamond

A diamond symbolizes love, as in a diamond ring, as well as hardness and endurance. It may also symbolize wealth. A lost diamond, especially a ring, may reveal concern about a love relationship. A gift of a diamond depends on who is giving it and other circumstances. A diamond passed from a parent or relative could refer to an inheritance; one from a friend might indicate a wish to obtain the person's love.

digestion

Digestion could be a literal dream alluding to what you ate before going to bed. It can also signify spiritual nourishment or becoming more emotionally committed to your personal relationships. If you dream you are having trouble digesting something, think about what is going on in your life that you are not able to accept.

digging

What are you digging for? If it's something lost, you may be attempting to retrieve a part of your past. If it's a treasure, you may be delving into the unconscious—a treasure chest of knowledge. However, if you are burying something, it indicates a wish to cover up an act, hide your feelings, or obscure the facts of a matter.

dirt

When you dream about earth or dirt, you may feel "dirty" about some recent action. Or, you may be trying to bury feelings that are making you uncomfortable. If you have been stressed at work or in your life in general, you may be dreaming about the ground to symbolize your desire to "ground" yourself and your anxious feelings.

disappearance

This is a common dream in which you are searching for a missing person or item. If it's an object, you're merely coping with a trivial loss. If it's a person who is nowhere to be found, it means you long for a connection with this person. Perhaps you've had a disagreement and you want to make up, but your unconscious knows this may be impossible.

discipline

Being disciplined in your dreams could refer to how you feel about yourself or others. Are you getting things done the way you should? If not, you may feel you need to punish yourself.

disinfectant

Disinfectant in your dreams can refer to cleaning up your own life. Do you feel dirty about particular emotions you're experiencing? Are you comfortable with your own sexuality? Using disinfectant could also show you are attempting to deal with bad situations in your waking life.

dismemberment

Dismemberment, in a dream, refers to breaking apart before putting things back together. It suggests joining the pieces of your own life puzzle.

disobedience

A dream about being disobedient signifies that you're feeling too many restrictions in your life right now. You want to rebel and break free.

diving

To dream of diving into a body of water may indicate you are about to dive into something in your waking life that has strong emotional content for you. On a deeper level, a diving dream may symbolize an exploration of the unconscious.

doctor

A doctor can indicate healing or a healing guide. For some people, a doctor in a dream might symbolize mainstream thinking as opposed to alternative health options. Dreaming of a doctor may also mean you need to visit one but are afraid to go.

dog

Dreaming of a dog can mean you're seeking companionship, affection, or loyalty. Dogs are beloved around the world. In animal companions, such as dogs and cats, you may see qualities that reflect ones you would like to have yourself. In your dream, notice how you interact with the dog. Is it friendly or wary? What color and breed is the dog? How do you feel with the dog? Most often, unless you are afraid of dogs, they symbolize friendship, unconditional love, and loyalty. If you are dreaming of dogs, you might see these qualities in yourself or another person. Or you might desire a romantic partner who has these qualities.

doll

Dreaming of a doll refers to childhood thoughts and memories. Is the doll in good condition? If so, it means you're feeling good about your past. If it's in poor shape, it's a sign you need to heal certain issues from your past. Also, think about any situation or relationship in your life in which you feel you are being toyed with or treated like a toy.

dolphin

Because it resides in the sea, a dolphin may be considered a messenger of the unconscious or a guide to the unconscious realms. You may be diving into your unconscious. What do you fear? What do you hope for? Because a dolphin is at home in the water, you may feel emotionally balanced. Dolphins are also playful, so your dream may be telling you that you need light, playful experiences in your life.

door

A common dream symbol, doors can indicate an opening or a new opportunity at hand. A closed door suggests something is inaccessible or hidden, or that an opportunity has passed by. If a door is broken, something may be hindering you from taking a new opportunity. The condition of the door, the material it's made of, and any markings that appear on it often provide clues about what lies behind it or about your perception of reality.

doorbell

If you dream you hear a doorbell ringing, your unconscious is trying to get your attention to let you know something new is arriving in your life. If you are ringing a doorbell in your dream, you are trying to get someone's attention.

dove

A dove in a dream is always a lucky symbol meaning peace, affection, love, and prosperity. Notice where the dove goes. Is this the direction of your heart's true desire?

dragon

Dragons refer to intuition and psychic ability. You may know that something is about to happen, but you don't want to admit it. Dragons also represent authority and power. How do you feel about the dragon in your dream?

drawer

A dream of a drawer or putting something into a drawer signifies putting aside foolish pursuits and dealing with the current situation. You may dream of drawers when you'd like to keep a part of yourself hidden from the rest of the world. If you take something out of a drawer, analyze the object to determine what part of yourself you're now ready to share with people.

dream

To have a dream that you're dreaming usually indicates you're having a lucid dream. In these dreams you can learn how to control outcomes and steer things toward positive results.

drinking

Symbolically, water is related to the unconscious and emotions. Drinking may suggest you are being nourished or thirst for emotional involvement. As a metaphor, drinking spirits may suggest a search for spiritual sustenance. For an alcoholic or someone who is close to an alcoholic, a dream of drinking alcohol may be a warning.

driving

Driving signifies a need to take the wheel and gain control of your life. If you're driving and the car swerves out of control, or the accelerator is stuck in place, it's possible your unconscious knows you don't yet have the skills to get where you want to go. The dream may also warn that you are being reckless or moving ahead too fast.

drought

Generally an unfavorable omen in a dream, droughts represent the absence of life or the drying up of your emotions. Are you with someone in the dream? Maybe an unresolved issue between you and someone you are close to is leading to a quarrel or separation.

drowning

Drowning in a dream signifies a deep-rooted fear of delving into your unconscious mind or your deep emotions. You are emotionally overwhelmed at this time in your life, or fear that if you give in to your emotions they will overwhelm you. The more you express and process your emotions, the less overwhelming they will seem.

drugs

Many times, dreams about drugs are literal—you're under their influence. But being offered drugs in a dream usually refers to negative influences around you. Who is the person offering you the drugs? Drugs can also indicate that a part of you wants to be released from responsibility.

drum

Dreaming of a drum or drumbeats may relate to a primitive urge or the universal heart. Alternately, a drum could symbolize communication, magic, or even an entrepreneurial spirit, as in "drumming up" business.

drunk

You often dream of being drunk when you've had too much to drink in real life. If you dream of seeing a drunk, it could indicate you feel you're being foolish and indulgent in a current situation.

dwarf

Dwarves are traditionally associated with magical powers. Dreaming of a dwarf could be an extremely fortuitous sign. On the other hand, a dwarf can symbolize a stunted condition. If growth is limited in your waking life, your dream may advise pursuing an alternate path.

dying

Dreams of dying represent the end of an emotional state, relationship, or situation at hand. To dream that you are going to die suggests inattention to a particular aspect of your life that requires your focus. If you dream of other people dying, you fear the qualities you possess that you also recognize in these individuals are passing away.

dynamite

If you dream of dynamite, you fear a potentially explosive situation. Are your repressed emotions about to explode? Examine other features in the dream to determine where the problem lies.

E

eagle

The eagle, soaring high in the sky, can symbolize a spiritual quest. It can also stand for combat, pride, courage, and ferocity. Eagles are traditionally associated with nobility. They also can represent a father figure or the sun.

earrings

Pay attention to the type of earrings in your dream. Are they cultured and demure, like pearls, or fun and large, like colorful hoops? If they're conservative, it may be you're longing to change the way people see you. If they're outrageous, you may be worried about the way people see you or you seek a larger role in life.

ears

A dream of human ears can indicate you need to watch what you say. Ears can also call attention to something. Listen carefully to what's going on around you.

earth

The earth is the ground underneath your feet. It is the soil in which all things grow. To dream of the earth signifies an awareness of the interconnectedness of all things. It also may indicate you need to be more grounded and stable in your relationships and/or financial matters. If you dream you are digging in the earth, you may be searching for stability and a strong foundation in some situation. If you dream of seeing the earth from space, you may be longing to return home, to be nurtured by a familiar setting. A dream of gardening and working in the earth suggests you are growing as a person and planting seeds you want to blossom. If you dream of someone who's "earthy," you might want to connect with a part of you that is more comfortable with your physical nature. If you dream someone is "down to earth," you consider that person, or an aspect of yourself, to be real, honest, and trustworthy. Dreaming of the earth is usually a positive, healthy sign.

earthquake

Dreaming of an earthquake might suggest your personal, financial, or business matters are unstable. Is something upsetting taking place in your life? Earthquakes can also have sexual connotations, such as the desire for sexual release. If there are other people in the dream, does one of them make the earth move for you?

east

East is the place where dawn breaks, thus it represents new beginnings. It is the symbolic and allegorical spring. If you are heading east in your dream, you may be about to embark on a new project or a new beginning in some area of life. Many South American shamanic traditions consider east the place of the visionary, home to the eagle, and symbolic of a new point of view or spiritual vision for yourself and the world. The sun rises in the east, so perhaps your "sun" is about to rise. A promotion or other positive development may be on the horizon for you.

eating

A dream of eating might suggest a craving for love or nurturance. It can also mean you are enjoying life or indulging in its pleasures. If you are the one being eaten in the dream, ask yourself if something is eating at you. Do you feel as if you are being eaten alive?

echo

To hear an echo in your dreams can mean you feel nobody is really listening to you or hearing what you're trying to say. Or, it could suggest that your feelings of loneliness are calling to you, encouraging you to connect more with others.

eclipse

An eclipse suggests a disruption of what's normal. When something is eclipsed, it means a period of activity has ended. Also, dreaming of an eclipse can mean cosmic forces are at work in your life.

eel

An eel, like a snake, can be a symbol of transformation, sexuality, healing, or hidden emotions. Take your cues from what the eel is doing in your dream.

egg

In the Jungian view, eggs represent wholeness, fertility, and new life. Eggs can also symbolize ideas that have not yet hatched. Finding a nest of eggs might indicate a waiting period, or that ideas are gestating. Financially, a dream about eggs can allude to your nest egg. What is the context of the dream? Is someone egging you on?

eight

Eight is the number of infinity, eternity, and universal abundance. A visually beautiful number, eight shows balance and symmetry. You may be about to make a major romantic commitment or celebrate an anniversary. Opportunities for financial growth may be on the horizon. Like seven, eight is a "luck" number, so good fortune is on the way if eights show up in your dreams. If you dream you are "behind the eight ball," you have missed out on a lucky opportunity or somehow are blocked from achieving success.

election

To dream of running for office means you'd like to have more authority and power in your interactions with others. It can also mean you don't feel you've been rewarded enough for your efforts. If you win an election in your dream, it symbolizes wonderful new changes are on their way.

electricity

Dreaming of electricity signifies drive and spontaneity—new life. It refers to a need to be more active. If you see something being electrified, it means you're aware of the inner battle you're currently having with igniting the passion in your life or your work.

electrocuted

To dream of being electrocuted signifies you may be shocked by the happenings around you. It also suggests you fear losing power in a close relationship or in your career.

elephant

The appearance of these large, solid animals may signify wealth, honor, and a steadfast character. As the elephants rule in the wild, their appearance in your dream may indicate you reign supreme in business and/or at home. How many elephants do you see in your dream? A herd of elephants may suggest great wealth, while a single elephant may represent a small but solid fortune. An elephant with its trunk held up is a symbol of excellent luck soon to come.

elevator

Rising in an elevator may symbolize a rise in status, such as a promotion, or a heightening of consciousness. Is the ascent rapid? Are you frightened? Exhilarated? A descent in an elevator might indicate a lowering in status or position, or a journey into the unconscious. A stuck elevator might suggest some aspect of your life is presently being delayed. A plunging elevator could indicate a rapid descent into the unconscious, and your fear of losing control in life.

elopement

If you have a dream of eloping, it's possible you're unhappy with your current love relationship and wish to run away. If you're happy in the dream, it could mean you're anxious for more stability in your emotion life and in love.

embarrassment

If you dream of being embarrassed, it indicates you're unsure of what to do next. It also signifies a general lack of overall confidence. Issues from the past that used to bother you have probably resurfaced in your life. Resolve them, and you'll stop having this type of dream.

embrace

To dream of embracing someone in a dream simply means that you have a new kind of affection for this person, or you see qualities in her that you would like to embrace in your own life. If you're forced to embrace someone, it means you feel pushed to a level of intimacy and connection prematurely.

embroidery

Embroidery, in a dream, can refer to departed loved ones or unfulfilled dreams of the past. Do you feel as if you've missed an emotional opportunity? Are you thinking about a relationship you broke away from in the past? This dream also refers to the little details in your life. What is it you are trying to weave together or create?

embryo

To dream of an embryo signifies beginnings and kernels of ideas you need to develop. It can also, of course, refer to birth, rebirth, and pregnancy.

empty

An empty room, cup, container, or object is a metaphor for the way you feel about yourself currently. You'd like to fill the object, simply because you're ready for things to go your way. This dream symbol also refers to boredom and loneliness.

enema

An enema, in a dream, indicates something is emotionally draining you. It could also stand for people in your life who depend on you financially. What do you feel is pulling you under?

enemy

Dreaming of an enemy you know in your waking life signifies that you long for peace with this person but believe it is not possible. An enemy you do not know in waking life usually refers to yourself—you are the enemy. Are you running from the enemy in your dream or facing him?

engagement

To dream of an engagement is usually a release or wish-fulfillment dream. Perhaps you long to have more security in your love life so you can plan for the future. This is also a good omen of positive social experiences to come.

engine

If you dream of putting together the engine of a car, it means your unconscious knows it needs to get down to basics—start over and rebuild things from the ground up. This may refer to a business, or to your insecurities and doubts about current relationships.

entrance

An entrance in a dream refers to the choices you need to make. Do you walk through the entrance? Are you scared to go in? You may dream about an entrance when you're at a turning point in your life. To dream of making a big entrance signifies your need to be more socially proactive.

eruption

An eruption, in a dream, means you're holding back in your waking life. You need to release some angst and start things fresh. If the eruption occurs as a volcano, it can refer to repressed sexual desire.

escalator

Dreaming of an escalator suggests slowly climbing the ranks in either business or spirituality. Who is at the top of the escalator? Can he or she help you with your pursuit? Does this person have authority over you?

escaping

If you dream of making an escape, consider whether you are avoiding or need to get away from something in your life. Examine the people in your dream. Are you trying to get away from them? Do you need to confront them about something they've done?

eunuch

Whether you have this dream about yourself or about another person, it refers to you and harbored feelings of inadequacy. It could also signify guilt over how you've acted toward others around you.

evening

A dream that takes place in the evening suggests a situation in your life may be coming to a close. To dream of stars shining in the evening sky suggests hope and brighter times ahead.

evergreen

A dream of an evergreen—especially the word itself—may be a metaphor. To be "ever green" indicates wealth or at least financial stability. An evergreen or pine tree might symbolize hope or even immortality. A decorated evergreen or Christmas tree suggests giving or receiving gifts.

examination

If you dream of taking an exam, it might indicate a concern about inadequacy or failure. A stack of tests could suggest you feel you are being tested too often. You feel that someone is judging you. Look at the surrounding elements in the dream. If you forget to go to class in your dream, it suggests you are worried about being unprepared.

exchange

To dream of exchanging one thing for another indicates a recent change in your way of thinking or even your style—the way you present yourself to others. What is it you're exchanging? Notice the people around you in the dream and how they act toward you.

excrement

A dream of excrement can be a good omen. First of all, it can nourish new ideas and beginnings. It also signifies ridding yourself of what you no longer need to start out anew. In rare cases, it can refer to feelings of being dirty (see *dirt*).

execution

If you're about to be executed or about to witness an execution in your dream, it refers to the current sadness and heaviness of heart you feel. If you're depressed, seek professional help. In rare cases, execution can also refer to the end of the old, and a new start, in terms of a way of life.

executive

Dreaming of being an executive in your dream is usually quite literal. You may long for more power and authority in your career. In some cases, this also refers to having more stability in your home and family life. Or it reveals your desire to feel in charge of what is going on in your life.

exhaustion

More often than not, this is a literal dream referring to your current physical health. It may be time for you to take a break or go on vacation. Also, it can refer to feelings of being overly drained emotionally.

exhibitionism

Exhibitionism, in a dream, is healthy. It signifies a willingness to take things on with open arms and to show the world your vulnerability. In some cases, exhibitionism also refers to an affinity for more sexual adventures. It suggests you feel free of the constraints of society or age.

exile

To dream of being in exile usually represents one of three things. You could feel you're being left out or punished by a social circle or relationship you long for. Or, it can mean you feel judged or criticized. Another possibility is that you just feel alone right now.

expedition

To set out on an expedition signifies an openness and willingness to have new adventures—both with travel and in your relationships. It's a good sign for positive experiences soon to come.

explosion

A dream of an explosion could be an attempt by your unconscious to get you to pay attention to a matter of concern. An explosion may suggest a release or an outburst of repressed anger, or an upheaval in your life.

eye(s)

Eyes have been called the windows of the soul. If you dream of your own eyes, you may be opening up to a new way of seeing things in your waking life or to a heightened sense of your own intuition and inner wisdom. If you get something in your eye or your eye is bloodshot or otherwise unclear, something is obscuring your ability to see a situation clearly. If you are looking deeply into another's eyes in the dream, you feel you are seen and known for who you really are—or you wish that were so.

eyeglasses

Eyeglasses (or contact lenses), in a dream, refer to seeing the world more clearly. Your unconscious is trying to tell you to take a good look around. If eyeglasses are handed to you in the dream, you are being given the opportunity to expand your range of vision. You need to pay more attention to what is going on in your life right now.

F

face

If you see your own face in a dream, this is a symbol for the face you show to others and the world. Your face is your identity in the world. It represents the most public aspect of your persona. In the dream, notice the expression on your face. Are you smiling? Angry? Sad? The dream most assuredly will be trying to reveal something that hides beneath your the public "face." If the face is the main element of the dream and you dream you are turning away, you may be having difficulty facing a situation or behavior in yourself or others.

Facebook

If you dream you are on Facebook, you want others to be able to get to know you. If you are distressed in the dream by being on Facebook, you worry that you have revealed too much of yourself or are losing your privacy in some situation or personal matter of importance.

facelift

To dream of having a facelift signifies you'd like people to see you in a different light. What is it you imagine they feel toward you? On rare occasions, dreaming of a facelift can be a literal dream—you fear becoming and looking old.

fairy

Fairies are light, ethereal creatures of whimsy, fun, and guidance. Dreaming of fairies could indicate you want to embrace a lighter, more magical part of yourself or connect more deeply to nature and the spirit realms. Fairies can also be messengers or tricksters. Look at the situation or events in the dream to see what the fairies are trying to tell you about your life right now.

falcon

Dreaming of a falcon represents spiritual awareness and rising to new heights. It also indicates freedom from the burdens of society. In some cases, a falcon can signify news soon to come. If you feel a strong, positive connection to the falcon, it may be your totem.

falling

Falling is a common dream symbol and usually an expression of concern about failure. The dream could be a metaphor for falling down on the job. In most falling dreams, the dreamer never lands. If you do hit the ground, it could mean you've struck bottom in a matter. If you are unharmed, the dream may be suggesting that you won't be hurt by something you perceive as a failure.

famous

To dream of being famous signifies you long to be in the public eye and to be rewarded for your previous efforts. This dream can be a release dream or a wish-fulfillment dream.

fan

A mechanical fan moves air and, as such, represents spiritual guidance. It indicates clearing the air and clarifying your thinking. Fans in dreams may symbolize your need to go with the flow now and take things as they come. If you dream of followers who are fans of yours, you desire recognition for your accomplishments, or you feel supported in your creativity and work by many people in your life.

fat

A dream of being fat might indicate a concern about your diet. It could also be a metaphor either for wealth and abundance, or for overindulgence.

father

The appearance of your father can have many connotations, depending on the context of the dream and your relationship with him. Typically it represents a need for advice in a troubling situation or the need to protect yourself in some situation. Someone in your life may have qualities that remind you of your father.

father figure

To dream of a father figure in your dream represents the need for more stability in your life. It could also be your unconscious telling you to be wary of the current situation you're facing. If you have bad feelings about this father figure, you may doubt your place within your own family. Are those around you treating you with respect?

feather

To dream of a feather floating through the air bodes well. Your burdens will be light and easily mastered. To dream of an eagle feather implies your aspirations will be met.

February

A dream of this short winter month might suggest you feel the need to retreat from the world. Perhaps you are depressed with the amount of time things are taking to manifest in your life. If you love the winter and winter sports, this could be a dream of pleasure and anticipation of some of your favorite activities. The dream's setting or this time of year may indicate when you are at your best and happiest.

feet

You get around in the world on your feet. Feet enable you to move forward in life, so when you dream about your feet, notice whether they are bare or in shoes. Bare feet may signify you are comfortable and feel free about whatever situation is currently going on in your life. If you are having difficulty moving your feet in the dream, think about where in your waking life you may fear moving forward. If your feet are steady in the dream, you feel confident and comfortable with your ability to get where you need to go in life.

fence

A dream of a fence can indicate that you feel "fenced in." A fence can block you or it can protect you. If you are "on the fence," the dream might suggest you are undecided about something.

fever

To dream you are suffering from a fever suggests a needless worry over a small affair. Be patient, and it will work itself out. This dream may also be a response from your body letting you know you are getting sick and that you actually have a temperature.

field

To dream of green fields, ripe with corn or grain, indicates great abundance. If you dream of plowed fields, you are getting ready to plant the seeds of your future. If you dream of lost crops, you fear some endeavor will come to naught. Perhaps you are ready to harvest all that you have created with your hard work and attention to detail. If so, enjoy!

fig

Figs are one of the sensual symbols. A dream about figs can refer to all things erotic—desire, sex, sexual need, and longing. Who is eating the fig in your dream? A fig also signifies hidden pleasures you should take advantage of. They're waiting for you.

fight

To fight in a dream may represent a conflict or the need to resolve an issue. Are you winning or losing a fight? Are you fighting with a loved one? Pay attention to other details in the dream so that you may interpret it better.

filing

To dream of filing signifies a hidden need to separate your feelings and emotions from a potentially difficult situation. It could also recommend getting better organized in your life.

fingers

Fingers, in a dream, refer to touch, emotion, accusation, warmth, and communication. In order to determine the meaning of the dream, take note of what you're doing with your fingers or how the other person is using them. Translate this literally, and then look for other symbols in the dream.

fire

Fire is a primal universal symbol, deeply embedded in the consciousness of all living beings. It represents rebirth, containing within itself the power of consumption and regeneration. Think about all the ways you use the imagery of fire in your daily life. If someone "lights a fire" under you, he is trying to get you going on something, but if someone "lights your fire" she ignites your passion. When you dream of fire—even the flame of a candle—you are being asked to come alive in some area of your life.

Your subconscious is trying to connect you to that vital, primal energy of inspiration, life force, and passion. Fire is generally a favorable symbol, so long as you are not burned. Alternately, fire can symbolize destruction, purification, illumination, and a spiritual awakening. Look for other metaphors. What are you getting fired up about? Are you (or another figure in the dream) concerned about being fired or getting burned?

fire engine

A symbol of distress and ultimately of protection, a fire engine indicates worry over an important matter at hand with the hope that help is on the way.

firefighting

To dream of fighting flames suggests hard work is required before you'll achieve success. If you are trying to put out a fire or are watching others put out a fire, you fear an emotional issue or situation will get out of control and you would rather make it go away.

fireplace

Fireplaces signify warmth, comfort, financial stability, domestic happiness, and a longing to increase your social status. Examine the aspects of the dream to determine which meaning fits for you. Sitting in front of a fireplace with a friend or loved one means you'd like to be closer, emotionally, to this person.

fireworks

A dream of fireworks suggests a celebration, a joyous explosion, or a release of repressed feelings.

fish

Fish are at home in the water, so dreaming of fish relates to your emotional life. Fish swimming can symbolize exploration of the unconscious or something that lies below the surface. The Jungian interpretation is that fish symbolize a spiritual quest. Fish in dreams also represent good intuition, so trust your gut. Fish also refer to the month of February/March and the zodiac sign of Pisces.

fishing

To dream of fishing signifies a need to examine your emotions and to delve deeper into your unconscious. Because fish also refer to your intuition, you might be fishing for a solution to a problem—you already know how to solve it.

fit

Dreaming of being physically fit is a good indication that you're feeling psychologically good about yourself. This can also be a wish-fulfillment dream—you'd literally like to look better and be more fit.

five

Five is the connecting number—the swing number between the four basic symbols and the higher numerical vibrations. It reflects the shift from the more purely personal numbers of 1, 2, 3, and 4 (self, duality, mother, and father) toward the transpersonal experiences reflected in 6, 7, 8, and 9 (others, spirituality, eternity, and cycles). As such it usually represents change when it shows up in a dream. Change is unpredictable and can be for good or ill, so notice what's going on when five comes into your dreams. Five can also represent the struggle between freedom and discipline, and can give you important messages about how you approach goals and tasks. If you are giving someone "high fives" in your dream, you are celebrating an accomplishment or shared success.

flag

Your unconscious is aware of social issues around you. Are political issues irritating you? Perhaps you long for less confusion and more cohesiveness in a partnership. A flag can be a warning in a dream. If you dream there is a "flag down on the play," then there is something inappropriate about your actions or someone else's in a situation. Similarly, if you dream about seeing "red flags" in your dream, you are being asked to proceed with caution in that area of your life. Flags are also used to communicate and denote something of importance, so reflect on how the flags are showing up in your dreams to determine the meaning for you at this time in your life.

flames

To see flames in a dream represents the need for purity and purification of thoughts and deeds. Take note of what is on fire to determine the exact meaning. Flames can also refer to hidden passion or a crush you prefer not to admit to.

flint

Striking flint can represent fickleness or a little devil in you waiting to get out. It can also refer to love and marriage, or to a spark between you and another person.

flirting

If you're flirting in your dream, you are trying to attract something new into your life. Who are you flirting with? If it has a positive outcome, it could be a wish-fulfillment dream rather than a prophetic one.

floating

This can be an astral dream—your spirit actually could be floating. This is a very positive sign of good things to come; it means happier, more hopeful, and easier times ahead.

flogging

To be flogged in a dream signifies you feel you should be punished for something you've done or for treating someone badly. To see someone flogged in a dream indicates the need to settle some emotional issues in your life.

flood

A dream of a flood might suggest you are being overwhelmed by emotion. Or, your awareness of the unconscious aspects of your being may be rising. A dream of flooding can also warn that personal matters are spilling over into other areas of your life.

flower

Flowers have universal connotations of celebration, love, and ceremony. If you dream of dead flowers, however, you are dreaming about a part of yourself or your life that has passed. If you dream of flower buds, you are opening to new experiences or aspects of yourself. If the flowers are in full bloom, you feel confident and fulfilled at this time in your life. Flowers represent your own unfolding, so think about what in your life is flowering, blooming, or past its peak. The type of flower will also have particular associations. Think about the color and type of flower and the connotations you have to determine what the dream's message is for you.

fly (insect)

You may be experiencing some pesky setbacks that are causing disappointment now. Try to be patient. It may take a little longer, but things should go as planned. If you dream of being bitten by a fly, you are being annoyed by someone in your circle of acquaintances.

flying

A flying dream may suggest you are soaring, or flying high, as a result of a successful venture. Flying can also symbolize breaking free of restrictions or inhibitions. Flying itself can be a joyous experience in a dream, no matter what the symbolic meaning.

fog

Dreaming of foggy conditions indicates a lack of clarity in some aspect of your life. Fog can also symbolize something hidden or something you're not seeing. Keep in mind that fog is usually short-lived. When it lifts, you will gain a new sense of clarity.

foliage

A dream of foliage signifies concerns in love and in financial security. If the foliage is lush and green, it indicates good times ahead. If it is wilting, it may portend problems soon to come.

food

Because food is essential for survival, a dream of food has to do with nourishment—ideas, relationships, material well-being, and so on. It also suggests you are acknowledging new ways of looking at things and incorporating them (digestion) into your life. Pay attention to the foods you eat in the dream—are they healthy and nourishing, or bad for you?

fool

To dream of a fool advises you to take a chance on something risky in order to be successful. It means a leap of faith is necessary for you.

footprints

Footprints may signify you long to emulate someone who is close to you. Perhaps you'd like to be as successful as that person or possess some of his qualities. It may also be a sign that you can see where you need to go in life but are not yet ready to step into those impressions.

forehead

A forehead in a dream signifies worry over a particular issue. Though things may be tough right now, this dream means you'll soon find a resolution to the problem at hand.

forest

A forest suggests an exploration of the unconscious. It can also symbolize a need or desire to retreat from everyday life—to restore and revitalize your energies through nature. To dream of a lush forest in complete foliage may mean prosperity and pleasure, although finding yourself in a dense forest could signify you feel lost emotionally.

forgery

Deceptive people may be around you—watch out! This symbol could also indicate contracts are not as they seem. Read the fine print. Forgery can refer to unexpected money, such as an inheritance or lucky lottery number.

forked line/fork in the road

You'll have to make a decision soon. This dream indicates you should choose the simplest route for now.

fortune-teller/fortune-telling

You are looking for answers of a mystical nature. You have anxiety about the future and want to be reassured. What is it you are concerned about? Seek out the help of people you trust.

fountain

A dream of a fountain can suggest longevity and virility. Water is related to the emotions and unconscious, and a fountain can indicate an emotional surge. Also, a dream of a fountain can recommend examining your emotions. What is the condition of the fountain? A fountain with clear water suggests vast possessions and many pleasurable emotions. A dry and broken fountain symbolizes emotional emptiness. A sparkling fountain in the moonlight can indicate a hidden emotional pleasure.

four

Four symbolizes masculine, father energy. It is the number of stability, structure, and foundation. Even the appearance of the number, with its square 90-degree angles, suggests structure and support. When four shows up in a dream, consider issues of fatherhood or with your father. This may be a message about your own stability and security in life, including financial security.

fox

If you're currently arguing with someone, a fox dream may be a warning not to speak. Silence will help you gain control over the situation. Also, be careful of the people around you. Someone may not be as honest and forthcoming as she seems.

fragrance

To smell a fragrance in your dream is a sign of happiness to come and good luck in love. It can also indicate a visitation from a loved one on the Other Side who wore a particular scent. If so, enjoy the reconnection.

fraud

Dreaming of fraud can be a warning about yourself or others. Who is committing fraud in the dream? If you're the one committing fraud, it's possible you've shown a side of yourself to someone and now feel vulnerable.

freedom

A dream about freedom can mean two completely opposite things. It could indicate you feel repressed and are longing for more freedom to do the things you'd like to do. It might also mean you are currently feeling good about the freedom you're experiencing in life.

freelance

To dream about freelance projects can be literal—you're involved or would like to be involved in these types of undertakings. It could also refer to the autonomy you'd like to express more often. Creative ideas should come to you more freely now.

friends

If you dream of a gathering of your friends and they are all happy, you are feeling connected to others and happy with that support and connection. If you dream of a gathering of your friends who are sad and gloomy, you are feeling disconnected at this time in your life. You might want to reach out for support.

frog

Frogs are transformative creatures—remember the fairytale about the prince who was turned into a frog? They start as tadpoles, grow legs and arms, and develop lungs. To dream of a frog may imply a major change or transformation in your life. Because frogs live part of their lives in water, a frog may also symbolize a leap into the unconscious.

frost

Frost, like ice, may represent a cold emotional state, your own or someone else's. To see a friend or lover in frost could mean chilly feelings regarding the relationship.

frostbite

If you dream of frostbite, it could indicate a part of you feels stuck in a current situation or love relationship. It could also mean you're not expressing yourself as well as you could or should.

fruit

Fruit, in your dreams, refers to health, long life, and knowledge. Are you yearning to take a class? It may be a good time to do so. Sometimes, fruit in dreams can be your unconscious giving you a literal warning to eat more healthfully.

fugitive

If you're on the run in your dream, chances are you're running from yourself. What aspect of your life are you unhappy with? Being a fugitive also refers to running away from your problems in love, at home, or at work.

funeral

Rather than death, this usually refers to saying goodbye to a way of thinking or a way of life. It indicates change and transformation. In rare cases, it can refer to worry about growing older.

fungus

Fungus in your dream can refer to an actual physical problem. It can also symbolize a situation in your life that's growing out of control.

funnel

Funneling liquid from one container to another refers to moving emotions, perhaps between you and someone else. You may be picking up the emotions of someone close to you or vice versa. Some people have this dream when their bladders are full in real life.

fur

Dreaming of fur indicates warmth, nostalgia, and friends from long ago. Have you recently seen a friend from your past? Fur in dreams can also suggest you are feeling luxurious at this time in your life.

fur coat

Dreaming of a fur coat doesn't necessarily mean you want one. Even if you're against the manufacture or ownership of a fur coat, its presence in your dream signifies luxury and easy living.

furnace

A furnace usually relates to security in your life and relationships. Lighting a furnace might refer to new love and the possibility of the relationship growing in intimacy. An unlit furnace can mean you fear you will be unable to provide the necessary fuel to accomplish your goals in life.

furniture

The meaning of this dream depends on how you feel about a particular piece of furniture. If you dream of furniture from your childhood, you may be reliving issues from the past. If it's a comfortable piece of furniture, you might long for more comfort or warmth in your home life.

fury

To be in a fury in your dream indicates a certain anger you feel toward yourself with regard to recent decisions you've made. If you feel fury toward another person in your dream, you may harbor resentment toward him. You'll need to deal with this soon.

fuse

If a fuse blows in your dream, this refers to repressed anger you have toward someone. It can also signify unexpected, startling news to come.

G

gambling

A dream of gambling suggests taking a chance. If you are winning, it may bode well for a risky business deal or even a new love relationship. If you're watching others win, the game may symbolize fear of taking a chance. Whether you should be more daring or play it safe depends on other factors in the dream.

games

In order to translate this dream, notice what kind of game you're playing and whether you win or lose. If it's a board game, you may feel a bit insignificant in your current dealings. If you win, it's a good omen of what is to come. If you lose, you may feel as if others are playing with you.

gang

If you encounter a gang in your dream, it means you're feeling nervous about a situation you're currently in, and the need to escape is great. You may also feel that others have "ganged up" on you and you are trying to hold your own in the situation. Confront the problem, and you'll cease having this unnerving dream.

garbage

To dream of garbage suggests a need to get rid of old, worn-out ideas or excess baggage in your life. Ask yourself if you are clinging to something or some condition you no longer need.

garden

Dreaming of a garden sometimes indicates a need to bring more beauty into your life. It may be a metaphor for personal or spiritual growth. Or, it might suggest a desire to cultivate a new talent or to move into a higher realm of awareness. A garden with lots of weeds may symbolize a need to "weed out" old ideas so your spiritual self can blossom.

gardener

A gardener in your dream represents a person who takes care of things and enables them to sprout and grow successfully. These could be relationships, financial endeavors, or personal happiness. Who is the gardener? Do you know this person in your waking life? Chances are he or she has a positive influence on your life. If you are the gardener, you are actively tending to the details of your life.

garnish

In a dream a garnish on top of a dish signifies the ultimate details in terms of your soul. Because food relates to spiritual nourishment, the garnish is the final touch. This is a sign that you're getting your life together—and it's going well.

gate

A gate may represent a portal from one state of being to another. Is there a gatekeeper in your dream? Do you meet the gatekeeper's criteria for passage to the next level?

gather

What are you gathering in your dreams? Flowers? Books? Whatever you're gathering is what you hope to reap from your efforts. Take note of the object, and think about the associations you have with that item to understand what it is you are trying to pull together in your life.

gathering

To dream you're in a gathering can mean many things, depending on what type of gathering it is. Is it a happy occasion? If so, it represents a time in your life when you are enjoying socializing with others. If not, you may be feeling emotionally connected to others who are going through a difficult time.

ghost

An apparition or ghost appearing in a dream may suggest that something in your life is elusive or out of reach. If a person who has died appears in a dream, consider your past relationship with that person and what he symbolized in your life. A ghost of a living relative or friend in a dream may mean someone you know is not as fully present as you would like him to be in your life. Or, if that ghost appears haggard, it may indicate a part of you that you fear is disappearing.

giant

Dreaming of a giant can mean two things. If you're scared of the giant, you're aware of problems looming over you that you're unwilling to face.

If the giant is friendly, it could mean your life is about to expand in a big way.

gift

If you're given a gift in your dreams, it's a good sign. You probably feel you're being rewarded for a job well done. If your gift is broken or damaged, however, you may feel you're not getting enough attention from loved ones. If you are giving the gift, you want to share more of yourself with others.

girl

To dream of a little girl can signify a longing for innocence or purity in your life. It could also refer to femininity. If you see yourself as a little girl, it means you're feeling vulnerable lately and may want to be taken care of. Perhaps some childhood experience is influencing your behavior in your current life situations.

glass

Glass suggests separation and passive observation. Looking through glass in a dream may indicate something is clouding your brightest hopes. Receiving cut glass in a dream may mean you need to look at a situation from several different angles. As you do so, the pieces of the puzzle will fall into place.

glassware

Glassware represents your home life. If the glass breaks, it could indicate a recent or upcoming dispute at home. If the glass is beautiful or if you're drinking from it, it indicates stability and good luck with family matters.

glider

Flying in a glider signifies hopefulness and optimism toward the future. Possibly, you feel like you've been liberated recently from an oppressive situation. This could also refer to the positive progress of a new love in your life.

globe

A globe, in a dream, signifies wisdom, world consciousness, and politics. It can also refer to upcoming travel. A globe is a circle, which signifies wholeness. You're searching for completion in a project or venture.

gloom

If the scene around you in your dream is gloomy, you probably feel this way about your current state of affairs. What's depressing you? Look to the other figures in the dream and examine whether or not they're positive influences in your waking life.

gloves

If you dream of wearing gloves, regardless of the weather, it means you feel the need to protect yourself from something you are accepting into your life. To dream of old, ragged gloves suggests you may feel unprepared and unable to properly protect yourself. To dream of finding a pair of gloves may indicate you are being offered protection through serendipity.

glue

Glue, in a dream, may signify your wish to bind something or someone to you. Do you want to be closer to someone? If you dream the glue is an annoyance, perhaps you feel stuck in a current situation or believe someone is not sticking to a promise he made you.

goat

A goat signifies nature, femininity, and care-giving. If the goat is eating in the dream, it means you long to find more solid ground in your relationships. The goat also refers to the month of January and the zodiac sign Capricorn.

gold

Dreaming of gold jewelry, coins, or a gold object indicates success is forthcoming. To dream of a room filled with gold suggests you feel very blessed and abundant in your life right now. If you dream your gold is not real, you are feeling deceived by someone or in some situation in your life.

gold dust

Seeing or feeling gold dust usually indicates a sprinkling of good fortune. Alternatively, the dust could mean that something treasured is crumbling and you fear the loss.

Google

If you dream you are googling you are looking for a piece of information you feel you don't have. If you cannot find what you are searching for, you feel the knowledge you seek is eluding you.

goose

A goose is often associated with a golden egg; dreaming of one is a symbol of abundance. On the other hand, a goose in the oven or on fire suggests that your goose is cooked—you're in trouble. Alternately, a big goose egg can mean "zero" reward for your efforts.

gossip

If people are gossiping about you in your dream, you're concerned with your recent behavior and are worried what people may think of you. If you're the one gossiping, you may feel unable to open communication with someone in your waking life. This person could also have qualities you don't like, qualities that are also within you.

grains

Grains indicate abundance, birth, and rebirth. They also refer to the start of a new project or undertaking. Dreaming of grains can also signify abundance and fruitfulness in financial ventures.

grandmother

Notice the aspects of this dream. Are you dreaming of a grandmother who has passed on? If the dream is vivid and in color, chances are you're having an astral visit with her. Perhaps she wants to let you know she's fine or she has advice for you. If you dream of someone else's grandmother, you probably long to be close to a maternal figure.

grandparents

A dream about grandparents may signify that you're looking for recognition and approval of your current efforts. If your own grandparents have passed away, check to see if this is an astral dream. Normally, you will receive visits from the Other Side from one grandparent at a time.

grapes

Grapes in a dream indicate fun, joyous times ahead. Don't be so pragmatic—go with the flow. Be spontaneous and things will turn out for the best. Grapes also indicate enjoyment of life's physical pleasures and nature's abundance. If you are upset with someone, you could have "sour grapes" toward that person.

grass

Dreams set in meadows or tall grass have a mystical, fluid quality to them. You may be in a period of new growth in your life and are in the process of discovering different aspects of yourself. If you are barefoot, you feel part of whatever is happening. If you dream you are lying in a meadow in an idyllic setting, you feel in the flow of events and secure with the natural and instinctual side of yourself. Dreams about awakening sensuality often involve tactile imagery like soft grasses, wildflowers, color, and light, so think about where you may need to reconnect with your natural sensuality.

grave

Like many dream symbols, a grave is one that grabs your attention, especially if it's your grave. A grave may portend a death, but not necessarily a physical one. It may mean you're leaving the old behind, moving on to something new. As a metaphor, a grave suggests you may be dealing with a grave (serious) matter.

grease

This is a warning to watch where you're going in some situation in your life. The road ahead could be slick and slippery. If another person is involved, make sure you can trust him. Take time to plan and prepare if you are embarking on a new venture. The dream may mean you want to move things along faster and are looking for ways to "grease" the wheels so you can achieve your goal as quickly as possible.

green

Green is the color of plants and is associated with the heart chakra. It is the integrating or balancing point in the rainbow of colors. The color of money in many nations, green in a dream is often associated with abundance on the material plane. If you dream of green, you could be experiencing feelings of jealousy toward another person or situation—the "green-eyed monster" may be present. With the expanding consciousness toward green living, you may desire to be more in harmony with nature and her resources. Green is also a color of healing, growth, money, and new beginnings. It suggests positive movement.

grief

Grief, in a dream, can be a good thing because it helps you deal with a problem you're facing in waking life. Normally, you are actually suffering from something harsh in both the dream and in real life. The dream is helping you release the emotion.

grocery store

Dreaming of a grocery store refers to the many upcoming choices you need to make. Take note of what you purchase in the store. Is it a practical food, a staple such as rice or corn? Or is it a fun, sweet food such as cookies or cake? This is a warning about making the choices that best support and nurture you.

grotesque

Dreaming of something grotesque refers to a fear you have within yourself. What is grotesque in the dream? What does it signify for you? If a part of yourself is misshapen or grotesque, you feel a quality you possess is negative or unhealthy and becoming visible to others.

group

Dreaming of a group can have two meanings. How do you feel toward this group? Are you included or excluded? You may feel left out in your personal relationships if you long to be part of this group. If the group annoys you, it means you resent having to join or follow the pack.

growing

Growing, in a dream, refers to your emotional state. Are you the one growing? Are you watching something grow? If you're growing straight and tall, it's a sign of positive things to come. If your growing is distorted in some way, it means you'll have some struggles, emotionally, but that you'll come out of it a better, stronger you.

guard

Seeing a guard in your dream may signify that something you deem valuable is being kept away from you. What is beyond your grasp? Does it have to do with emotions or with a valuable object? Most likely, the thing you crave most is affection or love from a person close to you.

guest

Having a guest in your house can signify two things. Is this person someone you know? If he is, it's someone you'd like to bring closer, within your circle. If the guest is a stranger, you'd like to feel freer with your choice of friends and within your social circle.

gun

A gun in your possession can symbolize protection, but it is also a sign of aggression. If you shoot yourself, the act is what's important, not the gun. Think about where you might be shooting down other people's ideas or even your own opportunities.

gushing

Gushing water or fluid often refers to release—mostly sexual. For a woman to dream of gushing water indicates repressed sexual desire. Gushing water from a fountain can also mean upcoming joy and happiness.

gymnastics

Performing gymnastics in a dream signifies you're feeling happy and liberated—or that you'd like to feel this way. If you're watching gymnastics, it indicates a longing for simpler, happier times.

gypsy

Gypsy dreams can translate differently, depending on how you feel about the gypsy. A gypsy can signify mistrust, misunderstanding, and misplaced values. But she can also symbolize adventure, freedom, and spontaneity. Analyze how you feel toward the gypsy, and you'll get to the root of these issues.

H

hail

To dream of being in a hailstorm, or to hear hail knocking against the house, represents being besieged by a troubling matter, thoughts, or emotions. Know that you cannot be hurt by your own strong emotions, so express and release them. If you fear being hurt by another's emotions, you need to talk with that person about how his emotional outbursts are affecting your life.

hair

To dream you have a beautiful head of hair and are combing it indicates you are concerned with your appearance and the public self you show to the world. To see your hair turn unexpectedly white suggests sudden grief or shock over a situation. For a man to dream his hair is thinning might be a literal dream of a fear of baldness. For either sex, dreaming of losing hair reveals fears of losing your attractiveness or growing older.

hallway

A hallway can signify many things, but it usually refers to the many choices (doorways) along your path. If a hallway is empty, without doorways, it means you feel your path was chosen for you. If the doorways are open along the way, it means that you haven't yet found your way—but you will.

halo

Dreaming of a halo indicates a longing to return to innocence and spiritual purity. What is it in your life that you feel needs refining? Chances are, you're dreaming of a person or place from the past that you once deemed perfect.

halter-top

A dream of putting on or wearing a halter-top refers to a need to celebrate youth. Or, perhaps you're too caught up in the need to be beautiful, and your unconscious is aware of this. How far will you go to stay young?

hammer

A hammer may suggest strength or power. However, because it can be used for either constructive or destructive purposes, the way the hammer is used is the key to its meaning in the dream.

hand

A dream of a hand (or hands) is open to numerous interpretations, depending on what the hand is doing and the surrounding circumstances. Shaking hands is an act of friendship or an agreement. Hands folded in prayer may suggest you are seeking help or pursuing religious or spiritual urges. A grasping hand may reveal a fear of death. Something important could be "at hand." Beautiful hands signify feelings of great honor and rapid advancement. Ugly and malformed hands point to disappointment and poverty. A detached hand represents solitude—

people may fail to understand your views and feelings in a matter. Burning your hands suggests you have overreached your abilities and will suffer some loss because of it.

handbag

If you dream of a handbag, it indicates that you're trying to work out day-to-day problems. You're concerned with the details—appointments, bills you have to pay, and so on. A lost handbag means you feel you are losing your identity.

handyman

A handyman fixes things or makes repairs on behalf of someone else. When you dream of a handyman it may signify that you feel some aspect of your life is not being fulfilled and you need help to fix whatever is wrong. You don't feel you can fix the problem on your own, so ask for help. If you are the handyman, you feel you are good at helping others with their problems. The dream might also mean you'll be asked to help someone soon.

hang

If you see someone being hanged in your dream, you are afraid of being judged without the chance to explain yourself. If you dream you're being hanged for something you've done, it means you have enormous guilt. This is a warning to stop being overcritical of yourself.

hangover

To dream of a hangover signifies you've been overdoing some aspect of your life that's unhealthy. It could be smoking too much or even drinking too much. Your unconscious recognizes this as a vice you would do better without.

happy

To dream of being happy signifies you're optimistic about what is to come. It also means you're aware of the positive energy surrounding you now. Go with it. Luck is on your side.

harbor

To dream of a harbor suggests you are digging into your subconscious for answers to a current situation. You long for peace, safety, and tranquility in your life. You want to feel secure in your emotional life.

harem

To dream of being in a harem can mean two things: either you long to be more open sexually or you fear your partner is being unfaithful. To see a harem may signify that you're now open to try more creative things in life—perhaps exotic ones.

harvest

A harvest represents completion and abundance, and it may indicate that your reward is due. As with all symbols, personal connotations are important. For instance, if you grew up on a farm, a harvest dream could mean a longing to return to the past or to simpler times.

hat

A hat can suggest concealment, as in "keep it under your hat." Dreaming that you have a feather in your hat indicates achievement. A tall hat signifies responsibility and authority.

havoc

If you dream there is havoc or bedlam around you, you're feeling overwhelmed in your life right now. If you're causing the havoc in your dream, it means you are aware that others deem your behavior less than satisfactory.

Hawaii

A dream of Hawaii or things associated with Hawaii is most likely a wish-fulfillment dream. Perhaps things have become too staid and predictable in life. You long for some fun and excitement. Maybe it's time to take a trip?

hawk

A hawk is a creature with keen sight. A soaring hawk in a dream might suggest the need for insight. It also might mean you should keep a hawk's eye on someone or a situation.

head

Dreaming of a human head could indicate that you are "ahead," or successful, in a matter of importance. A head also symbolizes a source of wisdom.

hearse

If you dream of seeing a hearse, it may indicate you sense some problems ahead that you feel could be deadly. If you dream of riding in a hearse, it signifies that you're saying goodbye to a certain part of yourself. Be ready for new things to come.

heart

To see a heart might relate to romantic inclinations. Is there a heartthrob in your life? Alternately, the image might suggest you need to get to the heart of the matter. On the negative side, if your heart is bleeding, it may mean you are sad or that excessive sympathy is becoming a burden for you, the recipient, or both.

heaven

If you dream of heaven, it could mean you're aspiring to new heights in your love life or career. Examine who else is in the dream and what that person is doing there.

heel

The heel of your foot or shoe may symbolize vulnerability, as in the Achilles' heel story. It might also stand for an oppressive situation, as in "under someone's heel." Are you dealing with someone who is not trustworthy? He or she could be the heel in your dream.

heights

To dream of being afraid of heights signifies that you're not doing enough in your career. You may have a fear of success, and consequently your own ambition is being thwarted. If you love heights, then you are soaring to new heights in some aspect of your life, or you are gaining new perspective on a situation or relationship.

helmet

Wearing a helmet in a dream denotes protection. The helmet could also symbolize a need to guard your time, thoughts, or ideas.

hemorrhage

To dream of hemorrhaging denotes that your life force is being sapped by a situation or person in your life. Someone or something is emotionally draining you and you feel your energy is being depleted.

hermaphrodite

To dream of a hermaphrodite could mean two things. Either you're trying to unify the different sides of yourself, or you've been presented with two choices and you have an important decision to make.

hermit

Dreaming of a hermit is a sign that you need to be patient and wait for things to right themselves. Now is not the time to take action. It also means you enjoy the time you spend alone, and that it is time to listen to your inner wisdom.

hero

To dream of a hero signifies you'd like more recognition in your career. If you dream you are the hero, it means you're feeling good about yourself and can sense that things are now going your way.

hiccup

Most likely, some plans you had or will have in the near future have been thwarted and you're searching to find out why. Hiccupping, in a dream, also refers to making too much out of trivial matters.

hiding

If you're hiding in a dream, it signifies that you're embarrassed or may feel guilty about some of your recent behavior. It could also point to a desire to get away from the rigors of daily life.

high tide

To dream of a high tide symbolizes that a change, usually favorable, is in order—the tides are turning.

hill

If you dream of going up a hill, it's your unconscious telling you that you need to strive for more in life and love. If you dream of going down a hill, it may be that you're afraid of setbacks to come.

hitchhiking

To dream of hitchhiking is a message that you've been too dependent on others. You've relied on them to get you where you want to go, and now you need to take more responsibility for your actions. It may also be a warning that you've put yourself in danger in some situation and that you should be more careful in the near future.

hitting

If you dream of being hit in a dream, it means you feel others are taking advantage of you and are judging you harshly. If you dream of hitting someone or something, you may have resentment or anger bottled up and you need to express it.

hog

A fat hog in a dream may suggest abundance, whereas a lean, hungry hog may foretell of a troubling situation. If the hogs are wallowing in mud, the indication might be that you've lowered your standards regarding a matter, or that you are groveling. A squealing hog suggests something distasteful has occurred or will soon occur.

hole

Seeing a hole in a dream can symbolize a fear of the unknown. It may also refer to sexual desire and the need for sex in order to feel complete. A hole in your clothing indicates financial concerns.

holiday

Dreaming of a holiday is usually a wish-fulfillment dream. Perhaps things have been a bit boring lately or a little too hectic. This is the way your unconscious says you need to take a break.

home

To dream of a home usually points to how you feel about your life at the time of the dream. It can also refer to family life in general. Was the home in your dream cozy or a mess? Did you feel good in it? Who else was there?

homesickness

Being homesick in a dream is usually quite literal—you long for the way things were in the past. It can also portend a call or visit from someone you once knew and haven't heard from in a while.

homosexuality

Dreaming of being homosexual rarely has to do with your sexuality, unless this is a particular concern for you. More likely, the dream describes an emotional part of you that you've recently discovered. It might also mean you fear being different in some way.

honeymoon

A dream of a honeymoon can be a literal, wish-fulfillment dream. But dreaming of a honeymoon can also refer to a partnership in business. It's a good sign of positive things to come. If the honeymoon goes badly, it could be that you're nervous about the intentions of a new person in your life.

horse

A horse symbolizes strength, power, endurance, majesty, and virility. A man dreaming of a horse might desire virility and sexual prowess;

a woman might be expressing a desire for sexual intercourse. Riding a horse suggests you are in a powerful position.

hospital

Finding yourself in a hospital suggests a need for healing or a concern about your health. Seeing someone else in a hospital might indicate that the person is in a weakened condition. If you work in a hospital, the dream may relate to work matters. In the latter case, other circumstances in the dream should be examined to interpret its meaning.

house

Houses are common forums for dreams. Overall, you can think of a house in your dream as representing you or your life in the larger context. If you dream you are in your childhood home, perhaps your subconscious is using that location to let you know whatever is happening in your current life has its roots in your childhood experiences. If you dream you are in a hotel, you might feel you are not "at home" in some part of your life. Think about recent events and situations where you might have felt out of place or not totally comfortable with what was happening. If you dream you are in an office, almost assuredly you are processing experiences and emotions about your work life and career. Discovering new rooms in a house or following secret passages in an old house can indicate you are exploring the unconscious. This can also mean you are discovering new parts of yourself. A small house might suggest a feeling of confinement. If a house is under construction, it could symbolize growth. If it's dilapidated, the dream might be telling you that improvements are needed in some part of your life.

hugging

To dream you're hugging a stranger suggests you crave affection. If you know the person you are hugging, the interpretation will depend on your relationship to that person.

humidity

Dreaming of humidity represents an oppressive situation, either at work or at home.

hurricane

Destructive and unpredictable, hurricanes in dreams can have different meanings depending on the context. A coming hurricane symbolizes torment and suspense. Possibly, you're trying to avert failure. Looking at a hurricane's debris suggests that others will save you from calamity. If you dream you are in a house that is shattered by a hurricane, or you are trying to save someone caught in the rubble, it may mean your life will suffer many changes; you won't find peace in domestic or business matters. To see people dead and wounded as a result of a hurricane suggests you are concerned about the troubles of others.

I

ice

Ice in a dream may symbolize your emotional state or someone else's. Are you being given an icy reception? If you are in a tenuous situation, you could be skating on thin ice. In a sexual context, you could be acting coldly toward your partner (or vice versa). To dream of ice floating in a clear stream signifies an interruption of happiness. Ice is frozen water, so think about where your emotions can't flow freely, and release the blocks.

iceberg

To dream of hitting an iceberg in your dream means that things have been rocky emotionally, or you sense they soon will be. It's a good indication that, though there are obstacles to overcome, you'll be all right if you look for the warning signs and process your emotions as they emerge.

ice cream

A dream of ice cream, especially melting ice cream, may suggest that obstacles are being removed and there is reason to celebrate. If ice cream is your favorite dessert, the dream suggests you're being rewarded or have reason to treat yourself. It can also represent a desire for sexual fulfillment.

icicles

Icicles represent danger, or your concern about a matter that is hanging over you in some way. To dream of icicles falling off trees or the eaves of a house may suggest that some emotional misfortune will soon disappear. If you feel your own or another's emotions are hanging over you, it is time to confront the problems, deal with the emotions, and process them.

idiot

Seeing an idiot in your dream signifies your unconscious is aware that you're about to make a very foolish decision. If you dream of being an idiot, it means your self-confidence is low right now and you need to do something to bolster it.

illiteracy

Dreaming that you can't read or write has two meanings. Either you're having trouble expressing yourself in waking life, or there's a breakdown in communication with someone close to you.

illness

If you dream of being ill, ask yourself if you're in need of being cared for or pampered. This dream might also be a message to watch your health.

immortality

To dream of being immortal signifies your need to rise up to your own and others' expectations. Also, this dream can point to anxiety or an acute fear of getting older.

impersonation

To dream of impersonating someone, or that someone is impersonating you, refers to envy you may be feeling toward someone to whom you're close. Also, it signifies that your sense of self is being threatened in waking life.

impotence

A dream of impotence means you feel insignificant and powerless in some area of your life. Rarely does this dream actually refer to sexual problems.

incest

A dream of a sexual encounter with someone within your family is not necessarily a warning about incest. Examine your relationship with the person in the dream. If you've recently been alienated from this family member, the dream may be an expression of your love or need for love in a shocking way that will catch your attention.

indifference

This dream is indicative of how you think others view you. If someone is indifferent toward you in a dream, it could mean you worry this is how he really feels. Your unconscious may be letting you know that he does truly feel indifferent toward you. If you are indifferent toward someone or some situation, think about whether or not you wish to continue that relationship or project. Instead, put your energy toward something that has greater meaning for you.

indigo

Indigo is the dark, blue-black color of the night sky and is associated with the sixth chakra, the place of intuition and mysticism. It symbolizes the subconscious, the bridge between spiritual and physical reality. It is a color of deep mystery, the unknown, and psychic energy. When indigo shows up in your dreams, you may be opening to intuitive wisdom or experiencing psychic or precognitive dreams. Pay attention when indigo appears, as it could be alerting you to hidden information not obvious in your waking life. If you dream of someone wearing indigo, you may need to be wary—hidden aspects may not have been revealed yet.

infants

Infants signify new beginnings in life. You may be at the stage of a new venture where you are starting to explore your world and grow in your development.

infidelity

Many times, dreaming that your partner is being unfaithful is simply a fear you have of being abandoned or cheated on in waking life.

However, sometimes this is a warning sign that the deed is actually being done.

inheritance

Dreaming that you come into an inheritance is a good sign of opportunities soon to arrive. The dream suggests you'll be successful in your pursuits if you shoot for the stars. Dreaming of disinheritance denotes rough times ahead. If you dream of a will or making your own will, you are eager to create a legacy for others.

initiation

A dream of initiation suggests a new path is opening for you. It could be a career change or advancement. Often, initiatory dreams relate to a spiritual quest.

injured

If you dream of being injured, it refers to your current emotional state. Perhaps someone has used harsh words with you lately or has let you down in some way that has affected you deeply.

inquiry

If someone keeps asking something of you, in a dream, chances are you're aware you need to get this particular thing done. If you answer her, it means you've decided to go ahead and do it. If you don't, it means you're not willing to deal with it yet, but you know you need to.

insects

What's annoying or "bugging" you? If you dream of ants, you may be feeling "antsy" about a matter (see *ant*). Most insects in dreams are about your fears or frustrations. And, almost all represent little problems, behaviors, or situations that are annoying you but have not risen to the level of a major irritation. You can look to your own associations with the particular insect showing up in your dream to better understand the particular issue that might be the source of the irritation. Think of minor annoyances that come up during the day (rather than major difficulties), and you'll be on the right track.

insults

To be insulted in your dream means you are being hard on yourself. What are the insults? Do you feel this way toward yourself? Many times, if you're insulting someone in your dream, this is how you feel toward the person you're insulting.

intercourse

Many times, this dream is about wish-fulfillment and release. If you'd like to be more adventurous in life, you might also have this dream. The partner in the dream is less important than how you feel about the actual lovemaking. You may be desirous of greater intimacy and connection with someone in your life.

interview

Being interviewed in a dream is similar to taking an examination. It suggests you feel you're being judged. If you're surprised by the interview, it may indicate you are feeling unprepared in a business or family matter.

intestines

Dreaming of intestines relates to your courage. Often someone who's courageous is described as having "guts" or a bold action is considered "gutsy." This body part symbolizes strength of will and the gumption to move ahead in the face of adversity. Notice in the dream how you feel about the intestines and the level of your intestinal fortitude. Are they strong and healthy, or weak?

invalid

A dream of an invalid may indicate that you (or someone else you know) feel weak or incapable of living independently. It's an indication that you need to take charge of your life.

invisibility

To dream that you're invisible is metaphoric. You may feel you're being ignored by others and would like to be recognized more for who you are than who others think you are.

invitation

If you receive an invitation in your dream, it could mean you'd like to get out more and be more social. If you send out an invitation in your dream, you're looking for guidance from someone close to you.

ironing

Ironing in a dream signifies getting all the little things done in your life—paying bills, going to the doctor, running errands, and so on. Ironing can also refer to turning things around and making them go more smoothly.

island

An island can be viewed as an exotic place or as a separate, isolated land. Dreaming of an island might mean that a vacation is due, especially if going to the islands refers to your vacation destination. Alternately, finding yourself on a desert island may suggest you are cut off from others or from your inner self.

itching

If you have an itch in waking life, it could translate into your dream. As a metaphor, itching in a dream refers to little nagging problems you need to deal with as soon as possible.

ivy

Dreaming of ivy growing on trees or a house indicates you are adding to what you have. You are experiencing beautiful growth on top of what you have already brought into being. If the ivy is taking over and you are concerned in the dream, it indicates something in your life is taking over—you need to cut back and regroup.

J

jail

A jail may indicate you're feeling restricted or confined. You fear being punished—or, you may believe you should be punished. Dreaming of being a jailer suggests the desire to control others or to gain more control of your own life. In some cases jail dreams may refer to a past life. Who was your jailer? Do you know him in this life?

January

To dream of this month may mean you are ready for new beginnings. The new year begins in January, and it is a time of resolutions and change. Think about what in your life you want to change and make a plan to do so.

jaws

Do you feel like you're under attack? Jaws can be the entry point to an archetypal journey into the underworld. Such a dream might also translate as a disagreement with a close friend, family member, or partner. If your jaw is stiff in a dream, you might be repressing things that you need to communicate.

jealousy

Who are you jealous of in the dream? Is it someone you know or is it a stranger? If it's someone you know, this may be a literal dream. If it's someone you don't know, perhaps you are feeling a strong sense of inadequacy. Pamper yourself.

jewelry

In a material sense, jewelry can symbolize affluence, but look to other aspects of the dream for confirmation. Jewelry can also stand for inner wealth, self-worth, values, psychic protection, or healing.

jewels (gems)

Dreaming of jewels signifies good luck to come. To dream of owning emeralds means you may inherit property. Dreaming of a sapphire denotes continuous good fortune. Diamonds represent fidelity and commitment in love. Think about what the particular gem means to you. Your dream may even be telling you that wearing that gemstone might be good for your vibration.

job

Dreaming that you are at work may indicate you're overworked. You may be deeply focused on some aspect of your job, or you might want to work harder and achieve more.

joke

If you're the butt of the joke in your dream, you may feel you're being taken advantage of or that people are talking badly about you. If you're telling a joke in your dream, you're trying to lighten a situation or provide comic relief.

judge

If you're the judge, the dream suggests you have a choice to make. A judge can also represent justice or fairness. Alternately, a judge may stand for a part of you that criticizes your ideas or behavior. Or perhaps you're concerned that you're being judged. Who is judging you?

juggler

Dreaming of a juggler or having a dream in which you're juggling implies that you've been spreading yourself too thin lately. You might be trying to juggle a number of things in your waking life. It also indicates worrying about finances. Concentrate on one thing at a time.

July

A dream that takes place in this month symbolizes relaxation and freedom from responsibility. July is vacation time, the celebratory time of summer, so you may need to take a break or make time to get outside in the sunshine and relax.

jumping

Pick your metaphor. Are you "a jump ahead," "jumping to conclusions," "jumping the gun," or "jumping for joy"? A series of jumps may be the take-off point for a flying dream. A great leap can also symbolize success or achievement, "a leap of faith."

June

June is often associated with weddings and graduations. This may be a time in your life when you are celebrating a love relationship or feeling you have "graduated" in your personal growth and development.

jungle

A jungle may represent a hidden, dark part of yourself that you've been avoiding. Your unconscious might be advising you to explore this part of yourself. The dream jungle may also represent a great, untapped fertility for spiritual growth within you. Or, it might symbolize a situation in your life that is incredibly dense and complex, and through which you'll have to find your way.

junk

If you dream of junk or clutter, ask yourself if you're clinging to the past—to things or ideas that are no longer useful. If something you value appears as junk in a dream, it may indicate that you need to reassess your values.

jury

Being in front of a jury in your dream simply means you feel that someone is judging you. To be on a jury indicates that you have an important decision to make.

K

kangaroo

To see a kangaroo may suggest you're hopping mad about something. It could also mean that you have the ability to "hop to" a particular matter that is pending.

karate

To dream of karate indicates one of two things: either you feel that someone is opposing you and you need to defend yourself emotionally, or you have recently felt physically in danger and you want to be prepared.

ketchup

To dream of ketchup signifies a certain element of sweetness in your life that you've been ignoring. Possibly, you've been too hard on someone close to you. Learn to open up to this person, and your life will be better for it.

key

A key can stand for a part of yourself that you've locked away, or something you can now access because you have the key. Such a dream may also indicate you hold the key—the answer—to your own concerns.

kicked out

To get kicked out of a place denotes sadness about not fitting into a group or social situation. In waking life, this may also mean you push people's buttons or limits too much and too often.

kicking

Kicking, in a dream, represents hostility and anger. Are you the one kicking or is someone kicking you? Kicking also indicates a desire to get revenge on someone who has wronged you.

killing

A dream of killing someone is not a warning that you might turn into a killer. Instead, the meaning is more likely a symbolic act of aggression. Who do you kill in the dream? What bothers you about this person? The dream may symbolize killing off an unwanted part of yourself, and the person you kill might portray characteristics you wish to eliminate.

kindergarten

If you see a kindergarten in your dream, it may mean you're sick of people's childish behavior. If you have children, dreaming of kindergarten often indicates you want the best education for your own children. To dream of being in kindergarten suggests you long for simpler times.

king

A king is a ruler and a powerful authority figure. Dreaming of a king may mean you seek status or support. The king may represent your father or some other powerful figure in your life. If you're the king in your dream, the indication is you have achieved a high level of authority or are a highly capable individual.

kiss

A kiss suggests a romantic involvement, but it can also be a metaphor, as in "kiss and make up" or the "kiss of death." For married people to kiss each other symbolizes harmony in domestic life. Notice whether it is dark or light outside during the kiss. The former suggests danger or an illicit situation, whereas the latter represents honorable intentions. To dream of kissing someone on the neck symbolizes a passionate inclination toward that person.

kitchen

For most people, the kitchen connotes the "heart" of the home. This is the place where you were nurtured with food and sustenance in childhood, and where you still nurture yourself and your loved ones. If your dream is set in the kitchen, think about how you are nourishing yourself or feeling nourished (or not) by the people and events in your life. The kitchen is also a place of connection and bonds of family and friendship. Here you might chat with neighbors and friends. Therefore, kitchens in dreams can symbolize intimate conversations you might have had or want to have with others—or even with yourself. When you dream you are in a kitchen, think about what you were fed (thoughts, beliefs, feelings, events) growing up and how you feed yourself today. Most often the kitchen represents nourishment of an intangible kind and lets you know where you need to better care for yourself. Perhaps you are feeling uncared for in a situation or relationship in your waking life. Notice what you're doing in the kitchen. Alternately, a kitchen might suggest that something is in the process of being "cooked up," such as a new project.

kite

Flying a kite in your dream usually refers to a work or social situation that is taking off—you're finally having success with it, or you're just about to. If someone in your dream tells you to "go fly a kite," you feel dismissed by others in some area of your life.

kitten

To discover kittens in a closet or a basement suggests the awakening of hidden aspects of yourself. Kittens can symbolize new ideas and projects.

kneeling

Kneeling down in a dream usually means you feel guilty. It also indicates that you hope someone will accept your sincere apology. You may feel that a situation in your life will "bring you to your knees."

knife

A knife is a symbol of aggression. It's also a phallic symbol. Examine the other aspects of the dream. Are you being stabbed in the back? Do you hold the knife, or is someone threatening you with it? A rusty knife may symbolize dissatisfaction, a sharp knife means worry, and a broken knife represents defeat.

knight

A knight signifies honor and high standing. Are you searching for a knight, or are you acting like a knight? Knights are armored and therefore might represent protection—or that you feel a need for protection.

knitting

Knitting, in a dream, can refer to the small details in life. It might also symbolize peace within the home and with family. A dream about knitting may mean you are putting together the fabric of your life.

knob

A knob appearing in a dream may imply you need to get a handle on a matter. Knobs also signify a means of passing from one room to the next, or from one way of life to another.

knot

Dreaming of knots suggests you're all tied up about something—worries and anxieties are troubling you. You may feel as if you're tied in a knot. Alternately, if you or someone close to you is tying the knot, the dream might signify concern about an upcoming marriage or a desire for marriage.

L

laboratory

A laboratory is a place where experiments are conducted. The implication is that you are unsatisfied with a present situation and are experimenting with something new. You might be testing a relationship with someone.

labyrinth

A dream of a labyrinth may indicate that you feel trapped in a situation or a relationship and are looking for a way out. It may also refer to the intricacies of a spiritual journey.

lace

Dreaming of lace might indicate romantic feelings or a strong desire to feel more feminine. If a man dreams of lace, he might have feelings for the woman wearing the lace. Or, he could be acknowledging a softer side of himself. Lace has intricate patterns, so think about any relationships in your life that might be more intricate than they need to be.

ladder

Are you going up or climbing down the ladder? An ascent may symbolize a higher step into an inner realm or a promotion to a higher status in your career or social standing. A ladder also means you should be patient—destiny is guiding you.

ladle

Serving something in a ladle in your dream indicates you may feel restless. You may be annoyed with your job as a caretaker of others. The dream signifies a need for change and less responsibility. Take a break.

lagoon

Lagoons symbolize doubt and confusion regarding an emotional matter, or a stagnant emotional situation.

lake

In the Jungian world, lakes and other bodies of water stand for the unconscious or emotions. In one interpretation, the dreamer who dives into a lake is returning to the womb. In another, the dreamer explores the unconscious. But if neither interpretation fits you or your situation, examine the other elements in the dream. Is the lake clear or muddy? The former suggests lucidity and clarity of purpose, whereas the latter may represent muddled feelings or uncertainty about a matter at hand.

lamb

A lamb may stand for gentleness. It can also suggest vulnerability, as in "a lamb to the slaughter." Or it may be a spiritual symbol, as in "sacrificial lamb" and "lamb of God." However, a dream of a lamb may simply indicate your love of animals. On another note, is this animal your totem?

lamp

A lamp, like a lantern, represents light or illumination and suggests you are searching for truth.

lance

A lance, by Freudian standards, is a phallic symbol, one of masculinity and aggression. Who is using the lance in your dream? Do you have intimate or aggressive feelings toward this person in waking life? Do you feel you need to defend yourself in a situation?

landing

Dreaming of landing in an airplane, for example, indicates your wish to finish a current project successfully. If the landing goes well, it's a good sign that it will.

language

Hearing another language spoken may indicate a desire to meet more people and, perhaps, to travel to foreign lands. It may also signify that you feel you don't understand something or someone in your waking life. Perhaps you feel lost in foreign emotions or events.

lantern

Holding a lantern or seeing one in your dream means you'd like to shed some light on a current issue. Perhaps you're aware that you're not getting the whole truth.

lap

This is a symbol of security, the "lap" of luxury. To dream of sitting on someone's lap signifies safety from a troubling situation. To dream of a cat in a lap represents connection and comfort.

lasso

If a lasso is used on you, it means someone or something is holding you back. If you're the one using the lasso, you are trying to capture an opportunity that you feel would be good for you.

launch

To launch a boat—or perhaps a space rocket—in a dream signifies the successful start of something new. Usually, it refers to new ideas or financial projects. Examine how the launch goes to see how your new endeavor will fare.

lawsuit

Dreams of legal matters suggest you feel you are being judged.

leeches

Leeches are nightmarish creatures that suck blood. Is someone in your life draining your energy or resources?

legs

Legs are frequently seen in dreams, and interpretation depends on the context. Overall, dreams of legs are about mobility and flexibility. A wounded leg might indicate inability to move forward at this time or that you feel your ability to get where you want to go is compromised somehow. Legs can also relate to your standing in the world, so think about how you view your position at work or home. Dreaming that your own legs are clean and shapely means you feel good about your abilities to support yourself.

leopard

Leopards are hunters, great climbers, and creatures of the night. What part of the leopard do you wish to emulate? If the leopard is attacking you, something from your shadow side needs to surface. You need to face your fears. If someone close to you is in your dream, you may feel that person is not as constant or committed as you believe—he may "change his spots" and hurt you emotionally in the process. If you dream of a leopard in a cage, you may feel your true nature is restricted at this time.

letter

A letter sometimes symbolizes a message from your unconscious to you. If you're unable to read the letter, look at other aspects of the dream for clues. An anonymous letter may signify concern from an unspecified source. Blue ink indicates steadfastness and affection. Red ink may suggest suspicion and jealousy, and a letter with a black border may represent distress or a death of some kind. Receiving a letter written on black paper with white ink may suggest feelings of misery and disappointment over a matter. If this letter is passed between husband and wife or lovers in a dream, concerns about the relationship may be present. A torn letter may mean concerns that hopeless mistakes could ruin your reputation.

lightning

A dream of lightning indicates a flash of inspiration or sudden awareness about the truth of a matter. Lightning can also mean a purging or purification, or fear of authority or death.

lion

Lions are kings of the animal world and powerful hunters. A lion is also the symbol of the constellation Leo, so a lion in a dream may symbolize someone in your life who is born under the zodiac sign Leo. A lion in a dream may be calling you to claim your own power. If you are being attacked by a lion, you feel helpless and vulnerable in some situation in your life. If the lion is in a cage, you are afraid of your own power and feel it needs to be held back. Release the lion and empower yourself!

living room

The living room is the main room in most houses where you greet your guests and socialize. Usually when you dream you are in your living room, you are dreaming about the image you project in the world. This dream might be concerned with how you want other people to see you. Depending on the emotions and actions in the dream, you may feel you are being judged unfairly. Perhaps who you truly are and the image you want people to have of you are inconsistent. The feelings and actions in the dream, as well as the other people present in it, will reveal specifics. What is surfacing about your public image?

loss

To dream of losing something in a dream often means your unconscious is working out the loss of something very real in your waking life. What do you feel you're parting with? Is it a healthy thing or something you actually still need? The thing you lose in the dream is often not literal; it's a symbol for the actual lost object, relationship, or opportunity.

lottery

To dream of a lottery signifies taking a chance or throwing your fate to luck. If you dream of holding the winning number, then luck and good fortune regarding a matter at hand may follow. To see others winning in a lottery suggests you wish good fortune for those you know.

luggage

Luggage stands for your personal effects or what you carry with you on a journey. What happens to the luggage in your dream? Lost luggage might indicate concern about your identity or about being prepared for the journey. Stolen luggage might suggest you feel someone is interfering with your attempt to reach a goal.

M

magic

This dream could point to the magical aspects of creativity or, on the darker side, to deceit and trickery.

mailbox

A mailbox symbolizes sending and receiving communication. Think about what you want to communicate and to whom. An overstuffed mailbox means you have been ignoring the little details of day-to-day life. An empty mailbox means hoped-for communication has not come.

man

Whether you are male or female, a man in your dream represents a part of you. Notice the events in the dream and the man's actions to understand the dream's message. For a woman, dreaming of a man often means she is being asked to embrace a more assertive part of herself in order to accomplish what she wants in life. If you fear the man in the dream, perhaps you fear a part of yourself could hurt others.

manuscript

A manuscript represents the collection of your hopes and desires. To interpret the dream, note the shape or appearance of the manuscript. Is it finished or unfinished? Are you at work on it? Did you lose it?

map

You're searching for a new path to follow, or are being guided in a new direction. What countries or regions are depicted on the map? What do these areas represent to you? These could provide clues to the dream's meaning.

March/march

March marks the beginning of spring—a time of new beginnings and new growth. If you dream of March, it may be your birthday month. Or, the dream may mean you are looking forward to new beginnings in your life, or to a sense of renewal and rebirth. If you dream you are marching or being forced to march with others, you may feel you are following someone else's lead or that you don't have control over the direction your life is taking. Are you following your own dreams or someone else's?

mask

A mask hides your appearance and your feelings from others, but the dream may signify that you are hiding your feelings about a particular matter from yourself. If another person(s) is wearing a mask, perhaps the dream is warning you that he is not being truthful.

May

May is the season of flowers and Mother's Day, so a dream of May can indicate you are thinking of your own mother or want to become a mother.

medicine

Taking medicine in a dream can be a potent symbol of healing your wounds. It also suggests that you have to "take your medicine" and do what is necessary or required of you.

merry-go-round

A merry-go-round suggests that you are going around and around in life and never moving ahead.

meteor

A meteor or falling star may indicate that your wish will come true. Or, the dream could suggest you are engaged in wishful thinking. Look at the other elements in the dream to decide which possibility is true for you.

microphone

A microphone may symbolize the desire to communicate your ideas more forcefully or to a broader audience. You may wish to perform or to find a way to make your opinions heard.

microscope

A microscope symbolizes the need or wish to find something that's out of sight or hidden from you. A microscope allows you to bring into clear vision something that your natural vision might miss, so think about what needs clarifying in your life. Also, think about where in your life you might feel that you are being "put under a microscope" or otherwise judged or evaluated in a way that has you feeling uncomfortable. If you are the one looking through the microscope, you may be too tied up in meaningless detail and missing the big picture, or conversely, you may need to dig into the details to find out the truth of the situation.

milk

Milk symbolizes nurturing. It can also represent strength and virility. To dream of milk portends prosperity and happiness. To dream of giving milk away may mean that you are too generous for your own good. Dreaming of sour milk means you are not nurturing yourself in the way that you need.

mist

Like fog, mist indicates a period of temporary uncertainty. Seeing others in a mist may mean things are not clear in your relationships with these people or in some situation involving others.

mistletoe

To dream of mistletoe signifies connection, celebration, and happiness in love. If you dream of kissing someone under the mistletoe, you desire greater intimacy with this person, or this person possesses a quality you wish to embrace.

money

Money represents energy, power, freedom, security, and influence. Think about what money means to you. Dreaming of gaining money suggests abundance; losing sums of money symbolizes a draining of physical and emotional resources. To dream of stealing money indicates you feel you need to get power and security from others.

moon

The moon represents feminine energy, nighttime, mystery, and duality. Your emotions might be running high right now. Try not to make too many impulsive decisions. Wait until you're calmer. The moon also indicates feelings about a relationship and the mysteries of the human heart. Dreaming is very active during the moon cycles, and if you dream about the moon, notice the phase. Is the moon full, shedding clear light along the path? Or is it a new moon representing the start of a new chapter in your life or in a particular situation? If you cannot see the moon in your dream as you search the night sky, then you are in the dark about some situation.

morning

Morning represents a fresh start or a sudden, positive change of fortune. To dream of a cloudy morning indicates that heavy matters may overwhelm you.

mother

To see your mother in a dream means you are connecting to qualities in her or in your relationship that you need at this time in your life. Perhaps you want to be mothered now. What is the context in which she appears? Think also about your feelings toward your mother and any unresolved emotions or issues between you. This is a perfect time to heal old wounds. If your mother has crossed over, you may be receiving a loving visitation from her.

mother-in-law

A dream in which your mother-in-law appears suggests that you are looking to deepen connections or to resolve problems with her. Think about the qualities in your mother-in-law that you admire or that trouble you. You will find these same qualities in yourself. Perhaps your dream is asking you to become less engaged in someone else's life; allow her take more responsibility for herself.

motorcycle

In a dream, a motorcycle is like a car in that you should notice the model, make, size, and any other pertinent details. Motorcycles are associated with the rebel, so you might feel the need to rebel against some part of your life. A motorcycle can also symbolize freedom. You might feel burdened with responsibility in your daily life; at night your desire for freedom and a carefree life emerges.

mountain

A mountain represents a challenge. If you're climbing the mountain, you're working to achieve your goals. Descending a mountain suggests that things are easier now and your future success may be ensured.

mule

Mules are known for their contrary behavior, as in "stubborn as a mule." To dream of a mule suggests that you may be acting in a stubborn manner that others find annoying. Mules are also work animals. Consider whether you are rebelling against some aspect of your job or career.

murder

Murder symbolizes repressed anger, either at yourself or others. If, in your dream, you murder someone you know, consider your relationship with that person. If you're the murder victim, the dream may symbolize a personal transformation.

music

Music in a dream symbolizes emotional matters. Consider the type of music you heard and how you related to it. Did it fill you with joy? Did it make you sad or angry? Did you recognize the tune? If so, does it connote a particular event or time in your life, or convey a message?

N

nail

A nail in a dream can have a variety of meanings. To "nail it down" suggests putting something together or holding it together. If you "hit the nail on the head," your intuition is right on the mark. If you step on a nail in your dream, it's a warning to be more aware of your surroundings. If you break a fingernail, you may need to take better care of yourself, physically.

naked/nudity

Being nude in a dream can symbolize a wish for exposure—to be seen or heard. It can also relate to a need to bare the truth. Alternately, a dream of nudity can have sexual connotations and suggest that you are no longer inhibited. Dreaming of being naked in your daily life means you fear embarrassment or exposure.

name

Hearing your name called in a dream can mean one of two things: either someone is trying to get your attention in waking life, or you are trying to alert yourself to something important that is happening around you. It may also be that your guides are attempting to contact you.

napkins

Napkins are used during mealtime to keep yourself clean, so this dream corresponds to the part of your life that nurtures and feeds you. If the napkins are dirty, you are not feeling nurtured in your life right now. If the napkins are clean, you feel you have the resources to feed your inner being. On the other hand, it can indicate you need to clean up your life in some way.

navigating

To dream of navigating a spaceship, boat, or other craft indicates a desire to come out on top in a current situation. This dream says that, although there will be obstacles, if you're careful, you can find your way and navigate through obstacles.

neck

A neck can be a sexual symbol related to the slang term "necking." It can also represent taking a chance, as in "sticking one's neck out." Alternately, if there is pain related to this part of the body, someone or something might be a "pain in the neck."

necklace

To dream of receiving a necklace signifies a pleasant gift that highlights your ability to speak for yourself. To dream about losing a necklace may mean you're afraid you will lose the opportunity to express yourself. This can also be a literal dream—you fear losing a particular necklace. If the necklace is too tight around your neck, you may feel closed off in your expression.

needle

A dream of a needle and thread might indicate that a matter is being sewn up or that a deal is being completed. A needle might also suggest that someone is needling you. To dream of threading a needle symbolizes you are trying to find an opening in your life.

neighbor

If you dream of a neighbor, think about the qualities you either like or dislike in her. These qualities reside in you as well, so pay attention to the events in the dream to figure out the message.

nest

A nest is a symbol of home and might indicate a desire to return home. If you are moving, it might relate to your concerns about your new home. If there is an egg in the nest, the dream might relate to a concern about your savings or "nest egg." To dream of a nest full of eggs is a good omen. An empty bird's nest may denote worry about tough times ahead or sadness about your own "empty nest," aging, and being alone.

newspaper

If you dream of a newspaper, chances are you feel out of the loop and your unconscious is urging you to be more on top of things. This is also a good sign that news is on the way.

night

A night setting for a dream might suggest something is hidden or obscured. Nighttime in a dream suggests a lack of clarity. There might be a need to illuminate something.

nine

Nine is the number of completion and the ending of cycles. It also signifies accomplishment. You may have attained a goal. If so, celebrate and acknowledge yourself and your achievements. You may be experiencing an end to a career, lifestyle, relationship, or even to an outdated way of thinking. The number nine encourages you to let go of what no longer serves you. When nine shows up, ask for support to easily release what is meant to move out of your life. If you are "dressed to the nines" in your dream, you have reached the pinnacle of elegance and opulence.

north

North is the place of dormancy, winter, and hibernation. It is also the compass point for direction in life, the reference point for finding your way in the world. You follow the North Star. If you are searching for "true north" in your dreams, you might be trying to find your own core of integrity. If you are heading north, it might be a fallow time when you can rest and regenerate. In Native American traditions, north is the place of the elder or ancestor, and of wisdom; it represents retreat and healing.

nose

A nose can be a symbol of intrusive behavior, as in "sticking your nose into someone else's business." Dreaming of a nose may suggest someone else is interfering in your life or that you are being nosy.

November

November is the time of Thanksgiving and a return to hearth and home to prepare for the winter. A dream that takes place in November could suggest going within and reflecting on all you are grateful for in your life.

nurse

A dream of a nurse suggests you are being healed or are in need of healing. It also implies a desire to be pampered or nursed. The dream could relate to a relationship or a project that you are nursing along.

O

oak

An oak tree represents strength, stability, endurance, truth, and wisdom. A dream of an oak may suggest that you have established a strong, proper foundation.

oar

An oar can represent masculinity and strength; it dips into the water, which symbolizes the emotions. To row vigorously suggests you are moving through an issue or situation quickly and aggressively. If you have only one oar and are rowing in a circle, it might suggest frustration with a lack of forward movement in life.

oasis

An oasis suggests you've arrived at a place of comfort and sustenance—that you are being nurtured. Or, it might suggest that you're taking a break from your journey or have succeeded in reaching a destination on the journey. Alternately, the dream might imply that you need a rest or vacation.

objects

If there are many objects in your dream, you need to analyze each object and the symbolism around it. Many times, the objects represent how you, the dreamer, feel about yourself.

obstacles

Obstacles in dreams always translate metaphorically. In other words, you have placed a burden or problem in front of yourself, and all you need to do is step back and see the picture more clearly in order to solve the dilemma.

ocean

The ocean often represents the emotional setting of your life. The context of the dream is important here. Sailing through rough seas suggests you are capable of dealing with life's ups and downs. Large waves can also represent untapped powers, strong emotions, or the unconscious. Catching a large fish in the ocean can suggest opportunity or that you are delving into the wealth of your unconscious. To be lost at sea may mean you need direction. To be anchored in the ocean might indicate you have found a place in life.

October

October is the harvest month, so to dream of October portends success. New friendships or business affairs will ripen into lasting relationships.

odor

If you smell an odor in your dream, it could be literal. You might smell an odor in waking life and it filters into the dream. Otherwise, good odors signify good luck and bad odors signify the opposite.

officer

An officer, whether military, police, or otherwise, represents an authority figure. Dreaming of an officer, especially if you don't know the person, can suggest a fear or wariness of authority figures or a need for guidance from an authoritative person.

oil

A dream of oil represents great wealth or inner wealth, if you are pumping crude oil to the surface. Using aromatic oils in a dream can represent sacred matters. A person associated with oil might be slick, or a smooth talker.

old man

If the old man guides or directs you in some way, he is, in Jungian terms, an archetypal figure. If the man appears to be weak or injured, he could symbolize some part of yourself that requires attention or someone in your life who needs your help. The dream may also advise you to redefine your beliefs about aging.

old woman

In Jungian terms, an old woman is an archetypal symbol of feminine power, or the gatekeeper between life and death. If she is weak or injured in your dream, she may represent a part of yourself that needs attention, or someone in your life who needs help. She could also represent your own inner wisdom—the sage crone.

one

The number one almost always represents new beginnings, whether it shows up alone or in combination with other numbers. It is the initiator, usually a very positive indicator that you are moving in a new direction in life. It also signifies divine unity. You become one with another. One can indicate a time period such as one month or one year.

operation

To dream of an operation could mean you're worried about some aspect of your health and you'd like to become more physically fit. It also represents change from a current situation.

orange

Orange is a joyful color linked with the second chakra. The second chakra is the place of your emotions, childhood experiences, and sensuality. It is associated with your emotional nature, water, creativity, and propensity toward addictions. Orange is a bright color that connotes warmth, connection, and affection. If you are dreaming of orange, you may be revisiting issues from childhood or opening up your creativity. Because orange is associated with childhood, a dream about the color orange might encourage you to be playful in the way of the child, especially in creative pursuits. When the second chakra is healed, you are in balance, so orange can also represent balance and harmony.

oven

An oven might represent a gestation period. It also symbolizes the womb and feminine energy. A dream of an oven could relate to a pregnancy or a creative project you have in the works.

owl

An owl represents both wisdom and mystery, and is a symbol of the unconscious. If you hear an owl screech in your dream, it could mean that unsettling news is coming. If an owl is your animal totem, listen to your own inner wisdom and you will know what to do.

ox

An ox is a steadfast, strong, and hard-working creature associated with stability and wealth in many cultures. To dream of an ox implies strength and endurance, and an ability to carry on against great odds.

P

painting

If a wall is being painted in your dream, the act may suggest something is being hidden or covered up. Pay attention to the color(s) as they can add information about the dream's meaning. Painting at an easel may indicate you are ready to express your artistic or creative talents.

paper

To see papers piled high indicates a certain level of stress in waking life. Perhaps you feel you aren't taking care of your responsibilities. If you're signing papers in the dream, it indicates you'll soon have a decision to make—and you'll make the right one.

paradise

If you dream you're in paradise, you are happy and content at this time in your life. Notice what is around you in your paradise—people, animals, scenery, and so on. Your dream will give you valuable information about what creates feelings of happiness and contentment for you.

park

Dreaming of a park may suggest a wish to relax and enjoy life. Walking in an unlit park at night may mean you are delving into areas of darkness and danger, or that you are pursuing hidden or mysterious matters. If you are parking your car, you may need to take a break from your journey at this time. If you are unable to find a place to park your car, you feel you cannot stop working right now, even though you are tired and need a break.

party

To dream you are at a party suggests a celebration is in order. If you are concerned about a particular matter that remains unsettled, the dream may indicate a favorable resolution.

peacock

A dream about this bird suggests you have a reason to be proud, just as the peacock displays its colorful tail feathers to get attention or show power. Alternatively, it could mean that someone you know is arrogant and unduly prideful. Pay attention to your emotions in the dream to interpret the meaning.

pearls

Pearls are gems hidden in oysters, which come from the sea. When you dream of pearls, you are dreaming of finding hidden "gems" within yourself, particularly of an emotional nature. If someone gives you pearls, you are receiving wisdom from your higher self or someone else whose opinions you trust. Let your inner gifts shine!

pepper

If you dream of pepper burning your tongue, it could mean you feel hurt by sharp words recently spoken—by yourself or someone else. To sneeze from pepper in a dream indicates that something in your life is irritating you and you want to get rid of it.

photograph

Because a photograph is an image of a person or object rather than the real thing, a dream of a photograph hints at deception or falseness. If you recognize a person in a dream photo, be aware that a part of you doesn't think the person is being authentic and open with you. To dream of seeing yourself in a photograph may indicate nostalgia for the past. Or, you may feel trapped by an image others have of you that is not who you truly are.

physician

A physician appearing in a dream might indicate that healing is at hand. A physician is also an authority figure who might be offering a diagnosis on some matter. Sometimes, a physician may take the form of a trusted friend who isn't a doctor but whose nurturing traits are healing.

piano

Music in general represents joyous or festive feelings. Note the condition and type of music coming from the piano. A broken piano symbolizes a need to reconnect with your creative, joyful side and to express all the aspects of who you are.

pill

Taking a pill in a dream suggests you may be required to go along with something unpleasant, but positive results should follow. If you're taking a birth control pill, it's a warning to pay attention to current sexual activities. This might also mean you don't feel ready to embark on a new stage of life and want to prevent it from happening.

pilot

A pilot symbolizes someone soaring high in the sky. He's in control in spite of the fast pace. A dream of a pilot may mean you're in the pilot's seat concerning some issue in your life. Because air symbolizes the mind, the issue may involve intellectual pursuits or communication.

plane

See *airplane*.

planet

Seeing a planet or visiting another planet in a dream may indicate a new adventure, a new way of thinking, or a new dimension of creativity.

plums

If you dream of ripe plums, you are feeling nurtured in life. If you are gathering plums in your dream, you need only do a little work to secure your heart's desires. Receiving or eating a plum could indicate a "plum" opportunity is coming your way.

polar bear

Polar bears live in the frozen water and, as such, may symbolize a need to delve into old, frozen emotions to find the truth in a situation. Because polar bears are white, they blend in completely with their background and hunt from under the cover of this camouflage. Think about where in your life or relationships you are hiding or camouflaging your true feelings. Like other bears, polar bears are creatures of great beauty and strength. Where do those qualities exist in yourself or others? Polar bears are facing extinction, so the dream may contain a message that some part of you that resembles the qualities of a polar bear may be killed off by your current life circumstance.

police

Police officers represent authority; they uphold the law. A dream of police may serve as a warning against breaking the law or bending rules. It might also suggest a fear of punishment. Alternately, the dream may indicate a desire for justice.

pond

A pond signifies tranquility and a placid outlook—either your own or that of a person in the dream. Your emotional life might be calm and peaceful right now.

pregnant

If a woman dreams of being pregnant, it could indicate a desire for a child or the onset of an actual pregnancy. A pregnancy could also symbolize something new coming into your life—an idea or project that is gestating.

president of the United States

Not as uncommon as it may seem, a dream of talking with the president of the United States may represent an interest in lofty ideals or political matters, or a strong desire to be a politician.

priest

A priest represents a spiritual authority serving as a guide. Alternately, a priest might symbolize a dictatorial figure or one who judges and condemns. A dream of a priest may indicate the need to follow or eschew conventional religion. Look to surrounding details for clarification.

prison

Constraint and restriction are implied by this dream symbol. If you see yourself at work in a prison, the dream might suggest you've limited your creativity or that you feel it's difficult to escape your job for a better one.

professor

A professor may represent knowledge, wisdom, and higher education.

prophet

A prophet provides knowledge, guidance, and perhaps a peek at the future. The symbol may also indicate that you need guidance.

puddle

Stepping into or stomping through puddles represents a parting or clearing away of emotional troubles, with good times to follow. To dream that you are just wetting your feet in a puddle may mean you only want to dip into your emotions a little bit.

pump

To see a pump in a dream suggests energy is available to meet your needs. A functioning pump could also symbolize good health. A broken pump signifies a breakdown or disruption in the usual way of doing things.

puppet

A dream of a puppet might indicate that you feel manipulated in some aspect of your life. Alternately, if you are behind the puppet or holding the strings, the dream may mean you're acting in a manipulative manner.

Q

quarantine

If you dream you are being quarantined you feel restricted by others. You may also believe you have been unfairly set apart in some way. You fear some part of your life or your behavior is unacceptable to others and needs to be healed.

quarrel

A dream of a quarrel may indicate that inner turmoil is plaguing you. If the person you're quarreling with is someone you know, look at your relationship with the person and see if you can identify the area of disagreement. The dream may hold clues to help you resolve the differences.

queen

Both an authority and a mother figure, the queen is an archetypal symbol of power. If you are the queen, the dream may be suggesting a desire for leadership. If someone else is the queen, the dream may indicate you see the woman as capable and powerful.

quest

A dream of a quest may indicate a desire to achieve a goal or embark on an adventure.

quicksand

A dream of quicksand indicates you need to watch where you are headed. If you're already in the quicksand, you're probably mired in an emotional matter and feel as if you can't escape. The dream could refer to either business or personal matters.

quill

A quill or fountain pen is a symbol of masculinity and signifies you need to follow your heart's desire. It's also a sign to stay steadfast in your convictions.

quilt

A quilt suggests warmth and protection. A patchwork quilt symbolizes joining together various aspects of your life to form a protective covering.

R

rabbit

The rabbit is a symbol of fertility and magic, like the rabbit pulled from the magician's hat. Although fertility could relate to the conception of children, it might also concern financial abundance, the success of a particular project, or other matters. A white rabbit may signify mystical experiences.

race

If you are racing in a dream, perhaps you're involved in an overly competitive situation or you're in a rush. The message might be that it's time to slow down and relax.

rain

A fresh downpour symbolizes washing or cleansing away the old. Alternately, a rainy day may indicate your emotions are gloomy right now. To hear the patter of rain on the roof may signify domestic bliss, while seeing a downpour from inside a house may represent feelings of sadness and loss. Seeing it rain on others may mean you feel emotionally tied to the fortunes of others.

rainbow

Usually seen after a storm, a rainbow in a dream may mean that favorable conditions will arise after a brief storm. Seeing a low-hanging rainbow over verdant trees may signify success in an endeavor.

ram

A ram is the zodiac symbol for Aries, so if you or someone you know are born under the sign of Aries, the ram may represent that person. If you dream of a ram charging you with its head down, it indicates you feel under attack. If the ram is close to you in the dream, it may indicate the attack is near or that you will have little time to react. A ram charging from a distance suggests you will have time to respond to the situation. Consider whether someone in your life is trying to "ram" something down your throat. If the ram is quietly grazing in a pasture, the indication could be that you have powerful allies on your side.

rapids

Rapids represent danger and a fear of being swept away by emotions.

rat

Rats are cunning survivors who live underground and near water. Dreaming of a rat or rats may suggest the deterioration of a situation. Or, someone might be behaving like a rat toward you. What are your own associations with rats? Whether or not you are afraid of the rats in the dream will help to clarify the message.

red

Red is the most intense of the colors in the spectrum of the rainbow. It has the longest wavelength and is associated with the root chakra, the spiritual center of your connection to the physical world and to nature. Red represents vitality, energy, and physical stamina. It can also refer to anger as in "seeing red." Because red is the color of blood, it can symbolize the life force. If you dream, for example, that you are bleeding, look to see what situation in your life is sapping your energy and vitality. If you are wearing red in your dream, you are feeling vital and alive in the situation described by the dream. Red is also the color of passionate love and sexuality, so when you dream of red you may be dreaming of the passion you have for someone or something in your life. Red often indicates the dream originates from the deepest level of your being.

referee

A referee in a dream can symbolize an inner battle, or it can relate to conflict in your daily life. Can you identify the issue? If so, weigh the two sides, negotiate, and reach a settlement. Sometimes working with an unbiased third party can help.

religion

To dream of religion—discussing it or practicing it—indicates that you may be evaluating your spiritual path. Religion is dogmatic, so you may be going through a period in which you are revisiting beliefs or feeling rigid in your belief system. You may see others as rigid in their beliefs and think they don't accept you. If your religion is an important part of your life, you may be receiving guidance or comfort in your dream from your spiritual beliefs.

ribbons

Ribbons are often associated with gifts, beauty, and decorations. As such they are usually happy portents when they appear in a dream. If you are trying to tie some ribbons together, you are in the process of pulling together various aspects of yourself and your life. If you are decorating your home with ribbons, you are adding beauty to your life in small ways. Look at the colors of the ribbons to find more meaning.

rice

Rice is the dietary staple of the majority of the world's population. A symbol of fertility and good fortune, rice in a dream signifies your ability to feed and nurture yourself and others. If you dream you are throwing rice at a wedding, you are sending good wishes for a happy life.

river

A dream of floating down a river might indicate an inability to control where you are going. Or, it could mean you are at ease and confident about going with the flow. Are you allowing surrounding circumstances to direct your life rather than taking charge? A dream of a surging, frothing river may relate to deep-seated emotions that need to be processed. In mythology, a river sometimes symbolizes death or passing from one state to another.

road

A road is a means of getting from one place to another. What is the condition of the road in your dream? A smooth and straight road suggests the path ahead is easy. A road with dips and curves may indicate you need to be aware, flexible, and ready for change. A roadblock suggests there are detours or obstacles in your path.

rose

A rose symbolizes the feminine and is associated with romance, beauty, and love. A dream of someone handing you a rose may indicate an offering of love.

ruins

To dream of something in ruins suggests the deterioration of some condition in your life. Keep in mind that when things fall apart, an opportunity to rebuild inevitably appears. If you are planning a trip, especially one to another culture, a dream of ancient ruins could symbolize the adventure of the journey ahead. Alternately, it could mean you have the ability to access knowledge or wisdom from the past.

running

When you run in a dream, you may be in a hurry to reach a goal or to escape from something (usually yourself or a current dilemma). The dream may indicate that you're rushing around too much and need to rest. Are you running alone or with others? The former may symbolize that you will overcome your competition in business matters, while the latter may represent participation in a joyous occasion. If you dream of running for exercise, it means you are moving toward a pleasant and successful life. Running and not getting anywhere indicates a feeling you've lost control of a certain situation in your waking life.

S

sacrifice

To see yourself sacrificed or making a sacrifice in a dream suggests you're giving up something important for the sake of others. Closely examine your feelings about the matter. Decide what changes, if any, need to be made.

sailor

A dream of a sailor suggests that you are working on a ship. Symbolically, it could mean you are working on matters involving the unconscious or your emotions (see *ship* and *water*).

saint

A saint in a dream indicates you're being guided or are seeking guidance from a higher source. Pay attention to what he says or does, and take his advice.

salt

Dreaming of salt generally indicates unpleasant situations or unhappy surroundings. Are you due for a move or a change in career? It could also mean you need to spice up your life.

school

A school dream may indicate you are gaining a deep level of knowledge or that your unconscious is processing lessons from your waking life. What happens in the school is important to the interpretation. If you're late to class or show up to take a test without ever having gone to class, you feel unprepared for something in your life. If you're looking for a school or classroom, you may be searching for the best way to continue your education.

scissors

Is there something or someone in your life you want to cut off? Scissors also indicate a need to "cut it out." Or, the person with the scissors may be acting "snippy."

scrapbook

Scrapbooks are full of things from the past that are filed away and forgotten. Note the other details of the dream. Are you viewing a scrapbook with someone? What are you placing in the scrapbook? The dream may suggest an unpleasant situation that needs to be put in the past.

sea

Dreams of the sea represent unfulfilled longings or the ebb and flow of emotions. If you dream you are "at sea," then you might be feeling lost in some situation in your life. If you are dreaming you are unable to see land, then you might be feeling emotionally overwhelmed by some situation in your life and unable to see how to resolve it. Think first of your emotional life. Because the sea is deep, expansive water, the emotions coming up may be very deep within you and extremely important.

September

September is the first month of autumn and the time when many children return to school. Therefore, this symbol could indicate a harvest period, a time of decline, or a search for knowledge depending on your feelings and the actions in your dream. Think about what you associate with September, including the holidays Labor Day and Rosh Hashanah, the Jewish New Year.

seven

Seven is the number of spiritual attainment, connection to the Divine, and luck. There are seven days in the week, seven sacraments in the Roman Catholic faith, seven chakras in the Hindu and Buddhist traditions, seven notes in the musical scale, and seven colors in the rainbow. Even in mythology and folklore, the number seven shows up repeatedly (for example, Snow White and the seven dwarves). If seven appears in your dreams, expect good luck that has a spiritual foundation. Meditate on the number seven to understand how you can best develop and work with spiritual energy in your waking life.

shadow

Dreaming of your shadow may suggest you need to address hidden parts of yourself. Perhaps you do not accept these darker aspects of your personality and project them onto others. The dream may also mean you need to incorporate the shadow side into your psyche.

shaking hands

A handshake marks either a new beginning or an ending to a situation. Are you saying farewell to someone in a dream? Then perhaps you are saying goodbye to a matter at hand. If you're meeting someone new, you might be embarking on a new venture or relationship. To dream of shaking hands with a prominent leader may mean others hold you in high esteem.

shaving

Is there something in your life that needs to be cleaned up or removed? To dream of shaving yourself connotes you are in charge of your future. Shaving with a dull razor suggests a troublesome or painful issue. A clean-shaven countenance indicates a smooth journey.

sheep

Do you perceive yourself as one of a flock? This can be a comforting image in terms of being part of a community. Or, it may indicate you lack individuality or the will to strike out on your own.

shell

A shell usually symbolizes a womb. Depending on the circumstances of the dream, it can portend the birth of a child or a new project. A shell can also represent protection. Is it time to emerge from your shell?

ship

Because a ship travels on water, the dream may signify a voyage through the unconscious or a journey involving your emotions. Consider the state of the ship and the condition of the water in your interpretation. To see a ship in a storm may indicate your concern over a tempestuous or unfortunate affair, either in business or personal matters. To dream of others shipwrecked may mean you feel unable to emotionally protect friends or family. If you dream that you are shipwrecked, then you are feeling at the mercy of your emotions and powerless to successfully navigate the situation. You might be burning out from overwork or chronic stress, so take time to consider where in your life you are feeling powerless to create positive change.

shoes

Shoes are a means of moving ahead. Shiny, new shoes might suggest a journey is about to begin. Well-worn shoes, on the other hand, might indicate you are weary of the journey or that it is near completion. Mismatched shoes could mean the journey is multifaceted. Consider the old cliché, "If the shoe fits, wear it."

shovel

A tool for digging, a shovel in a dream may indicate you are searching for something or are about to embark on a quest for inner knowledge. A shovel might also represent labor or hard work ahead. A broken shovel could mean you are experiencing frustration in your work.

shower

To dream of taking a shower may symbolize cleansing or spiritual renewal. It might also signify a bonus, reward, or blessings being showered upon you.

sickness/illness

If you dream of being ill, ask yourself if you're in need of care and pampering. This dream might also be a message to watch your health. A sick family member represents some issue that is troubling your domestic life.

singing

Hearing singing in a dream signifies a pleasant and cheerful attitude. You may hear promising news soon. If you are singing in the dream, note the type of song you are singing.

six

Six is almost always associated with career, so notice what is happening with your work life when six shows up in your dreams. Six was the number of days it took to create the world according to the Bible, therefore some spiritual texts associate it with worldly pleasures and the imperfection of humankind. Often six symbolizes romantic relationships, whereas the number two describes all types of relationships. Six is the sensual lover aspect. If in your dream you are at "sixes and sevens," you are scattered and need to organize your thinking around a particular situation.

skating

Dreaming of skating may signify you are gliding over a matter at hand, or you may be skating on thin ice. Make note of all the aspects in the dream. Are you headed toward something? Are you skating away from something? Skating can be liberating, but it can also be frightening if you're not sure how to do it. (See *walking* and *running*.)

skull

To dream of a skull and crossbones is a traditional sign of danger and possible death—a warning. If you just dream about a skull by itself, notice the feelings in the dream. Most likely this is a dream about personal transformation (like dreaming of a corpse or dying), not about death. One skull looks just like another, so think about where in your life you might be feeling a loss of your unique identity, or where you might have "lost face."

sky

Dreaming of the sky symbolizes hope, vitality, and a creative force.

smoke

If you dream of smoke filling a room, it suggests a situation is being obscured. On the other hand, if the smoke is clearing, clarity is imminent.

snake

A snake is an archetypal image that can have numerous interpretations. According to *Medicine Cards: The Discovery of Power Through the Ways of Animals* by Jamie Sams, and certain Native American teachings, snakes represent transmutation. Snakes do not always have a negative connotation; they also symbolize healing. A snake coiled around a staff is a symbol of health and medical practitioners. Are you afraid in the dream? What associations do you have in your waking life about snakes? Consider your feelings and the events in the dream before making a final interpretation. Analyze your dream and what's going on in your life to see what makes sense for you.

snow

Snow can represent purity if seen in a pristine landscape. Because snow is a solidified form of water, it can also stand for frozen emotions. If the snow is melting, frozen feelings are thawing. To find yourself in a snowstorm may represent uncertainty in an emotional matter or sorrow at failing to enjoy some long-expected pleasure.

south

South is the place where daylight is the longest and the brightest, where the sun most evenly bathes all equally. It equates with summer. South is also a metaphor for declining fortunes. If you are "heading south" in a dream, you might be experiencing a reversal in your plans. In astrology, the south relates to childhood, your heritage, and the past. If you dream of returning to the south, you may be revisiting your past or past lives. In some South American shamanic traditions, the goal of the south is to shed the old and the past so the present can come into being.

spaceship

A spaceship in a dream may suggest a journey into the unknown or a spiritual quest.

spear

Thrusting a spear at someone in a dream may represent an effort to thrust your will on another person. If the spear is hurled over a field or toward a mountain or an ocean, the dream may mean you are making a powerful statement to the world (see field, *mountain*, or *ocean*).

spider

Spiders may symbolize a careful and energetic approach to your work. Most likely you will be pleasantly rewarded for your labors. To dream of a spider spinning its web signifies your home life will be happy and secure. A dream of many spiders means good health and friends. Spiders also represent creativity, so you might be experiencing a need to express yourself creatively at this time in your life. If you are afraid of spiders, you fear something happening in your daily life will trap you.

square

A square shape represents solidity and a strong foundation. If you dream of squares, you may need to be precise in your work or personal life. You might be building a strong foundation in some area, or trying to "square things" with someone else if you've had a misunderstanding or dispute. If you are called "square" in your dream, you may feel left out of a group or that you don't fit in somehow. If you are hiding in the corners of a square structure in your dream, you may feel "cornered" in some way and want to protect yourself. A square can also represent equality and balance, as no one side is longer than any other. If you dream of a town square, you may be feeling the need to get together with others for companionship and common activities.

squirrel

Squirrels are resourceful creatures that save and hide food to get through the cold months. To see these creatures in your dream may mean you need to "squirrel" away some of your resources in preparation for leaner times ahead.

stairs

Climbing a stairway in a dream can mean you are on your way to achieving a goal. Descending a stairway, or falling down one, might indicate a fall in prestige or economic status. To sit on a step could suggest you are pausing in your everyday life to consider where things stand.

statue

Dreaming of a statue or statues could signify a lack of movement in your life. Statues are also cold and can symbolize frozen feelings.

stillborn

To dream of a stillborn infant indicates a distressing circumstance or a premature ending to a new venture.

stone(s)

Stones, rocks, and boulders in dreams can have various meanings depending on the circumstances and feelings in the dreams. A stone can represent a person in your life whom you feel you cannot reach on an emotional level. Someone could be "stone cold" to what you desire. Or, you may have withdrawn emotionally from a relationship and your dream imagery is letting you know that your feelings have gone cold for that person. If, in your dream, you are dodging stones, think about whether you feel attacked on some level in your day-to-day life. Because stone is hard, dense, and enduring, it can also represent qualities of strength, endurance, and solidity—you may feel that someone in your life is a solid person or that you yourself possess these qualities. If someone is being stoned in a dream, you may be receiving an intuitive message that someone you know is addicted to drugs or is feeling victimized. Work with your own connotations about stones to come up with the interpretation that works best for you.

storm

To dream of an approaching storm indicates emotional turmoil in some aspect of your life. Dark skies and thunder may also warn that danger is approaching. Alternately, a storm could symbolize rapid changes occurring in your life.

suffocation

To dream of being suffocated may have to do with the way you're sleeping. Is your breathing being obstructed in some way, by a cold, asthma, or a blanket? If not, it's possible you fear being bossed around or caged in. Other people or circumstances may be suppressing your expression.

suicide

A dream of killing yourself probably is a symbolic reflection of what's going on in your conscious life. Such a dream might reflect a personal transformation, divorce, career change, or other major life shift. You are essentially killing your past—becoming a new person.

sun

Dreaming of the sun is usually fortuitous. The sun symbolizes light, warmth, and energy. In Native American lore, the sun represents the father or the masculine principle.

swimming

A dream of swimming suggests you are immersed in an exploration of emotional matters or the unconscious.

sword

A sword is a symbol of strength and power. It also can cut to the bone. Dreaming of a sword might suggest that aggressive action is required.

T

table

To dream of an empty table might suggest a concern about a lack of possessions. A table laden with food may symbolize a time of abundance.

tambourine

The appearance of a tambourine symbolizes a need for fun and joyful expression.

tattoo

Traditionally, tattoos were associated with the strange and exotic, although they are much more commonplace today as means of self-expression. To dream of seeing your body tattooed suggests you want to wear your true beliefs and feelings in a way that can be seen and known by others. You may also feel a need to express your originality and uniqueness, and to stand out from the pack. If you dream you are a tattoo artist, you may want to help others express their unique gifts and talents.

teeth

Dreaming of teeth is one of the more common and shared dream experiences. Interpretations can range widely depending on what is happening to the teeth in the dream. On the most basic level, you show your teeth when you smile or feel comfortable enough with another person to relax. Teeth are part of your appearance, so if you dream of losing your teeth or that your teeth are dirty or damaged, you are having an anxiety dream in which you are worried about how you appear to others. Teeth also enable you to take in nourishment, so you may be receiving information about your ability to nourish yourself or to digest some situation in your life. If you dream you are biting something, you might desire to "get your teeth into" a project or situation at work. If you dream your teeth fall out, this is an expression of anxiety. Think about what is causing anxious feelings or where you feel your might be seen as inadequate.

telephone

A telephone might symbolize the attempt to contact the unconscious. If the phone is ringing and no one answers, the dream might suggest you are ignoring the call of your unconscious. If you have trouble hearing the person on the other end of the line, it suggests you're having problems communicating in a relationship.

tent

A tent provides shelter and is usually associated with camping. A dream of a tent could indicate you need a getaway—a retreat from everyday life.

texting

Texting in a dream signifies a desire to communicate. You are trying to get your message across to someone. Notice the emotion associated with the action. If you are frustrated and can't get your text message the way you want, perhaps you feel unable to communicate with a particular person in your waking life.

thaw

Thawing represents a rebirth or a return to pleasant conditions. To dream of seeing ice thaw may mean something or someone who's been giving you trouble will soon yield. Your emotions or feelings in regard to old injuries or resentments can also be thawing.

thief

If you dream of someone stealing something, the implication is that something is being taken from you. It could be a boss or colleague who is stealing your energy or ideas rather than an actual theft of goods. If you're the thief, the message may be a warning that you are taking what you don't deserve and should change your ways.

thirst

A dream in which you are thirsty suggests you are in need of nourishment —physical, mental, or emotional. To see others relieving their thirst suggests nourishment may come from others.

thorn

A thorn may represent an annoyance of some sort, such as "a thorn in your side."

three

Three is the number of the triangle, the trinity, and the mysteries of body, mind, and spirit. Three almost always represents creative self-expression and nurturing mother energy. If three shows up in your dreams, ask yourself what creative projects you are being prompted to begin or continue. If you are dreaming about a relationship and three shows up, beware of a triangle. This symbol can also portend a pregnancy.

tiger

Aggressive and fierce in the wild, these animals in a dream may mean you feel threatened at this time or fear repercussions for your actions. However, if you see yourself fending off an attack, this may mean you will be extremely successful in your ventures. If you dream you have a tiger by the tail, you are conquering your fears and feeling empowered in your waking life.

tornado

Swift and terrible agents of destruction in nature, tornadoes in dreams suggest your emotions concerning a particular situation could be hurtful to you and others.

torrent

To dream of a seething torrent of water suggests profound unrest in your emotional state or that of another person in the dream.

totem

This is the term for your animal or spirit guide. Usually, your totem is the animal to which you have the deepest connection. If you're afraid of an animal in your dream, it is not your totem.

tower

To dream of a tower could symbolize vigilance, as a watchtower, or punishment or isolation, as a guard tower. Dreaming of being in an ivory tower indicates you or the subject of your dream are out of touch with the everyday world. Usually a tower in a dream represents the realm of your mind, ideas, and beliefs.

train

A train symbolizes a journey. If the train isn't moving, the dream might be suggesting some impediment in your life. If you can't find your luggage, you might be concerned that you're not ready for this journey. If you are on a smoothly running train but there are no tracks, you might be concerned over some affair that will eventually be resolved satisfactorily. Traveling on the wrong train may indicate you're on the wrong track or going the wrong way.

treasure

A dream of a treasure may suggest hidden talents or abilities that you can now unearth. It could also indicate latent psychic abilities.

tree

When you dream about a tree it may represent a desire to be out in nature. A tree might also symbolize a part of your life, your body, or even your home. Trees in dreams may indicate whether or not you feel securely rooted in your life. Notice whether the tree has leaves, flowers, is in the process of shedding leaves, or is in the dormant stage during winter. Dreaming about a tree whose leaves are falling may be a message that some part of you or your life is in transition. You might be losing something that was an important part of you. A tree in winter, bare of leaves, may mean you feel exposed at the present time. Dreaming of a tree whose roots are exposed may mean you are being uprooted and are worried about your safety. Trees can represent your foundation and sense of security. They can even denote your family ancestry—your family tree. Notice the type of tree as well, as that may provide more information about the dream's message.

trial

A dream of being on trial suggests you are being judged or are afraid of being judged. Alternately, a trial in a dream could indicate you are judging others (or yourself) too harshly.

triangle

Triangles have many spiritual and mystical meanings. In relationships, triangles represent worries over unfaithfulness or betrayal. If you dream of triangles, you may have three projects or concerns with which you are dealing, and each may feel equally important. A triangle in a dream could represent the trinity, or body, mind, and spirit. You might feel you are caught in the middle between two people. A triangle has beautiful symmetry and harmony, so you may be in a period in your life during which you feel balanced and peaceful. Triangles in dreams can also indicate that you need to look at a situation from more than one angle to see the whole picture. If you dream of a pyramid, you may be dreaming of past lives or of a desire for greater mystical knowledge.

tricycle

A tricycle indicates you feel you need support to get where you want to go. Perhaps you need additional training to be successful.

triplets

To dream of triplets indicates greater success than anticipated. For a man to dream of his wife having triplets represents a happy occasion, overflowing feelings of joy, and good will. Triplets contain the symbolism of the number three, so read about the meanings for the number three as well as triangle to decipher your dream.

tunnel

From a Freudian perspective, a dream of a tunnel suggests a vagina, and a train entering the tunnel represents sexual intercourse. Usually, however, a tunnel shows you moving from one part of life to another, but you can't see the outcome yet. A tunnel may also be a link between two conditions. When you exit the tunnel, you will enter a new state of mind.

turtle

Although dreaming of a turtle might symbolize slow, painstaking movement, the shelled creature is also a symbol of spiritual development and patience. It could mean you feel at home wherever you go. If you dream the turtle is out of its shell, your dream might be telling you it's time to come out from under your shell.

tweet

If you hear a bird tweeting in your dream, most likely this portends a message (see *twitter*).

twins

A dream of twins may mean there are two parts to a matter of concern or two aspects to your personality. Read more about the vibration of the number two to gain more understanding.

twitter

If you dream you are twittering, then, like texting, you are trying to communicate with someone. If you dream you are trying to twitter and can't, you feel blocked in your ability to communicate at this time—even in short, brief communications.

two

Two is the number of relationship and partnership. When it shows up in your dreams it may be telling you something about your personal or business relationships, the opportunities and the challenges. Two is also the number of harmony and balance, as well as duality—of opposites. You may be asked to make a choice between two options.

U

ugly

If you or someone in your dream is ugly, you feel unattractive. Or, you don't like your own or another's behavior. This dream could point to an unhealthy trait that you or another possess. You may also fear rejection based on superficial criteria.

ulcer

If you dream you have an ulcer, something is eating at you. What in your waking life is bothering you? If the ulcer is bleeding in the dream, the situation is sapping your life force. Change the situation, or your reaction to it, if at all possible.

umbrella

An umbrella represents protection against adverse conditions. Because rain (water) symbolizes the emotions, this dream could refer to an emotional flood from the unconscious. If the umbrella is closed and a downpour is soaking you, it indicates you are open to your emotional needs.

underground

To dream of being underground often symbolizes contact with your subconscious. Other images in the dream will provide more meaning about the nature of the contact. How do you feel about the situation? Is there something you've been hiding that should be brought to the surface? Do you feel protected by the underground cavern or room? Or are you hiding or being held prisoner? Dreaming of an underground railway could indicate passage to another state of being—a personal transformation.

underwear

A dream of underwear may mean you are exposing something that is under cover or hidden. It could also indicate that you're bringing matters from the unconscious to the surface.

unemployment/unemployed

If you dream you are unemployed, this could represent literal events transpiring in your waking life at the time. More likely you are releasing fears that you won't have meaningful work or that the work you do won't support you. If you dream you are on an unemployment line, you feel you have to rely on others for your survival.

unicorn

To dream of a unicorn is always a good sign—it means happy circumstances will soon be yours. Unicorns protect you and cancel out the bad forces around them. To touch the unicorn's horn means you'll have luck for months. Dreaming of flying on a unicorn suggests you'll have true friendships and good health.

unicycle

Riding on a unicycle requires balance and skill. If you dream you are on a unicycle, you may be trying to achieve balance in your waking life. If you fear falling, it could refer to a project or situation that requires a great deal of finesse and skill that you are not confident you possess. Alternately, you're the "big wheel" and on your own.

urination

A dream in which you urinate may simply indicate that you need to wake up and go to the bathroom. Symbolically, the dream may represent a desire to eliminate impurities from your life.

V

vacuum

Dreaming you are vacuuming means you want to clean up something in your personality or your life. If the vacuum is clogged or not working properly, you feel unable to fix the problem at hand.

vagrant

Are you afraid of losing your home, stability, or livelihood? Perhaps you want to break away from social regimentation and responsibilities.

valuables

Uncovering valuables may symbolize the discovery of self-worth or inner resources.

vampire

To dream of a vampire may indicate that someone is draining energy from you or taking advantage of you. The message is to guard against people who take too much of your time or energy. To dream of battling and staking a vampire suggests triumphing over someone with harmful intentions.

vault

A vault usually holds valuables. Your ability to open it determines the nature of the dream. If you hold the key, the vault may be a symbol of wealth and prosperity. If you are unable to open it, the dream may signify that you are being frustrated in your effort to achieve wealth or a specific goal.

vegetables

If you dream you are growing vegetables, you are in the process of creating something healthy and nourishing in your life. If you are eating vegetables, you are feeding yourself vital nutrients and feel good about doing so. If you dream you or someone else "is a vegetable," you worry that you are not in control of your own destiny.

veil

A dream in which someone or something is veiled suggests you're hiding something or that something is being hidden from you.

veins

Veins are like tributaries that carry blood to the extremities. If you dream your veins are blocked, you feel your vitality or life force is blocked in a certain area—work, creativity, relationships, and so on. If your veins are discolored in the dream, you may not feel fully energized and alive; you aren't sending energy throughout all parts of your life.

ventriloquist

If you dream of a ventriloquist, you should beware of deception and fraud. Who are you letting speak for you? Find your own voice.

verdict

If you dream of a verdict, you feel judged and believe what happens in your life is up to someone other than you. If you deliver a verdict, you have strong ideas about what other people should do, and want to control someone else's behavior. You may also feel you are being treated unfairly in a situation. Or, you might believe you have done something wrong for which you need to be judged or punished.

victim

If you dream of being a victim, it may indicate you feel helpless in a particular a situation. If someone rescues you, the dream suggests help is available.

video

If you dream you are taking movies with a video camera, you are trying to hold on to memories of experiences that are important to you. If you see a video of yourself, you may feel other people aren't seeing your real self, just an image of how they expect you to be. If you are playing video games, you may be trying to best someone in your waking life. Or, you could be stuck in a repetitious pattern in a situation or relationship in which you feel games are being played.

violet

The color violet is the highest frequency and is associated with the seventh (or crown) chakra, the place of divine connection. This delicate, ethereal color reminds you that the physical world is transitory. If you dream of violet, you may be in the process of having a spiritual awakening or wish to open more to spiritual concepts in your daily life. Violet is also one of the colors of wisdom. If violet shows up in your dreams, you may desire to withdraw from the world and retreat within. You may be a "shrinking violet" and need to be alone, or you might experience fear about being center-stage in your waking life.

violin

A violin being played in a dream may portend a romantic interlude—a time of love and harmony. It can also mean that you or someone else is high-strung.

visitor

Encountering a visitor in a dream indicates that a new condition is entering your life. If you welcome the visitor, the change may be for the better. If you turn the visitor away, you're unwilling to change or you don't accept what is being offered.

voices

Dreaming that you hear pleasant voices indicates positive communications and connections with others. If the voices are angry, think about where you are frustrated or angry with yourself or others. If the voices are sad, you need to process and release sadness or grief.

volcano

The eruption of a volcano or a smoking volcano may suggest that your strong emotions are rising to the surface and need to be expressed before you explode.

vomit

To vomit in a dream may be a dramatic exhibition of a need to rid yourself of something or someone. You need to eliminate something you truly cannot digest—thoughts, events, emotions, behavior, situations, or relationships.

vulture

Vultures clean up what is dead. If you dream of a vulture, it might indicate someone in your life is just waiting for you to fail. Perhaps you are being asked to clear out what is dead and no longer useful from your life. It may be time to let go.

W

waiter/waitress

If you dream you are a waiter or waitress, you are most likely spending too much of your energy taking care of others rather than focusing on your own needs. If you are being waited on, you feel you are getting what you deserve and that others are there to help.

waiting

Waiting in a dream is a sign that you are not in control of whatever it is you want to happen. Perhaps you are waiting for someone else or waiting for a situation to change. Waiting usually brings with it feelings of impatience and frustration, so think about where you are waiting in life and what you can do to move things forward.

wake

If you dream you are at a wake you may be processing feelings of loss, or that an aspect of your life that you cherished has died. If you dream of people at your own wake, your unconscious is letting you know that other people are aware that some aspect of you has died.

walking

A dream of walking means you are on your way toward a goal. Notice where you are walking. Do you encounter any obstacles? Is your path easy, or are you having difficulty? Walking and not getting anywhere indicates a static situation you need to change.

wallet

A wallet carries personal effects, such as your identification. It also contains money and credit cards. If you dream of losing your wallet, you may have concerns about your sense of self or your finances. What happens in the dream and how you react can help you determine its meaning.

wallpaper

If you dream you are putting wallpaper on the walls, you are trying to conceal or cover up something. If the wallpaper has an outdated pattern that stands out in the dream, you may have inherited old habits or patterns from your family that don't really belong to you.

walls

Walls, like fences, can protect or block. Where are the walls and why are they there? If you need better emotional boundaries, you may dream of putting up a wall. You may also dream you are putting up a wall to keep someone from you, or that someone you know is putting up walls in your relationship. Fears of intimacy could cause you to wall yourself off from your own happiness. This dream might also suggest you need better boundaries in your relationships.

war

A dream of war could relate to reliving your past in the military. Whether you've served in the military or not, a dream of war might symbolize internal turmoil or a need to make peace with yourself or others. By examining other elements in the dream, you may determine the message behind the aggressive behavior. This could even be a past-life dream.

washing

If you are washing something in a dream, you may be attempting to cleanse or purify yourself. If a stain won't come out, the dream may relate to a concern about something from your past connected with feelings of guilt.

water

Water is another of the primal symbols deeply embedded in the collective consciousness. The symbol of water has to do with movement, rhythm, life-giving nourishment, and the ebb and flow of your emotional nature. If you dream of water, most likely your subconscious is using this primal symbol to help you understand and process emotional issues. Emotional release dreams almost always involve water imagery. Consider your emotional state when you have water symbols in your dreams. If you dream you are drowning, you feel overwhelmed emotionally at this time in your life. If you dream you are trapped in ice or snow, your emotions have hardened and you are having difficulty identifying and releasing them. If the water in your dream is warm, pleasant, and cleansing, you are feeling emotionally balanced at this time in your life.

A dream of water can also relate to the unconscious. In the Freudian perspective, water relates to sexual matters, usually the female genitalia (see *lake*, *ocean*, *river*, and *waves*). To dream of muddy water means your feelings about a certain person or situation are not clear. If the water is clear, you know what your heart desires. Rough water may connote problems communicating or getting along with a loved one.

waterfall

Water signifies the unconscious or the emotions, so to dream of waterfalls may represent a sudden or dramatic change in your emotional state.

waves

Waves symbolize the power of the unconscious. Enormous breaking waves may represent powerful emotions; gentle waves suggest a tranquil state of mind.

weapon

Weapons may signify you feel under attack or need to protect yourself. Consider who is holding the weapon and how it is being used to determine the dream's meaning.

wedding

A wedding unites two people, and dreams of weddings may indicate you're in the process of integrating the masculine and feminine aspects of your nature. This dream might also symbolize a union of ideas or another type of partnership or connection. Weddings are joyful, social occasions, so dreaming of attending a wedding represents a desire for celebration and connection with others. If the wedding doesn't take place, you fear a connection you are trying to cement in your life may not happen.

weeds

Dreaming of weeds suggests that something needs to be weeded out of your life. An overgrown garden might signify that something is being neglected in your life.

well

A well in a dream reveals that resources are available deep within you, although you may not be aware of them. To fall into a well symbolizes a loss of control regarding a matter at hand. A dry well indicates you feel a part of your life is empty and needs to be nourished. To draw water from a well denotes the fulfillment of emotional desires.

west

In many traditions west is the place of the adult and associated with the season of autumn. New life (the east) has moved through the ties of the past (the south) and come into full expression. Now it is time to move on. In the history of the United States, the west represented adventure, exploration, and the courage to move into the unknown. In the Peruvian shamanic tradition, west is the path of the warrior who has moved beyond fear and stands in harmony, balance, and peace. Because the sun sets in the west, something may be coming to an end in your life. Or you may be experiencing a peak in your professional or personal life, as west is also the place of attainment.

wet

As in the saying "you're all wet," wetness represents uncertainty or a lack of knowledge. Maybe someone is giving you bad advice about a particular situation. If something or someone is wet in a dream, emotion may be clouding the issue or the relationship.

whale

A whale is an enormous mammal, and to dream of one might indicate that you are dealing with a whale of a project. On the other hand, a whale dream may suggest you feel overwhelmed. Whales live in the water, so they can represent your relationship to the unconscious and the emotions.

whip

Being whipped in a dream refers to two things: you feel you deserve punishment for some transgression, or you feel someone is taking advantage of you undeservedly. If you dream of whipping someone, beware of your own manipulative or aggressive tendencies.

whirlpool

Water represents the emotions or the unconscious, so to dream of a whirlpool may indicate that your emotions are in a state of flux and can ensnare you unless you exercise caution.

whirlwind

A dream of a whirlwind suggests you are confronting a change that threatens to overwhelm you. Pay attention to the other aspects of the dream. Are you facing this danger alone or with somebody else?

wind

Dreaming of wind softly blowing means you may feel supported at this time in your life. If you dream you are walking against a brisk wind, it indicates you are courageous, able to resist temptations, and determined to get through obstacles in both your thinking and your actions. If, however, in your dream the wind blows you along against your wishes, it signifies you might feel you don't have control right now in a particular situation or relationship in your life.

window

If a window appears in a dream, it may symbolize a view of your life from the inside out. Are there changes you would like to make? If the view is illuminated, the outlook is bright. If you are on the outside looking in, you may feel you have been excluded from something.

wine

Drinking wine in a dream might be a sign of celebration. It can also represent an elevated or altered state of mind. In a spiritual sense, wine can symbolize a transformation. For an alcoholic or someone who has been affected by one, wine or other alcoholic beverages can signify a negative influence.

wings

Wings provide a means of transport. In a dream, they may suggest you will soar to wealth and honor, or that you feel supported by others in your life.

witch

The Halloween image of a witch might be symbolic of a scary or evil scenario. For those involved in Wicca or attracted to New Age ideas, a witch might indicate worshipping and respecting nature and the earth.

wolf

In Native American lore, the wolf symbolizes good medicine and represents the pathfinder—a teacher with great wisdom and knowledge. Dreaming of a wolf can be auspicious. Alternately, the wolf can be a symbol of a lone male aggressively pursuing a young female, as in the story of "Little Red Riding Hood."

woman

The appearance of different types of women can symbolize different things in a dream. Usually the woman will represent parts of yourself, whether you are male or female. Notice the woman's actions in the dream to further understand how she relates to your waking life. Other people in dreams almost always represent an aspect of yourself. If you know who the woman is in the dream, then think about the qualities of that person and which of those qualities you may possess or aspire to possess. Even if the woman in question has qualities you don't like, your dream will be showing you those qualities as part of your own shadow side. If it is a woman you don't know in your waking life, notice the actions and the feelings in the dream. A woman on her own is not an archetype, but if the woman is a mother, a virgin, a prostitute, or a movie star, for example, then you are connecting to the archetypical qualities of each of those symbols. In that case, you should reflect on where in your own life you may be emulating, or desiring to emulate, a particular archetype.

writing

Writing is usually difficult to read in a dream, so the message is often symbolic. Writing could serve as a warning, as in "the writing is on the wall." Writing could also suggest your inner self is seeking contact with your conscious self. Ancient writings in a dream indicate you are seeking knowledge from the distant past.

Y

yard

Dreaming of a yard may relate to your childhood—a time when you played in the yard. The dream may symbolize a longing for a carefree time, more personal space, or something to fill the vacancy of the yard.

year

If you dream of a year, it represents a time period for something in your life to complete or manifest. That time period may or may not be an actual year. In your dream, the "year" may just represent a longer period of connected time. A year is a single period of time that embodies the vibration of the number symbol of one. It is one unit, just as one day is a unit and one month is a unit. If you dream of multiple years, the important element is the number, not the duration of time (day, month, year). Pay attention to the number in that case and look up what that number symbol means.

yell/yelling

If you dream you are yelling at someone, it represents unexpressed anger or frustration either at yourself, another person, or a situation in your life that you feel unable to change. If you are being yelled at in your dream, you feel others are judging you. If you hear someone yelling from a distance in your dream, you may unconsciously be asking for help.

yellow

Yellow is the color of the sun, the life-giving force on the planet. It is linked with the third chakra, the place of your sense of self, your self-esteem, and your will. It is also often associated with an active mind, happiness, and the element of fire. If you dream of yellow, your mind may be particularly active right now. Or, you could be trying to empower yourself in your work and other areas of your life. Yellow is also associated with cowardice, the opposite of empowered will in action. If you dream that something treasured in your life is "yellowing," you may fear some aspect of yourself or your life is fading away.

yes

Saying "yes" to something in a dream or hearing or reading the word yes in a dream means you are ready to move forward in some area of your life. You feel positive about whatever choices you are considering at this time.

yoga

If you dream you are practicing yoga, you desire greater flexibility and physical ease in your life. Because yoga is a mind-body-spirit discipline, you may also be integrating these three facets of your life.

yoke

If you dream of a yoke or see yourself yoked in a dream, you feel compelled to do things for and/or with others. You may feel you can't rely on your own power alone or accomplish your goals by yourself. To whom do you feel bound? Where are you following the directions of others in your waking life? If you are experiencing a transition in your life, this transition may have been thrust upon you and is not one you like (for example, a divorce you didn't initiate).

youth

A dream of a youth might signify that younger people are energizing you. Seeing yourself as younger in a dream may point to youthful self-empowerment.

YouTube

Dreaming you are on YouTube means what is going on in your life is for public display. Notice your emotions in the dream. If you are happy about it, this means you desire to have a more public life. If you are worried, you feel parts of your life that you would prefer to remain hidden are being revealed.

Z

zebra

Dreaming of zebras galloping indicates you want to accomplish something quickly. Zebras are herd animals, so you may need to connect with others at this time. Zebras also have distinctive markings of black and white—are you seeing things only in black and white in some area of your life? Perhaps there are shades of gray to the situation.

zero

Zero is the empty space, the void, the unknown. When zero shows up in your dream, the answers you seek may not yet be known. You could also be experiencing emptiness in some area of life. On the positive level, you are ready to receive new gifts from the universe once you have allowed yourself to create open space in your life. Zero also forms a circle and can stand for wholeness and completion.

zip code

If you dream of your zip code, this dream is about your identity and the public persona you show the world. If you dream of a zip code you don't recognize, you may be moving. If you dream of a zip code from childhood, you may be experiencing situations or emotions at the present time that mirror similar experiences from childhood.

zipper

Zippers bring things together or keep things closed. If you dream you are trying to zip something up, you are trying to keep something in your life from opening up and falling apart. If you dream you or someone else is all "zipped up," you are reserved and have trouble being spontaneous. If you are told to "zip it," you may feel you can't express what you truly want to say.

zodiac

If you dream of the signs of the zodiac, you may be dreaming of particular people in your life whose birthdays fall in those particular signs. Or, the zodiac sign could indicate the time when an event will start or reach completion. If you dream about the entire wheel of the zodiac, you are receiving spiritual information about your energetic vibration in the world and the influences currently at work in your life.

zoo

A dream of a zoo might relate to a feeling of being in a cage. It could also symbolize chaos: "This place is like a zoo." Alternately, it could recall a time of recreation, relaxation, and pleasure.

Dream Groups

The following organizations, institutions, and publications are involved in dream-related activities.

The Alfred Adler Institute of New York

> 594 Broadway
> Suite 1213
> New York, NY 10012
> ⌒ *www.alfredadler-ny.org*

The Alfred Adler Institute provides training in psychotherapy and counseling along the theory of individual psychology as formulated by Austrian psychiatrist Alfred Adler.

American Society for Psychical Research

> 5 West 73rd Street
> New York, NY 10023
> ⌒ *www.aspr.com*

The American Society for Psychical Research conducts research activities into the paranormal, including the telepathic influences on dreams.

Association for Research and Enlightenment (A.R.E.)

215 67th Street
Virginia Beach, VA 23451

⌐ *www.edgarcayce.org*

A.R.E., also known as the Edgar Cayce Foundation, offers an extensive research library based on the recorded readings of famed psychic Edgar Cayce. A.R.E. hosts year-round seminars on a wide range of topics related to parapsychology, including dreams.

C.G. Jung Foundation for Analytical Psychology

28 East 39th Street
New York, NY 10016-2587

⌐ *www.cgjungny.org*

The Jung Foundation offers training and information on analytical psychology based on Jungian concepts. Archival material includes studies on archetypal symbolism.

Cleargreen, Inc.

11901 Santa Monica Boulevard
Suite 599a
Los Angeles, CA 90025

⌐ *www.cleargreen.com*

Cleargreen, Inc., was founded by Carlos Castaneda and his colleagues in sorcery to promote the teachings of don Juan Matus, a Yaqui Indian and sorcerer who taught dreaming techniques to Castaneda. The organization promotes seminars in which "magical passes," called Tensegrity, are taught. Cleargreen, Inc., also publishes a newsletter called Readers of Infinity: A Journal of Applied Hermeneutics.

Dream Network

1025 South Kane Creek Boulevard
Moab, UT 84532

⌐ *http://dreamnetwork.net*

Dream Network publishes a quarterly journal devoted to exploring the relationship between dreams and myths. Its stated purpose is to "demystify dream work and to integrate dream-sharing into our lives for the enhancement of our culture." Dream Network also provides information on ongoing dream groups.

The International Association for the Study of Dreams (IASD)

IASD Central Office
1672 University Avenue
Berkeley, CA 94703
🖰 *www.asdreams.org*

IASD provides an international forum for promoting research and dispensing information about the psychological and therapeutic aspects of dreams and their interpretation. The association offers a newsletter and sponsors study-groups, trainings, workshops, and annual conferences.

National Sleep Foundation

1522 K Street, NW
Suite 500
Washington, D.C. 20005
🖰 *www.sleepfoundation.org*

The National Sleep Foundation is an independent nonprofit organization dedicated to improving public health and safety by achieving understanding of sleep and sleep disorders, and by supporting education, sleep-related research, and advocacy.

Omega Institute for Holistic Studies

150 Lake Drive
Rhinebeck, NY 12572
🖰 *www.eomega.org*

The Omega Institute offers seminars taught by leaders in psychology, metaphysics, shamanism, the arts, and related fields.

Saybrook University Graduate School

747 Front Street, 3rd Floor
San Francisco, CA 94111
🖱 *www.saybrook.edu*

Founded and directed by Dr. Stanley Krippner, a renowned dream researcher and author, Saybrook is an accredited graduate school that offers pioneering approaches to health and wellness, as well as many opportunities to study dreams.

Sleep Research Society (SRS)

One Westbrook Corporate Center
Suite 920
Westchester, IL 60154
🖱 *www.sleepresearchsociety.org*

The Sleep Research Society fosters scientific investigation, professional education, and career development in sleep research and academic sleep medicine. The organization also publishes the journal *Sleep*.

APPENDIX B

Books and Web Sources

The following books may prove to be excellent resources for rounding out your knowledge of various disciplines that tie into a fuller understanding of deliberately working with your dreams and the Law of Attraction.

Books

Andrews, Ted. Animal Speak: *The Spiritual & Magical Powers of Creatures Great & Small*. St. Paul, Minnesota: Llewellyn Publications, 1993.

Barrett, Jayme. *Feng Shui Your Life*. New York: Sterling Publications, 2003.

Byrne, Rhonda. *The Secret*. New York: Atria Books, 2006.

Castaneda, Carlos. *The Art of Dreaming*. New York: HarperCollins Publishers, 1993.

Chopra, Deepak. *The Seven Spiritual Laws of Success*. Novato, CA: New World Library/Amber-Allen Publishing, 1994.

Csikszentmihalyi, Mihaly. *Flow: The Psychology of Optimal Experience*. New York: Harper Perennial, 2008.

Delaney, Gale. *Breakthrough Dreaming: How to Tap the Power of Your 24-Hour Mind*. New York: Bantam, 1991.

Eason, Cassandra. *The Art of the Pendulum*. York Beach, ME: Red Wheel/Weiser, 2005.

Ellerman, David. *Helping People Help Themselves, From the World Bank to an Alternative Philosophy of Development Assistance*. Ann Arbor: University of Michigan Press, 2005.

Faraday, Ann. *The Dream Game*. New York: Harper & Row, 1974.

Faraday, Ann. *Dream Power*. New York: Afar Publishers, 1972.

Fontana, David. *The Secret Language of Symbols: A Visual Key to Symbols and Their Meanings*. San Francisco: Chronicle Books, 2003.

Foster, Carolyn J. *The Family Patterns Workbook: Breaking Free from Your Past and Creating a Life of Your Own*. Los Angeles: Jeremy P. Tarcher, 1993.

Fox, Matthew. *Illuminations of Hildegard of Bingen*. Rochester, VT: Bear & Company, 2002.

Garfield, Patricia. *Creative Dreaming*. New York: Fireside, 1974.

Gimbutas, Marija and Joseph Campbell. *The Language of the Goddess*. New York: Harper & Row, 1989.

Godwin, Malcolm. *The Lucid Dreamer*. New York: Simon & Schuster, 1994.

Goldwell, Bruce, and Tammy Lynch. *Mastery of Abundant Living: The Key to Mastering the Law of Attraction*. Calgary, Alberta: Saga Books, 2007.

Growse, F. S., translator. *The Ramayana of Tulsi Das, Valmiki*. Allahabad: Ram Narain Lal, Publisher and Bookseller, 1966.

Harner, Michael. *The Way of the Shaman*. New York: Harper & Row, 1980.

Hicks, Esther and Jerry. *The Law of Attraction: The Basics of the Teachings of Abraham*. Carlsbad, CA: Hay House, 2006.

Hill, Napoleon. *Think and Grow Rich*. New York: Jeremy P. Tarcher/Penguin, 2005.

Jung, Carl G. *Memories, Dreams, Reflections*. New York: Vintage Books, 1961.

Jung, Carl G. *Man and His Symbols*. New York: Doubleday, 1964.

LaBerge, Stephen. *Lucid Dreaming*. New York: Ballantine, 1986.

LaBerge, Stephen, and Howard Rheingold. *Exploring the World of Lucid Dreaming*. New York: The Ballantine Publishing Group/Random House, 1990.

L'Engle, Madeleine. *Walking on Water: Reflections on Faith and Art*. Wheaton, IL: Harold Shaw Publishers/North Point Press, 2001.

Lewis, James R., and Evelyn Dorothy Oliver. *The Dream Encyclopedia*. Canton, MI: Visible Ink Books, 2009.

Losier, Michael J. *The Law of Attraction: The Science of Attracting More of What You Want and Less of What You Don't*. New York: Wellness Central, 2007.

Maxmen, Jerrald S. *A Good Night's Sleep*. New York: Norton, 1981.

McGuire, William, and R.F.C. Hull (Editors). *C.G. Jung Speaking*. Princeton, NJ: Princeton University Press, 1977.

Michaels, Stase. *The Bedside Guide to Dreams*. New York: Fawcett Crest, 1995.

Morris, Jill. *The Dream Workbook*. New York: Fawcett Crest, 1986.

Peale, Norman Vincent. *The Power of Positive Thinking*. New York: Fireside, 2003.

Perkins, John. *PsychoNavigation*. Rochester, VT: Destiny Books, 1990.

Perkins, John. *The World Is as You Dream It: Shamanic Teachings from the Amazon and Andes*. Rochester, VT: Destiny Books, 1994.

Ray, James Arthur. *The Science of Success: How to Attract Prosperity and Create Harmonic Wealth Through Proven Principles*. Carlsbad, CA: SunArk Press, 1999.

Roberts, Jane. *The Nature of Personal Reality: A Seth Book*. New York: Prentice-Hall, 1974.

Roberts, Jane. *Seth: Dreams and Projection of Consciousness*. New York: Prentice-Hall, 1986.

Roberts, Jane. *Seth Speaks: The Eternal Validity of the Soul*. New York: Prentice-Hall, 1972.

Sams, Jamie. *Medicine Cards: The Discovery of Power Through the Ways of Animals*. New York: St. Martin's Press, 1999.

Sanford, John A. *Dreams and Healing: A Succinct and Lively Interpretation of Dreams*. New York: Paulist Press, 1978.

Sheldrake, Rupert. *The Sense of Being Stared At: And Other Unexplained Powers of the Human Mind*. New York: Three Rivers Press, 2004.

Stasney, Sharon. *Feng Shui Living*. New York: Sterling Publications, 2003.

Too, Lillian. *168 Feng Shui Ways to Declutter Your Home*. New York: Sterling Publications, 2003.

Ullman, Montague, Stanley Krippner, and Alan Vaughan. *Dream Telepathy*. Toronto: Macmillan, 1973.

Ullman, Montague, and Nan Zimmerman. *Working with Dreams*. New York: Delacorte Press, 1979.

Villoldo, Alberto. *Dance of the Four Winds: Secrets of the Inca Medicine Wheel.* Rochester, VT: Destiny Books, and San Francisco: HarperSanFrancisco, 1990.

Villoldo, Alberto. *Island of the Sun: Mastering the Inca Medicine Wheel.* San Francisco: HarperSanFrancisco, 1992.

Walker, Barbara. *The Women's Dictionary of Symbols and Sacred Objects.* San Francisco, CA: Harper & Row, 1988.

Wattles, Wallace D. *The Science of Getting Rich: Financial Success Through Creative Thought.* New York: Barnes & Noble, 2007.

Weil, Andrew. *8 Weeks to Optimum Health, Revised Edition: A Proven Program for Taking Full Advantage of Your Body's Natural Healing Power.* New York: Ballantine Books, 2007.

Weil, Andrew. *Spontaneous Healing: How to Discover and Embrace Your Body's Natural Ability to Maintain and Heal Itself.* New York: Ballantine, 1995.

Williams, Strephon Kaplan. *Jungian-Senoi Dreamwork Manual.* Berkeley: Journey Press, 1980.

Web Sources

About.com
- http://altreligion.about.com/library /glossary/blsymbols.htm

International Association for the Study of Dreams
- www.asdreams.org

Center for Consciousness Studies
- www.consciousness.Arizona.edu /mission.htm

Self-Improvement-eBooks.com
- http://phineasquimby.wwwhubs.com

New Thought Library
- http://newthoughtlibrary.com/mulford Prentice/thoughtAreThings/title.htm

Christian Science
- http://christianscience.com

New Advent
- www.newadvent.org

Project Mind Foundation
- www.projectmind.org

Life Enthusiast Co-op
- www.life-enthusiast.com

Andrew Weil, MD
- www.drweil.com

Meetup
- www.meetup.com

Project Gutenberg
- www.gutenberg.org

Roosevelt Institute
- www.feri.org

Hinduism Today
- www.hinduismtoday.com

Pulse of the Planet
- www.pulseplanet.com

White Swan Records
- www.whiteswanrecords.com

Jean Houston
- www.jeanhouston.org

The Mary Baker Eddy Library
- www.marybakereddylibrary.org

Rupert Sheldrake
- www.rupertsheldrake.org

Assorted Worksheets

Worksheet 1: Nine Tips for Setting Intentions

This exercise is designed to help you clarify your desire to manifest an object. You know what you want, but if you were asked to describe that item in detail, could you do it? The universe will bring you exactly what you ask for, so it is important that you be specific. When you see something you want, you will perhaps remember only the general shape, maybe the color, and perhaps a detail or two. Use this exercise to establish a clear statement of your intention for manifesting a particular object by including as many details as possible.

1. Name the category of the material thing you most desire to manifest (for example, car, house, boat, jewelry, furniture, art, musical instrument, dishware, clothing, or electronic item).
2. Name the specific item make or style (for example, a car might be a Mercedes S-500; a musical instrument might be a Gibson folk guitar or a Stradivarius violin; an electronic item might be a Toshiba Satellite Pro laptop or seventy-five-inch plasma screen television).
3. What is its color?
4. What size and shape is it? If you don't know, find a picture of the object you desire on the Internet or in a magazine and cut it out. Knowing what it looks like will be important for your visualization exercises.

5. What does it taste like? Of course, this may not be relevant to the object you desire to manifest, but if it happens to be a 100-year-old bottle of Scotch, being able to imagine the taste will be important.

6. Does it have a scent? If so, write down your thoughts about what it smells like (new clothes or wooden instruments may have subtle scents, for example, whereas a piece of china probably will not have a scent).

7. What does it sound like? Sound may not be relevant for some objects, but for cars, musical instruments, or electronic equipment, sound is an important detail.

8. Mentally run your fingers over the object of your desire. How does it feel? What is its texture?

9. Now that you have employed your senses of sight, taste, touch, smell, and hearing in order to better imagine the object you intend to manifest, write a simple declaration of your intention. Here's an example to get you started.

I am elated to know that the Law of Attraction is in the process of bringing into my life the _____ that I deeply desire. I can see it clearly in my mind now (mentally imagine it) and am grateful (feel the gratitude) that it already exists in the realm of pure potentiality. I deserve this, am ready to receive it, and know that it is on its way to me and in the right moment it will manifest in my life.

Worksheet 2: Three Ways to Clarify and Refine a Vision

The Law of Attraction has no bias and does not differentiate between your positive and negative thoughts. It continually responds to your vibration. Words in a positive affirmation make you feel happy, excited, and anticipatory. When you affirm and visualize your desire for something in positive language and images, your feeling creates a magnetic vibration that draws the desired object into your experience. Use the following three techniques to clarify and refine your vision:

1. **Correct your declaration language.** Use breath work or meditation to move into a quiet, centered place in your mind where you can name and visualize the object, experience, or relationship you desire to manifest. Tell the universe what you want. Notice whether you used any negative words in your statement, for example: "I don't want any more bills." Check in with your feelings. How does the word bills make you feel? Most likely, it makes you feel negative. Rephrase your statement to include positive terms and get rid of words like don't, won't, and can't. Replace the negative statement with a positive one such as: "I desire financial prosperity and the means to easily meet my financial responsibilities." Now how do you feel? Notice the difference?

2. **Fix visualization problems.** The mind/body connection ensures you will experience feelings in response to your mental visualization. Let's say you need to attract powerful and influential people to your career path. Consider the imagery you are using to depict them in your mind. If you see powerful people as stern, harsh, and demanding, bringing into your life more misery, stress, and unreasonable deadlines and responsibilities, you most likely will feel apprehension and dread. Instead, imagine them as warm, friendly, helpful, generous, and wise associates, perhaps even mentors with a vested interest in helping you advance in your chosen field of endeavor.

3. **Eliminate any image that muddies or confuses your vision.** Perhaps you dream of having a trim, flexible, and muscular body, but you can't get rid of the extra pounds you gained during a pregnancy. You started a walking program with neighborhood friends and are now eating a healthy,

balanced diet, yet still the weight clings. In your mind, you see yourself in the bikini you wore when you were eighteen and you are doing affirmations. Why isn't it working?

The problem is that deep down on a subconscious level, you know you can never be eighteen with that same body again. Try taking a picture of yourself as you look today. Adjust your body size using scissors or a computer tool such as Photoshop. You want to create an image your mind believes is possible to achieve. Psychological experts say any time there is a struggle between the conscious and unconscious mind, the unconscious wins. You must convince yourself that a flexible and leaner body is possible for the person you are now. Start with a photo image and make it plausible. Paste that image on your refrigerator, bathroom mirror, and scale. Feel gratitude for each pound or inch lost and find positive ways to reward yourself as the Law of Attraction works with you to create a beautiful, strong, healthy, and leaner body.

Worksheet 3: Six Steps to Clear Blockages

Do you fear success? Are you going through the steps of deliberately manifesting and yet not seeing results? Perhaps you are subconsciously blocking the outcome you seek. Try these six steps to clear blockages:

1. **Cultivate positive feelings.** Imagine you have just received whatever it was you hoped to manifest. Using that moment as a point of departure in a journal entry, write about how you feel at having that object, situation, or relationship now manifested in your life. Remember, the Law of Attraction responds to feelings related to specific thoughts rather than the thoughts themselves.

2. **Feel worthy.** Redirect negative self-talk into positive statements. What are some of the reasons why other people (for example, your mother, father, spouse, lover, and children) love you? Make a list of all the lovable qualities and traits you have and why you are worthy to receive the gifts you seek from the universe. Love yourself and others the way you want to be loved and cultivate feelings of self-worth.

3. **Make every day the best day of your life.** If something goes wrong in your day, shift the energy of that moment as soon as possible. Don't go through an entire day with a negative attitude after breaking the handle off a china cup because you awoke late for an important early morning meeting. Listen to beautiful music, take a walk, lie down for a quick power nap, rejuvenate and refresh by doing some yoga or breath work, listen to a Law of Attraction CD, or offer a prayer of thanks to the Divine. You have phenomenal power in every moment of your life to change that moment, to shift the negative into neutral or positive energy, and to regain forward impetus.

4. **Focus on what you want rather than what you don't have.** Perhaps you can easily recount all the reasons why you don't own your own home, but you deeply desire to own a house. Make a list of all the positive reasons why you deserve it and how living there will change your life and the lives of your spouse, children, and pets. As a point of departure for writing about your hopes, dreams, and feelings of love and gratitude, imagine a celebratory meal with relatives, a holiday gathering, or a quiet peaceful moment in your own home. Take a mental snapshot of how

you feel after that writing exercise. Remember those positive feelings every time you move into feelings of lack.

5. **Fine-tune the direction and intention of your desires.** Be decisive when working with the law. Remember, it is always at work to bring you the things you mentally focus on, both positive and negative. Think of your mind as a canoe floating along the river of life, buffeted and buoyed by forces of energy (wind and currents) that you can't see. For certain, the canoe is going somewhere—perhaps places you like or don't. Instead of going with the flow, you have the "paddles" (your feelings and thoughts) to navigate in the direction you desire to go.

6. **Create space in your life for what you desire to manifest.** Consider that the new love of your life might not come until your current relationship has ended. If there is a lot of negative emotional baggage associated with the relationship you are in, you have to clear out those patterns of thought. Replace them with positive feelings of anticipatory excitement, hope, and expectation to attract the new love you desire and deserve.

Worksheet 4: Four Ways to Create a Vacuum for Manifesting

Release what isn't working in your life. Open your heart and mind to allow in new energy, relationships, and surprises that the universe may be ready to give you. Sometimes when the things you desire don't readily appear, you have to make space for them. For example, if a relationship has soured and counseling or other avenues for repairing it have not helped, it may be time to move on. Maybe your life seems stalled because your career has hit an impasse or your job doesn't inspire you. If everywhere you look things are broken, outdated, or not used, bless and release them. Here are four ways to start the process:

1. **Shift the status quo when the passion dies.** If you hate your job and want to find a new one, or you'd like to start your own business, tender your resignation. Bless and release the old work and get started manifesting your dream vocation. Feel the excitement of embarking upon a new path to a new dream. Brainstorm, write a business plan, figure out marketing, find funding, and set your dream into forward motion. When you do, you'll see how the universe puts the wind into your sails and pushes you quickly onto your chosen course.

2. **Clear the clutter from your life.** Energy flow is impeded when you are surrounded by clutter. Get that energy moving again by removing things that you no longer use, don't work properly, or are broken. Also put away pictures and the myriad things throughout your house that remind you of the demise of relatives and friends. Establish a special designated area in your home to honor them (for placement, read books about feng shui). Nourish relationships with helpful people and you'll open yourself to the inflow of healing, vibrant, and beneficial energy.

3. **Reprogram your thoughts.** Your outer life is a manifestation of your inner thoughts and feelings. When you release old patterns of negative thinking and replace them with powerful positive thoughts and expectations that make you feel hopeful and happy, you set into forward motion vibrations that can attract an abundance of good things to you. Do you desire love with a partner who is trustworthy, capable, and emotionally healthy? Examine your thinking to see why he or she is not already in

your life. Maybe the pain and drama associated with a previous relationship caused you to fear a future one. But if you can't imagine the possibility of a wonderful new love, how will it ever come to you?

4. **Learn to rely on your emotional guidance system of intuition or sixth sense to know when to let go.** If something is not right in your life, you may be overriding the signals from your emotional guidance system that warn you to steer clear or break away. The more you rely on your inner guidance, the more you will trust it when it warns you to shift direction. Sometimes just a little shift is all that is needed to create a vacuum for the abundance you seek.

Worksheet 5: Eight Visualization Exercises

Law of Attraction experts advocate using visualization when you are deliberately working with the law because you respond to the feelings created by positive mental images and thoughts. Choose one of the following topics and focus on, fantasize, and visualize as though you had already achieved phenomenal success in that area.

As you visualize (no negative feelings or thoughts allowed), focus on how you feel as you place yourself in your chosen scenario. Allow any/all details to unfold in your mind's eye. It's a little like daydreaming your way to success. Write down any insights or ideas for goals, timelines, and specific action steps to more quickly attain your desire.

1. Financial prosperity/wealth
2. Romantic love or partner
3. Birth of a child or pet project
4. Robust health
5. Peaceful life or an exciting life of travel and new experiences
6. Career advancement or establishing/running your own successful business
7. Meaningful and passionate work/journey in life
8. Spiritual advancement

Feel free to add your own special desire to the list. Reinforce your visualization work by doing one or more of the following:

- Write a desire/intention declaration or vision statement.
- Create a manifestation poster (using images, words, symbols, and statements clipped from magazines and glued to the poster) for what you want to create or manifest.
- Record in your journal all the positive feelings you experience whenever you visualize your desire actualized in your life.

Worksheet 6: Three Techniques for Dream Incubation

Dream work can inspire, enlighten, and amuse you, even if you have never done it before. The most important thing (besides remembering your dreams) is to know how to incubate a dream for understanding, insight, and guidance. When you are working with the Law of Attraction in an intentional way, you may find it helpful to incubate a dream to clarify whether you are on your path. You might discover you are obstructing the manifestation of something you deeply desire or the guidance you need to get what you want.

- Place a pad of paper and a pencil next to your bed. Even better, purchase and use a dream journal (any blank book will do).
- Upon awakening, remain in that sleepy state and notice how you feel from having the dream. Try to recall all the images you can about your dream.
- Without judging or analyzing your dream, write everything you can remember about the dream, especially your feeling and mood as you awakened.
- After you have recorded your dream, consult the dream dictionary to choose meanings for the symbols that make sense to you.
- Once you have interpreted all the symbols, actions, messages, themes, and any particularly potent images, rewrite the dream to expose its relevance and meaning. Meaning can be revealed in the layers of the dream or even over a period of time during which you dream the same dream again. Consult books about dream work to learn how to extract as much meaning as possible.

Incubating a dream requires a little preparation. Before going to sleep, do some breath work. As you breathe out, visualize dark negative energy that you've acquired during the day flowing out through the soles of your feet. As you breathe in, visualize white light or positive energy flowing in through your heart or head and filling your body. Ask for the dream you desire. Be clearly focused and specific, for example, "I open my heart and mind to receiving a dream about _____." Here are three techniques for dream incubation:

1. **Prepare and pray for the dream.** Ask your dreaming mind for exactly what you want. Don't try to incubate a dream after consuming heavy food or drink. Likewise, avoid incubating a dream when you are extremely tired, grumpy, or overstimulated by work or socializing. Take a hot shower or bath to wind down from your day. Make certain your bedroom is clean, with fresh linen on the bed. You should feel peaceful and ready to sleep. Place the necessary tools for recording your dream close by.

2. **Fantasize and explore every aspect of your dream topic until you can write out a short one-sentence dream question or goal.** During a meditation or quiet period, think about every aspect of the information you require or desire to receive from the dream. Clarity is essential.

3. **Open your heart and mind to any and all possibilities for information your dream (or dreams) may bring you about the topic in question.** Sometimes your dreaming mind may offer the dream in different ways on different nights. In essence, your dreaming mind brings you the information you desire sequentially, as if it were a flower slowly unfolding and yielding its secrets.

Index

We Have EVERYTHING® on Anything!

With more than 19 million copies sold, **the Everything® series** has become one of America's favorite resources for solving problems, learning new skills, and organizing lives. Our brand is not only recognizable—it's also welcomed.

The series is a hand-in-hand partner for people who are ready to tackle new subjects—like you!

For more information on the Everything® series, please visit *www.adamsmedia.com*

The Everything® list spans a wide range of subjects, with more than 500 titles covering 25 different categories:

Business	History	Reference
Careers	Home Improvement	Religion
Children's Storybooks	Everything Kids	Self-Help
Computers	Languages	Sports & Fitness
Cooking	Music	Travel
Crafts and Hobbies	New Age	Wedding
Education/Schools	Parenting	Writing
Games and Puzzles	Personal Finance	
Health	Pets	